THREE TIMES A GUEST

THREE TIMES A GUEST

Recollections of Japan and the Japanese, 1942–1969

Charles A. Fisher

CASSELL
LONDON

CASSELL LTD.
35 Red Lion Square, London WC1R 4SG
and at Sydney, Auckland, Toronto, Johannesburg,
an affiliate of
Macmillan Publishing Co., Inc.,
New York.

First published 1979

ISBN 0 304 30316 x

Photoset by
Rowland Phototypesetting Ltd.
Bury St. Edmunds, Suffolk

Printed in Great Britain by
The Camelot Press Ltd, Southampton.

CONTENTS

ILLUSTRATIONS

(Between pages 180 and 181)

MAPS

AUTHOR'S ACKNOWLEDGEMENTS

I wish to thank Messrs Methuen and Co. Ltd for allowing me to include an abbreviated version of the section entitled 'The Historical Setting' in *The Changing Map of Asia*, edited by W. G. East, O. H. K. Spate and Charles A. Fisher.

I also wish to thank the School of Oriental and African Studies for permitting me to include four of its maps, drawn by Mr A. De Souza, which have also been used in *The Changing Map of Asia*.

CAVEAT

Reminiscences, by definition, are inherently subjective, but those dealing with conditions in a Japanese Prisoner of War Camp (as in Part One of this book) are almost wholly dependent on fading memories of the spoken word. In this context, therefore, I must admit that I too share the view which Huckleberry Finn attributed to Mark Twain: 'There was things which he stretched, but mainly he told the truth.'

C. A. F.

INTRODUCTION

Ex Oriente lux?

In October 1968 Japan, which during 1941–5 had suffered the greatest disaster in its history, including both the virtual destruction of Tokyo and most of its other major cities, and the loss of its entire overseas empire, celebrated the centenary of the Meiji Restoration of 1868, which had marked the effective beginning of the new era of modernization, based on the introduction of Western science and technology. Nevertheless by 1968 this exhausted, devastated and down-at-heel country had become one of the economic giants of the post-war world, and its centenary celebrations, including a 'three-way hook-up' of Japan with the U.S.A. and the U.S.S.R., clearly implied that it now regarded itself as one of the three leading powers in the world.

Nor was this view without significant foundation for, thanks to its phenomenally high growth-rate during the post-Occupation period, Japan had by 1968 achieved the third largest gross national product in the world, surpassed only by the United States and the Soviet Union. Meanwhile its population, which had risen to over a hundred million, had attained a standard of living almost equal to that of Italy, and its capital, Tokyo, with over nine million inhabitants, was the largest city in the world. By any standards this transformation represented a prodigious achievement which stood in striking contrast to Freda Utley's assessment of Japan, *Japan's Feet of Clay*, less than thirty years previously, as a country of impoverished peasants, severely underfed children, deprived of proper education while often working long hours in factories, and women devoid of social—let alone political—rights, many of whom were treated as little better than beasts of burden in the coalmines.

Yet although the Japanese had every reason to be proud of their extraordinarily rapid economic advance, particularly since the Second World War, one of Japan's leading diplomats, Ichiro Kawasaki, was meanwhile writing a book, *Japan Unmasked*, which seemed to go out of its way to denigrate his own fellow countrymen. Thus, for example, he comments: '. . . the Japanese as a whole feel a deep inferiority complex towards foreigners, especially Caucasians. . . .' And, even more surprisingly, he elaborates:

> Of all the races of the World, the Japanese are perhaps physically the least attractive, with the exception of Pygmies and Hottentots. . . . Negroes in America and black Africans in South Africa are the targets of racial discrimination and even persecution. But even Negroes, their pigmentation of skin notwithstanding, are at least taller and straighter than the Japanese and perhaps have greater sex appeal.

This extraordinary antithesis between thoroughly justifiable national pride in their recent material and other achievements, and the surprisingly widespread feeling of racial inferiority on the part of a by no means insignificant number of Japanese individuals, most of whom had themselves contributed to Japan's 'great leap forward', appears at first sight to be not merely astonishing, but inherently—or at least potentially—psychopathological. And such a situation would become even more disturbing if the predictions of the economist, Norman Macrae, prove to be even approximately correct.

Specifically Macrae at the beginning of 1975 forecast that, if recent growth rates continued for another fifteen years or so, Japan would by the early 1990s surpass the United States to become the greatest industrial power on earth, and its by then 110 million inhabitants would on average be more than twice as wealthy as their 220 million American counterparts.[1]

Although, for reasons which will be discussed later in this book, I do not believe that Japan will achieve such economic pre-eminence by the 1990s, if in fact it ever does, there can be no denying that it will for the foreseeable future wield immense economic power, and indeed is already on the point of becoming one of the two or three major forces which will shape the destinies of the 21st-century world. For this reason alone it is surely a matter of paramount importance that the rest of us, and especially the peoples of the Western powers of North America and the European Economic Community, should make a far more serious attempt than we have yet done to understand the traditions, problems, and above all the thought processes of the Japanese.

As the result of a series of wholly unexpected coincidences I have

[1] 'Pacific Century, 1975–2075?', *The Economist*, 4 January 1975.

during the past thirty-five years spent three substantial periods as a guest—of one sort or another—of the Japanese nation, first in 1942–5 as one of their prisoners of war, secondly in 1961 as a guest of Gaimusho (the Japanese Foreign Ministry), and thirdly in 1969 as a Visiting Professor at the University of Hiroshima, under the auspices of Mombusho (the Japanese Ministry of Education).

Since much of what I saw and was told during these three periods—as well as on several briefer visits, most recently in 1976—proved to be of considerable relevance to the problem of understanding Japanese behaviour in the widest sense of that term, I propose in this book to describe and analyse what I learned from these three experiences, before attempting finally to present and explain the reasons for such conclusions as I have reached. However, before embarking on this somewhat formidable task, I shall try to explain how and why my interest in Japan originated and subsequently developed during the 1920s and 30s, well before I first set foot on Asian soil in 1941.

PART ONE

GUESTS OF THE IMPERIAL JAPANESE ARMY

Captivity in Thailand

For we would not, brethren, have you
ignorant of our trouble which came
to us in Asia, that we were pressed
out of measure, above strength, insomuch
that we despaired even of life.

2 Corinthians 1:8

1. ORIENTATIONS

I first became aware of the existence of Japan in the early 1920s, just after I had begun my education at the local primary school in the Staffordshire 'Black Country' town of Old Hill which, though of course I did not realize it then, was almost as squalid and depressed as some of the early industrial slums that I was later to encounter in Japan. However, my awareness of Japan was not awakened by anything that I was taught at school, but by my parents who were enthusiastic Japanophiles, although neither of them had ever been anywhere near eastern Asia.

What in fact had sparked off their interest was a combination of two quite different enthusiasms. At Cambridge my father's innate idealism had been aroused by a group of impressive young Anglican churchmen, and he had decided there and then to spend his life as a missionary, if possible in China or Japan where, he was convinced, the greatest challenge and also the richest opportunities lay. By contrast, my mother, the daughter of a Dundee mechanic who had risen to become the manager of a large cotton-spinning mill in Yorkshire, had caught the prevailing pre-1914 enthusiasm for the Anglo-Japanese Alliance, apparently as a consequence of her singing teacher's infatuation, not with her but with Gilbert and Sullivan's popular opera, *The Mikado*!

Meanwhile my father's hopes of becoming a missionary had been dashed within a year of their having been conceived. For, as an exceptionally versatile young sportsman, he had tried to get his 'blue' for both rugger and rowing at the same time, and permanently damaged his heart in the process. So the Mission's medical board turned him down, and he became a parish parson instead. Nevertheless his passionate interest in missionary activities remained with him for the rest of his life, and my mother turned our vicarage into a more or less permanently open house for missionaries and their converts from all over the world.

Among these last who frequented our home at one time or another, I recall some young Zulus; two Ugandan theological students, one of whom was the brother of the Queen of Uganda; an Iranian; and a Tamil from southern India. As a boy I was fascinated by the diversity of their features and colour, and my mother often used to amuse our friends by recalling the occasion when our Tamil guest—a Mr Aramugam—who was very black, had spent the night in our spare bedroom and she caught me the next morning surreptitiously examining his bed to see if his sheets were as black as mine were when—as all too often—I had gone to bed without washing myself.

It was in the context of our 'open door policy' that, some time in the early 1920s, our family made its first acquaintance with a real-life Japanese, Mr Paul Kanamori, a small, benign, elderly man, with an extraordinarily wrinkled yellow-brown face which instantly reminded me of the ageing apples that we stored each winter in our attic. With the advantage of hindsight I suspect that Mr Kanamori, at least in origin, was a typical Japanese peasant, for he was the living image of one whom I photographed in his ricefield in the Shinano valley some forty years later. Certainly Mr Kanamori was a remarkably active little man, perpetually cheerful and friendly, and we children took to him at once, thus decisively reinforcing our parents' belief in the excellence of the Japanese. As it happened, their view coincided almost exactly with that expressed in 1549 by the great Spanish Jesuit, Francis Xavier, to the effect that the Japanese were 'the best [people] that have yet been discovered' though, as an 'evangelical', my father would doubtless have been somewhat perturbed by this papist association, had he known of it.

During the early years after the conclusion of the Anglo-Japanese Alliance in 1902, the British were more than a little relieved to find themselves aligned with the Japanese, about whom, in fact, they knew very little, instead of—as had previously seemed more likely—with the Kaiser's Germany, concerning which many of them already knew more than they wanted to. In these circumstances it became fashionable to draw fanciful analogies between Britain and Japan, the 'two great island nations', each with long histories and—even more important—firmly established monarchies, which seemed to guarantee stability in an era of unprecedented and disturbing change. So Japan came to be called 'the Britain of the East', with Osaka and Kobe respectively cast as the Manchester and Liverpool of the East; the Japanese people became our 'little yellow brothers'; and a bibulous but inherently illogical custom grew up in Tokyo of coupling the toast to 'the Empire of the Rising Sun' with that of 'the Empire on which the Sun Never Sets'.

Although I am sure that Mr Kanamori never participated in such orgies, he was clearly not unaware of the prevailing trend in Anglo-Japanese relations and accordingly, throughout his preaching tour in England, was invariably billed as 'the Apostle Paul of Japan'.

In attempting further to encourage my younger brother Dennis and myself to share their interest in things Japanese, our parents at this juncture bought, as a kind of family Christmas present, what would nowadays be called a coffee-table book, namely Herbert G. Ponting's *In Lotus-Land Japan*, a large and lavishly illustrated volume, published by Macmillan in 1910. Ponting was one of the pioneers who attempted to develop photography as a form of art, and in Japan he found a rich and stimulating variety of subject matter, extending from exotic and wonderfully sensitive-featured craftsmen in ivory and bronze, to daintily demure geisha, communal bathing scenes, and the whole superb range of Japanese scenery from the *multum in parvo* of Seto Naikai the Inland Sea to such huge and violently active volcanoes as Aso San and Asama Yama, and above all—in every sense of that phrase—the extinct but sublime snow-capped cone of Fuji, which he photographed from every conceivable angle.

Shortly after returning from Japan Ponting went as photographer with Scott's expedition to the South Pole, and years later my old professor, the late Frank Debenham, who had been a geologist on that expedition, told us of the great contribution which Ponting had made to everybody's morale during the most exhausting periods of protracted cold and darkness, by showing them some of his Japanese pictures, particularly those of the most entrancing geisha!

Beyond any doubt it was Ponting's photographs—though not, at that stage, those of the geisha—which first really aroused my own interest in Japan, and by the age of seven or eight I had already made up my mind to visit that country and climb to the top of Fuji, which Ponting had excitingly described as being 'two miles above the clouds'. In part, however, the appeal of his book derived from the fact that, because it was so expensive, I was only allowed to handle it *if I was a good boy*, and even then, only on a Sunday afternoon, presumably because my hands might be a shade less dirty on the Sabbath than on other occasions. The trouble was, of course, that I was rarely a good boy on any day; and scarcely ever on a Sunday afternoon, after the exhausting experience of sitting through my father's long and incomprehensible sermon during the morning. So the number of occasions when I was able seriously to peruse Ponting's book for any length of time was very small, and doubtless for that very reason its contents remain more vividly etched into my memory than those of any other book I have ever read. 'Progressive' educationalists please note.

Thus by the time I was ten years old I, too, had become at least an incipient or embryonic Japanophile, even though I had as yet met only one solitary Japanese. However, this deficiency was now about to be remedied. For my father was beginning to be gravely alarmed about the growing pressure in certain quarters for revising the Church of England prayer book, and after a long and agonizing struggle with his conscience, he finally decided to leave the Anglicans and join the Baptists. And since, in typically Lancastrian fashion, he never did things by halves, he decided to change his country as well as his religious denomination, and so we all emigrated to Canada, where he had been invited to a church in Toronto. But even this was not the end; a few weeks later he received a 'call' to Winnipeg and while he was there, trying to size up the situation, he got a sudden invitation to become the pastor of a church in Vancouver. My mother, who found the prairie landscape dreary, and possessed a mind of her own, opted firmly for Vancouver, and thither, without further ado, we went. I have often wondered just how far we should eventually have got if an all-foreseeing Providence had not put the Pacific Ocean immediately to the west of British Columbia.

After an exhilarating journey through the Rockies, via the Canadian Pacific Railway, our first fitful glimpse of Vancouver, with drenching rain blotting out most of the harbour, and low clouds totally obliterating the surrounding mountains, was distinctly deflating. But a day or two later the whole scene was suddenly transformed by brilliant autumnal sunshine, and we all fell instantly in love with the place, an affection which, so far as I am concerned, has intensified rather than diminished during the forty-eight years which have passed since we left it.

In the first two weeks that we were there, while our parents were totally occupied in finding a house and settling into it, Dennis and I were left to our own devices, and we proceeded, at once and on foot, to discover first the docks and then Chinatown. If my father—let alone my mother—had had an inkling of some of the places we explored in those first two weeks, they would never have let us out of their sight again. Suffice it to say that by the end of the fortnight both Dennis, aged eight, and myself, twelve, knew Chinatown like the backs of our respective hands, and we had managed to get aboard—and to wander all over—an incredible variety of ships, from Japanese and other exotic coasters and smaller craft, to the Canadian Pacific's elegant 'White Empresses', from one of which an irate ship's officer unceremoniously hustled us ashore barely a couple of minutes before she sailed for Yokohama.

Along with thousands of other families from the 'old country' who had settled in British Columbia following the completion of the Canadian Pacific Railway in 1885, we were now more than half way to the supposedly mysterious East. Meanwhile more and more Chinese and Japanese had crossed the ocean in the opposite direction to settle in the Pacific coastlands of the United States and Canada, and it was here that my introduction to the realities, as opposed to the myths, of the Orient began.

However, while newly arrived British immigrants in Vancouver were apt to lump the Chinese and Japanese together, these two communities were largely isolated from one another geographically, and still more so socially. But although, so far as I can recall, there were no Chinese children at the Model School (not, needless to say, named after the character of its pupils) which Dennis and I attended, we had several Japanese classmates, and—perhaps because they all went on for another two hours' lessons at a Japanese school after our classes finished at 4 p.m.—all these young Japanese Canadians seemed to distinguish themselves above the rest of us in one way or another. Indeed the two girls in my class—Taka and Eiko, whose names for some curious reason I firmly remember—appeared to be very good at every subject in the curriculum, and especially so at Art (which I had hitherto known more modestly—and certainly more accurately—merely as drawing) while the boys, though not notably erudite, were pillars of the school's baseball team and hence of even greater distinction.

During our first winter in Vancouver my mother appeared to find further corroboration for her pro-Japanese convictions when she helped to organize a large Christmas party for a fascinatingly polyglot and polychrome assortment of children from the dockland area. The crucial moment came at the end of a boisterous but generally well-behaved evening, in which the concluding item was a game of musical chairs, whose rules had been carefully explained to those not yet familiar with them. When finally only one chair remained standing in the middle of the floor, an unexpected impasse suddenly occurred, as two dainty and exquisitely kimonoed little Japanese girls faced one another on opposite sides of the vacant chair, both bowing politely and profusely, but adamantly disdaining to grab the chair and sit on it! After the resultant crisis had extended over several baffling minutes a solution was eventually found by drawing lots. My mother returned home to tell the tale and, never being one to miss an opportunity of driving a useful point home, commented curtly how nice it would be if only Dennis and I would behave as politely as that.

Nevertheless disillusionment was swift to follow, for, however charming and hardworking the young Japanese Canadians might be, our British Canadian neighbours left us in no doubt that the Japanese community as a whole was distinctly less popular than its Chinese counterpart. Or, as an American lady had more pointedly expressed it:

> We like the Chinese but we don't admire them;
> We admire the Japanese but we don't like them.

The reason for this was not difficult to discover. For by the late 1920s it was clear that the Japanese were becoming increasingly obsessed with a desire to replace China as the leading power in Asia, a process which had begun with their victory in the Sino-Japanese War of 1894–5, followed in 1915 by their famous—or infamous—Twenty-one Demands, aimed at reducing China to the status of a Japanese satellite.

Against this background of steadily increasing expansionism, the British Pacific Dominions of Australia, Canada, and New Zealand were understandably concerned to prevent the renewal of the Anglo-Japanese Alliance, an attitude which moreover accorded closely with current American thinking. Thus, following the Washington Conference of 1921–2, the Anglo-Japanese Alliance was replaced by the innocuous Four Power Treaty between the British Empire, the United States, Japan and France. (It was in this context that the British decided to build the Singapore naval base immediately to the west of the limits prescribed by the Four Power Treaty for the establishment of further naval installations.)

Nevertheless the Washington Conference significantly lowered the international temperature, and within Japan the most critical event during the remainder of the 1920s was not a political but a seismic upheaval, in the shape of the cataclysmic earthquake of 1 September 1923, which almost obliterated the great port of Yokohama and caused even more extensive damage to the adjacent and much larger capital city of Tokyo.

In these circumstances the astonishingly prompt and characteristically generous assistance given, in particular by the American people and their government, not only helped enormously to relieve the immediate suffering, but also made a palpable contribution to the improvement of relations between the two countries. Thus, by the summer of 1929, when my father decided to take us all back to England after all, anti-Japanese sentiment seemed to be clearly on the wane.

Despite the fact that we had returned not to the industrial Midlands but to London, in which I had previously spent only two days, and was greatly excited at the prospect of living there permanently, even the young teenager as I then was could not but be struck by the extreme dullness and smugness of English suburban life by comparison with the vitality and dynamism that I had come to regard as normal in British Columbia. And as I was now beginning to take a real—if still very immature—interest in political affairs I was astonished at the degree of ignorance and unconcern which most British people seemed to show towards Japan and China. Admittedly the Japanese invasion and take-over of Manchuria in 1931–2, representing as it did both a new stage in the dismemberment of China and a body blow to the League of Nations, did cause considerable and widespread concern for a time, but its even more disturbing sequel in the second Sino-Japanese War, which broke out in 1937, was soon pushed into the background by the growing and more geographically immediate dangers associated with the continuing rise of Hitler, the antics of Mussolini, and the outbreak of the Spanish Civil War.

Nevertheless I must admit that, although by the summer of 1938, when I graduated from Cambridge, I had matured enough to be really—and thereafter almost continuously—concerned about the rapidity with which the European political situation was deteriorating, I was still sufficiently naive to share the prevailing British view that, whatever the Japanese might be up to, it could only be of peripheral concern to us. Moreover, even after the Second World War had broken out and I had given my name and qualifications ('if any') to the University Recruiting Board, I do not think my views underwent any significant change.

In the event I doodled over my research for well over half a year before I was called up to join the Heavy Artillery, only to receive a cancellation note a week later, since Dunkirk had apparently deprived us of any heavy artillery on which to be trained. A fortnight later new instructions told me to report to the Headquarters of the Suffolk Regiment at Bury St Edmunds, where I spent a peacefully bucolic summer before being sent in the autumn to the Artists Rifles Officer Cadet Training Unit to be processed into an infantry officer.

However, someone on discovering that I possessed 'geographical qualifications', whatever these might be, had in the meantime arranged for me to be transferred to the Royal Engineers Survey Training Centre at Fort Widley, near Portsmouth. During an intensely cold spell in the following winter, resulting from a combination of our exposed situation on the top of the Portsdown Ridge and a direct hit on our heating system by a German bomb[1], a spokesman from the War Office came down to lecture to us about the war in the Middle East and ended by calling for volunteers. Being both very young and unmarried I suddenly found all eyes homing in on me, and slowly, alone, and self-consciously, I raised my hand: after all, I told myself, the Middle East couldn't be as perishing cold as Widley. Ten days later I was astonished to find that I had been posted to Singapore. Geography has never been the strong line of the British army: not even apparently of either Royal Engineers Survey or the Geographical Section of the General Staff.

Yet even then I was not in the least surprised when everyone in my unit thought it all a huge joke. Whether I was assumed to have been putting on an act of bravado, or had been exceptionally cunning, or whether—most improbably—it was a case of virtue in volunteering having been rewarded, everyone, myself included, was convinced that I had fallen on my feet. Within a few weeks, after a brief and overdue spell of home leave, I should be on a long sea voyage to what everyone said was a marvellous country, with every imaginable kind of attraction and diversion, and as far removed as possible from any conceivable danger.

A few weeks later, after an unforgettable train journey across the Yorkshire hills and dales which I loved so well, we were transferred at Glasgow to the *Capetown Castle*, the luxurious flagship of the Union Castle fleet, now disguised outwardly, though much less so inwardly, as a troopship. As she steamed slowly down the Clyde estuary on a glorious midsummer evening, someone among the thousands of well-wishers cheering and waving to us from the shore bellowed through a loud-hailer the current catch-phrase of the comedian Tommy Trinder, 'YOU *LUCKY* PEOPLE'. We all laughed and cheered like mad at the obvious appropriateness of the gag, before descending to the palatial dining saloon to eat our fill of a magnificent dinner totally unmolested by rationing, and to explore the potentialities of what was said—and soon proved—to be 'one of the finest cellars afloat'.

*

For an ocean voyage extending half way round the world, and undertaken in the middle of 1942, our journey to Singapore was

[1]There was a certain wry humour about the fact that our air raid shelter was in fact the gelignite store. Presumably this was considered to be proof against any minor damage, but if it received a direct hit we should at least end our days with a monumental bang instead of a mere whimper.

surprisingly uneventful. As we were in a convoy our pace was slowed to that of the oldest and smallest tub of the lot, so that the overall journey took some twelve weeks. Since the *Capetown Castle* was an R.A.F. troopship, discipline—especially for officers—was more informal than it would have been under army control, a fact that was particularly appreciated by the small specialist detachments of army officers, including members of the Intelligence Corps, Service Corps, and Royal Engineers. The last of these, to which I belonged as a very young Second Lieutenant, was under the command of the most senior officer on board, namely Brigadier Ivan Simson, recently in charge of coastal defences in Scottish Command, and now on his way to take over as Chief Engineer, Singapore, where his particular specialist skills had suddenly become even more urgently needed than they were in Scotland.

Although I knew nothing about Brigadier Simson, apart from his rank and posting, I instinctively recognized him as someone totally unlike any other army officer I had ever met. Besides being extremely friendly and approachable, and a man of outstanding intelligence and sensitivity, he was intensely hard-working and lost no time in seeking out anyone he could find on board who possessed specialist knowledge or information about South-east Asia which might be useful to him, as a newcomer to that area whose crucial strategic significance was now becoming daily more apparent.

In addition to furthering his own education, however, Simson also persuaded many of the experts whom he had already got to know to contribute to a series of lectures which he personally organized for the officers' mess. Most of the best of these were given by some of the abler members of the small group of about ten Intelligence Corps officers, apparently representing the sum total of British citizens capable of speaking even a modicum of Japanese, who in 1941 were available for military service. By any standards they were a very mixed group, including one 'old Japan hand' who appeared to breakfast exclusively on whisky, though he was reputed to take a little solid food later in the day (thus reversing what was alleged to be the customary routine of the British Malayan planting community); one or two journalists covering the Far East; and a few—mostly relatively junior—staff members of banks, oil companies, and other international corporations operating in that same general area.

Although they inevitably came in for a certain amount of leg pulling over the Intelligence Corps badge, which depicted a drooping and indeterminate flower, somewhat inadequately flanked by a few nondescript leaves, and hence was unofficially said to represent 'a pansy resting on its laurels', several of the Intelligence Corps officers proved to be extremely impressive people. For besides, under further tuition, achieving considerable—in some cases outstanding—proficiency as interpreters, these particular individuals won intense admiration for their heroism in standing up for British and other Allied prisoners in some of the more terrible confrontations which were later to occur between our captors and ourselves.

However, as the presence of real experts seems automatically to tempt others with no such qualifications to assume that role, we also had our share of clowns, the most extraordinary of whom was an R.A.F. officer who offered to lecture on the interesting and undeniably topical subject of the fighting qualities of the Japanese. Modestly disclaiming any *real* knowledge of naval warfare, he limited himself to the air arm and the infantry, and began by assuring us that in neither of these respects had we anything whatever to worry about from the Japanese. In fact, he explained, it was now universally recognized that, owing to the slit eyes of the Mongoloids, it was quite impossible for a Japanese airman to use a bomb sight, and therefore to hit a target. Having thus disposed of the Japanese aloft, he then turned to their no less serious shortcomings at ground level, explaining that their abnormally low (and of course typically Mongoloid) body temperature meant that their reactions were correspondingly slow, and hence that they were virtually useless in the crucial infantry tactic of hand-to-hand combat!

Since by this stage I had had more than my fill of this curious concoction of racial pride and prejudice, I interrupted the lecturer to ask, 'What about judo? Isn't that the very embodiment of quick reaction?' He floundered and spluttered for a few minutes and then muttered that he would have to think about it. Next morning, having briefly indulged in what to him must have been a most unfamiliar activity, he came up to me on deck and said: 'I've got the answer, old boy: the Japs *had* to develop judo just because their reactions were so slow.' Thus relieved and fortified, we continued on our way to Singapore.

Meanwhile, however, a swift succession of major developments in the wider world had begun drastically to modify our earlier optimism about the military prospect in South-east Asia. On 22 June 1941 the Germans invaded the Soviet Union and, as this increased Japan's freedom of manoeuvre in eastern Asia, Japanese forces, which in 1940 had already moved across the border from southern China into Tonkin (the northern extremity of old French Indochina), now advanced southwards in July 1941 to occupy the area around Saigon in Cochinchina (the southern extremity of old French Indochina). This automatically brought the Singapore base, some 660 miles away, within direct range of Japanese bombers, less than a month before the *Capetown Castle* steamed into Keppel Harbour, Singapore. With French Indochina thus reduced to 'friendly' (i.e. Japanese) occupied territory, the so-called A.B.C.D. (American, British, Chinese, Dutch) front was hurriedly pieced together, but it was a front without a back, just as Singapore was now, for all practical purposes, a base without a fleet.

2. SINGAPORE: DECLINE AND FALL

Difficulties from which the regular forces are liable to suffer, owing to inadequate intelligence.

Chapter title in War Office Publication, *Small Wars*

For most of us who arrived there in August 1941, Singapore provided our first significant experience of British colonial rule, and after the squalor and degradation which we had glimpsed during our brief walkabout in the harbour area of Bombay, where the *Capetown Castle* had put in for a few days, the cleanliness, efficiency and vitality of the 'Lion City' proved to be positively exhilarating. (Legend has it that in the thirteenth century A.D. a Sumatran prince who had landed on the island of Temasek decided to found a new kingdom there. On seeing an unfamiliar animal, which he was told was a lion, he named the new kingdom Singapura, which is popularly supposed to mean 'City of the Lion'—though unlike the tiger, which was indigenous to Malaya until relatively recently, the lion has never inhabited this part of Asia. By the fourteenth century, the 'City of the Lion' already occupied a strategic maritime position foreshadowing that of present-day Singapore.)

Indeed, on first acquaintance Singapore seemed to epitomize all that was most positive in twentieth-century British imperialism. In so far as this was so, the credit for it must be shared between its far-sighted founder, Stamford Raffles, and the thousands of immigrant—predominantly Chinese—labourers who transformed his vision of what the island might become into a tangible reality. For Raffles was perhaps the most outstanding representative of a generation of early nineteenth-century English liberals, who saw the Industrial Revolution not in terms of 'dark satanic mills' but rather as an immense liberating force which could free men and women the world over from the drudgery of unremitting toil while radically improving the material circumstances of their everyday lives.

Having already seen for himself the stultifying effects of the mercantilist policies under which the Dutch East India Company still dominated the seaborne commerce of south-eastern Asia, Raffles was quick to appreciate the immense potential significance of Singapore, overlooking the maritime crossroads between the Indian Ocean and the South China Sea. Admittedly, at that time Singapore amounted merely to some 225 square miles of almost uninhabited equatorial jungle but, by planning his new port city carefully, and introducing liberal policies in respect of shipping, trade and immigration, he believed that this focal—though hitherto neglected—island could become what he characteristically called 'the emporium of the East'.

Thanks to the successful introduction of these policies Singapore subsequently became the capital of the Straits Settlements, which also included Penang and Malacca, and from these few footholds, together with Hong Kong which was acquired in 1842, the British not only dominated the main sea route through south-eastern Asia for a whole century, but also played a seminal part in the development of both modern tin-mining and large-scale rubber cultivation in the Malayan hinterland. Since both these commodities found their main markets increasingly in the United States, Malaya came to be known during the war years as the Empire's 'dollar arsenal', a name that for some reason greatly annoyed certain members of the top brass of Malaya Command Headquarters, which doubtless assumed that it alone commanded all arsenals—of whatever kind—within its geographical area.

But whatever it commanded in a military sense, Malaya Command H.Q., at the time when I joined its staff in August 1941, did not command any noticeable respect—let alone confidence—within Singapore as a whole, and indeed was most commonly referred to as 'Confusion Castle'. For the vision which, well over a hundred years earlier, had inspired Raffles and his associates, had long since faded away, and Malaya—a term which by the 1930s included both the peninsula and Singapore—was now being run by a breed of mostly myopic second-raters, who completely failed to see that so critically sited and crucial a base as Singapore had become, especially since the termination of the Anglo-Japanese Alliance, needed to be backed by a strong and united hinterland. Instead, however, Malaya, then with a total population roughly equal to that of Greater London, within an area virtually the size of England, comprised eight separate governments, a fragmentation which served only to aggravate the differences between its three main ethnic communities, namely the Chinese (45 per cent), and the Indians (9 per cent), both of whom were of immigrant origin, together with the local Malays (44 per cent) who alone could seriously claim to be *bumiputras*, or 'sons of the soil'.

Thus, as the result of a policy which at best can only be described as one of benevolent drift, no serious attempt had been made before the

Second World War to create among these diverse peoples a sense of common identification with the strategically exposed country in which they lived cheek by jowl with one another. Moreover, a similarly parochial attitude was adopted by the European population, which developed a curiously juvenile form of expatriate rivalry, particularly between the residents of the Straits Settlements (the original 'Colony') and the somewhat more recently created Federated Malay States, politically centred in Kuala Lumpur.

In the context of this make-believe world, it was scarcely surprising that acute rivalries were nurtured between Malaya Command, with its headquarters at Fort Canning on Singapore Island, and III (Indian) Corps[1], based at Kuala Lumpur. And, indeed, if rumour may be believed, even within each of these august clusters of exalted warriors there were times when G was barely on speaking terms with A, and neither would talk to Q, if they could possibly avoid doing so (G, A and Q refer respectively to the General, Administrative and Quartermaster Staffs).

Whether this depressing state of affairs should be attributed to some inbuilt tendency for all systems ultimately to degenerate beyond the point of no return it is impossible to say, but perhaps a less ponderous explanation may fit the Malayan case. In a public lecture by a distinguished former Governor of the Straits Settlements in 1882, the lecturer advised 'young men who repeatedly fail their examinations' to emigrate to Malaya. My own observations, scattered over several more recent decades, suggest that this advice has been extensively acted upon.

However, no such gloomy thoughts perturbed us when, in accordance with orders already received, we new arrivals presented ourselves at the office of the Chief Engineer (Brigadier Simson) at Fort Canning on the following Monday at 0900 hours for detailed instruction in the duties which we were about to assume. Within a few minutes the Brigadier, flanked by selected colonels and majors, joined us, and Staff Officer Personnel (S.O.P.—or 'Sop') acted as spokesman. Most of our draft presented no problem in typecasting, three of them being straightforward garrison engineers who were appointed to Singapore, Malacca and Johore, and two other routine appointments followed without any serious crisis. Then my case, as the new survey officer, came up and,

[1] For the benefit of those unfamiliar with the mysteries of the old Indian Army, it may help to recall the story about the wife of an Indian Army Officer who, trying to explain that her husband was not coloured, said 'It's just a case of a white officer with black privates.'

with a resounding chuckle, S.O.P. explained that, since there had never been a survey officer before, he hadn't the slightest idea what my duties were.

Much laughter followed this sensational disclosure, but the Brigadier, unaccustomed to such prolonged and irrelevant levity, snapped out sharply, 'Surely there are some files on the subject which he can read through?'

Carefully folding his tail between his legs, S.O.P.—who, curiously enough, did look like a cat—purred softly that there used to be a file about the formation of a Survey Company, but, as he hadn't seen anything of it for some months, he thought it was probably lost. This only aggravated the already tense situation, and amid a strained silence the Brigadier testily rang for the senior clerk. The latter confirmed S.O.P.'s statement but promised to carry out an exhaustive search which, he felt, would almost certainly yield something of interest to the new survey officer, though probably not the actual file in question.

Nothing further happened that morning, but shortly after lunch we were put in the picture by a large and rotund staff officer, who appeared to be the archetypal version of the 'well informed circle'. Details of the distribution, equipment, and capabilities of our various forces in Malaya slid off his tongue like honeyed kisses, and although, as he fully admitted, he knew little or nothing about the forces that might conceivably be pitted against us, he didn't hesitate to offer a string of highly ingenious speculations concerning them. Opinions, he concluded, were divided—or perhaps he said confused—over the possibility of a Japanese attack, though he for one was not inclined to rule it out altogether. If it did come, he was prepared to bet that, contrary to the orthodox view, Singapore would be attacked direct from both land and sea, and unless our air force received considerable reinforcements, we could expect a very sticky time. However, there had been alarms and excursions before, but the balloon had not gone up, so we mustn't take too seriously the alarmist stories which bobbed up from time to time.

Fortunately the senior clerk arrived at this juncture to say that the Survey file had been discovered, and I was forthwith told by the Brigadier to read it and write him a report on it. It was vintage Confusion Castle and made hilarious reading, though the best bits were the annotations. Thus, for example, 'What is a Survey company? Passed to you for information,' and the lucid reply, 'Something for making maps, they have them in India.'

Further perusal of the file led to my discovery that about a year previously a sudden desire had been expressed in Fort Canning for a Survey Company (perhaps by the officer who had been inquiring what it was). So a request was transmitted to India for one of these curious cartographic contraptions to be sent to Malaya, whereupon Delhi replied that they were rather short of them at the moment but instead were sending a colonel who would tell Fort Canning what they were all about. Apparently the colonel arrived unexpectedly, expressed himself forcibly on a few points, and then departed immediately for Java, leaving nobody any the wiser. However, on continuing to study the file I discovered that the Surveyor-General of the Federated Malay States and Straits Settlements (a civil, not a military, appointment) had helpfully stepped into the breach and offered to form, staff, train and equip a (military) all-Malayan Survey Company, and was willing to start on it at once, though he warned it would take several months to complete. This offer had been made some four months earlier, but although Fort Canning had since been giving the matter very careful thought, it had still not been able to discover precisely what the snag was, so no action had yet been taken.

However, now that several people had been made to look rather silly, it was felt that the best way of saving face all round was to let the Surveyor-General do the job, which he did magnificently, and the new Survey Company, composed of Malay, Chinese, Indian and Eurasian other ranks, officered by senior staff—mainly Australians—from the Federated Malay States and Straits Settlements Survey Department, was thoroughly trained and ready for action before the Imperial Japanese Army arrived in Malaya. Until the Survey Company was formed, however, my own responsibility was limited to maintaining liaison with the Survey Office in Kuala Lumpur, and since this was by no means an onerous task, for which I was immediately promoted to the rank of captain, the question came up as to what else I should do in the meantime.

Happily, the problem resolved itself, thanks to the timely intervention of a genial old colonel who invited me into his office one morning and offered me a tomato, as a preliminary to giving me a brief résumé of his life story. While at 'the shop' (Woolwich), he said, he had achieved distinction only by coming bottom in the final Survey examination, with the unfortunate result that whenever anyone came to his office and began to talk about survey matters he had no alternative but to apologize quickly and then go and wash his hands until the coast was clear, a state of affairs which was deeply embarrassing for all concerned. And so, he concluded, with a beaming smile in my direction, 'that's why we sent for you.' Nevertheless the Brigadier was still rather unhappy about my under-employment, but again the Colonel came to my rescue. 'Leave the boy alone,' he said encouragingly, 'he'll soon find something to do.' I did: I arranged to blow up an oilfield.

It came about like this. A letter arrived in our office one morning from the Garrison Engineer at Miri in Sarawak, asking for advice in preparing a scheme for the demolition of the oilfields at Miri, and found its way into the Brigadier's In tray about 8.30 a.m. From there it skipped with growing momentum through the In and Out trays of the colonel and two majors, before landing with a flourish on the desk of my room-mate, Captain Berrill, shortly after nine o'clock. Berrill, who in civilian life had been a concrete salesman, read the letter slowly and suspiciously, and began to make silly little drawings on his blotting paper, peeping at me from time to time over his spectacles, but receiving only a bleak stare in return. Presently, after a bit more sketching, he came across to me, explained the contents of the letter, and produced his suggested plan. Did I think it would work? Well, of course, as a survey officer I claimed no serious knowledge of demolitions, let alone of such tricky ones as these would probably be, but shortly before leaving England I had attended a morning's lecture on the subject, and spent the following afternoon blowing up bits of drainpipe in a deserted quarry, which—it seemed—was considerably more than Berrill had ever done.

One glance at his diagram showed quite plainly that the only destructive effect his peculiarly placed packs of gelignite were ever likely to have would be on the unfortunate chap who let them off. I was busily explaining this to him in words of one syllable when the Brigadier suddenly stalked in and demanded to know if the scheme had been prepared yet. 'Not yet, sir, I'm afraid,' replied Berrill blandly, 'it's a bit beyond me, but I think Fisher's got a few ideas.' 'Ah yes,' said the Brigadier, swivelling round at me, 'but—' as if this were the really difficult part '—can you put them into writing?' Having reassured him that I could write, I was thereupon ordered to have my letter drafted, typed and despatched within half an hour, as the matter was urgent.

Speaking strictly off the record, I had never in fact blown up an oil well before, and I soon discovered that it wasn't quite as easy as it might at first sight appear to be. The snag lay not so much in placing the charges as in calculating their appropriate size. *The Royal Engineers Pocket Book* gave innumerable formulae for blowing up rounds, squares and T-sections of steel, iron, concrete, wood, and various other things as well, but as regards concentric rings of steel pipes (of which oil wells appeared principally to consist) it maintained what seemed to be a strange but—I felt—significant silence.

However, I selected a number of formulae which seemed to approximate vaguely to the requirements, and from them I worked out a series of widely differing figures. I took the largest of these, just to be on the safe side, but somehow it seemed much smaller than I'd expected. So, after chewing my pencil for a time, I decided to follow the advice of the lecturer back in England: 'If in doubt, double the charge and make sure of the job.' I drafted the required letter, using the new figure, and then for a few minutes sat lost in thought. War was clearly coming to South-east Asia. It would be a war for oil. The Japanese would be bound to try to seize Miri . . . I should feel an awful fool if the war—with me inside it—were to drag on for years and years, all because my scheme had failed in the supreme hour of need. Manifestly this was my moment of destiny, the time above all others when I must trust my own judgement and stand firm, or cravenly capitulate. That did it. So, putting into practice what I believe the economists call the multiplier effect, I added a nought to the figure which I had already computed, and signed the letter, which was despatched immediately.

So far as I can recall, no more news from Miri ever reached our office, and indeed I had forgotten all about it until one evening, shortly after the first Japanese attacks on Pearl Harbor, Hong Kong and Singapore, I tuned in to a news bulletin from Delhi. After recounting a whole succession of increasingly dispiriting Allied reverses, the news reader's voice suddenly took on a quite different tone as he continued more or less as follows: '. . . We have, however, one very encouraging piece of news to report tonight, namely the unexpectedly successful demolition of the famous oilfield at Miri in Sarawak. So far as we can tell—though the situation is somewhat obscure at the moment—what remains of the installations appears to be of little—if indeed any—use, and it seems most unlikely that any more oil will be forthcoming from Miri in the foreseeable future. . . .'

During the several years that have elapsed since this escapade I have dined out—and usually distinctly well—in innumerable places in England and on the Continent, as well as in Canada, the United States, Australia, Singapore and even Thailand—purely on the strength of my spectacular achievement at Miri. But all good things have to come to an end, and a year or two ago the truth—if such it was—came out at last when a visiting officer, who happened to be passing through Singapore, opined that my letter of instructions had never reached

Miri, and the local sapper officer on the spot had accordingly done the job himself. *Sic transit gloria.*

Yet even stranger jobs than the Miri demolitions were tackled from the office which I shared with Berrill and Morgan, and no account of the Pacific War could be considered complete if it omitted the history—albeit a brief one—of Morgan and the goats. Morgan, who had travelled out with me, and had been taken off some very special work in order to become Staff Officer Royal Engineers, Singapore, was astonished one morning to find in his tray an urgent order to design and build temporary accommodation for a thousand troops who had just arrived at the docks, and were to be attached to the something or other Indian Regiment. Surprise gave way to mortification next morning, however, when he received the following note: 'Re mine of yesterday: for troops read goats.' Admittedly the distinction was a trifle academic, but Morgan, who was something of a purist, scrapped his plans and started again. He took a lot of trouble over those pens and, about a week later, he rang up the officer in charge of the goats to tell him that the desirable new residences were now ready for occupation. However, he had some difficulty in getting through because, as it happened, Officer Commanding Goats was simultaneously trying to get through to him to say that the goats were dying of some obscure disease, and could he dig pits to bury them in? 'Like hell,' replied Morgan, 'chuck 'em in the Straits of Johore.'

That might well have been that, but as things turned out it wasn't. The following Saturday night the Duty Officer, Fort Canning, was wakened from his slumbers to receive a Top Priority Message from R.A.F. Headquarters: 'A number of suspicious-looking objects have been sighted by our recce planes in the Straits of Johore. They are spherical in shape, with what appear to be four spikes protruding from their upper surfaces, and it is believed that they may be a new type of enemy mine. Recommend immediate investigation.' So, in the small hours, the senior ordnance officer was hurriedly pulled out of bed and despatched to the scene of action where, through the thinning morning mists of the Sabbath, he was uplifted by the sight of a large flotilla of upturned but extinct goats, with their legs pointing reverently skywards as if in a silent benediction, as they drifted slowly and peacefully down the Straits into the encompassing waters of the South China Sea.

It was only a short time later, before I'd properly found my way around Fort Canning—let alone Singapore and the rest of Malaya Command—that I had my first experience as night duty officer at Fort

Canning. On being notified of this I naturally asked for my instructions, but was merely told to turn up a few minutes before the day duty officer went off, and he would put me in the picture. However, when I got there, in good time, the day duty officer was already straining at the leash to dash off to an evening out in town, and his only reply to my request for instructions was, 'It's all in the Standing Orders book here. Just read it through—it'll tell you all you need to know.' Adding as an afterthought something to the effect that 'if in doubt ring fortress', he vanished into the night.

One glance at the Standing Orders book showed that it would probably take all night to read it through, let alone to assimilate its contents and, sure enough, before I'd read more than the first few pages the phone rang and a very imperious voice said, 'Police [or it may have been Customs] H.Q. speaking. I am carrying out a raid against smugglers along the foreshore of the Kallang-Siglap area at twenty-hundred hours tonight. Please make sure that all guns and searchlights are alerted. Is that clear?' While my head swam with visions of horribly mutilated corpses glaringly illuminated by whole batteries of searchlights, I replied shakily that the meaning was clear, though I didn't add that I'd no idea what to do about it. 'H'm,' came the voice again, 'you don't sound very sure about it. It's a serious matter—I don't want my men shot up. Get the arrangements made without any more delay.' And with that he rang off.

For what felt like an eternity my mind seemed to be a total blank. Then—what was the place the day duty officer said I should ring if I was in doubt? Barracks? No, that didn't sound right. Castle? No—Fortress??—or was that just another name for Confusion Castle? No—that's where I was—that at least was clear—no point in ringing myself up. Frantically I tried to find Fortress in the telephone book, but it wasn't there under F. Oh hell! And then, as I thumbed through the pages, the name Singapore Fortress suddenly appeared like an oasis in the desert. I pulled myself together, dialled the number, and back came a cheerful voice: 'Duty Officer Fortress. Can I help you?' Putting on my most nonchalant Cambridge style, I said: 'Oh, good evening, Duty Officer Fort Canning here. There seems to be some sort of a flap on about a raid against some smugglers—in the Siglang-Kallap area—or is it the other way round?—you know the place, of course?' (He did, thank God, and what's more he got it the right way round.) 'They're rather anxious not to get their chaps shot up. I suppose we ought to alert the guns and searchlights—and so forth. Do you happen to know who deals with this stuff?'

'Yes, old boy,' came the heartwarming reply, 'I do. Get yourself another drink and leave it to me.' I did; but not until I'd read Standing Orders through from cover to cover, by which time a sympathetically bloodshot dawn was lighting up the eastern horizon.

In retrospect all this seems utterly trivial and even faintly amusing. Nevertheless, to make a young newly-arrived subaltern directly responsible for vital decisions in the headquarters of the key military command in South-east Asia, at a time when the Japanese air force already had advanced bases within bombing range of Singapore—the supreme target in the entire area—still seems to me to have been curiously irresponsible, though unfortunately it was by no means untypical.

Indeed, in my capacity as liaison officer with the Federated Malay States and Straits Settlements Survey Department at Kuala Lumpur, I soon learned in no uncertain terms of the lack of co-operation with which the Surveyor-General, an outstandingly able man, who had been given the wartime rank of full colonel, had to contend at the hands of lesser men, though the treatment received by Brigadier Simson was even more disgraceful. As a member of Simson's staff, with whom he had often chatted in his informal but deeply penetrating way on our voyage to Singapore, and who now occupied an office close to his, I was often called upon to assist him in sundry tasks. While for me this was a privilege which I greatly appreciated, I nevertheless found it an increasingly traumatic experience to witness Simson's transition from astonishment through frustration to anger and disgust at the way in which virtually every proposal which he, as the expert deliberately selected for the task, put forward for strengthening the appallingly inadequate defences of Singapore and adjacent Malaya, was somehow or other prevented from being put into operation. Never in the whole of my life have I seen so great a man so deeply disillusioned and so shamefully let down by the inadequacies of those who should have supported him, and the only crumb of consolation is that now, after his death—well into his eighties—the truth about Simson, the greatest man I have ever been privileged to work under, is at last coming to light[1].

During the period I spent on the staff of Fort Canning there was an acute shortage of accommodation in officers' messes in Singapore, and accordingly I—along with most other newcomers—had to find civilian

[1] Noel Barber's *Sinister Twilight*, which gives by far the best account I know of the fall of Singapore, does full justice to Simson's efforts, against impossible odds, to persuade those at the top to open their eyes.

lodgings. Fort Canning was extremely embarrassed about this supposed hardship, for which we were compensated by lavish allowances, though the great majority of us who were not professional soldiers much preferred the freedom which this arrangement gave us. So a dozen or so of us from the *Capetown Castle* draft found very congenial accommodation together in a spacious and comfortable boarding house in River Valley Road, run most efficiently by a charming and positively motherly Australian lady.

Every morning at 7.30 Ah Kwong, my Chinese boy, would seize me tentatively by the big toe, in accordance with instructions received, and—pointing to a tiny banana sheepishly accompanying my morning tea—murmur 'flute'. My suggestion that I would prefer a couple of large clarinets produced only a vacant grin and the usual 'No savvy', so I ceased to press the point. All the house boys—Ah Kwong, Ah Hung, Ah Ling, Ah Ming and Ah Choo—were Cantonese, the Ah serving as a kind of diminutive and also providing a means of emphasizing an individual's name so that it was easier to call out. They worked hard and cheerfully and, when called, used to materialize instantaneously like Jeeves. Ah Choo in particular proved to be most adept at this, but unfortunately for him it was a virtue which carried within itself the seeds of its own destruction. For a certain Captain Russell, who suffered badly from hay fever, came to the boarding house, and from then onwards Ah Choo was kept perpetually on the run by false alarms. Irritation smouldered into anger, and anger into muffled rage, until, a few days later, open mutiny threatened. So Russell, who was a nervous little man and had recently seen a film about the Taiping Rebellion, took fright and departed, and life resumed its even tenor, punctuated by intermittent skirmishing between those of us who were sappers and those who belonged to the Dental Corps. I suppose we could have compromised and called both groups dental mechanics.

However, my duties as liaison officer with the (civilian) Survey Department necessitated fairly frequent absences from Singapore, as Noel Bridges, the Surveyor-General was anxious for me to have first-hand knowledge of every aspect of their work. Moreover, being a very clear-minded man, he insisted that I should learn the job in correct sequence, and I therefore began with a week in Kedah, in the far north-west of Malaya, where I accompanied a field survey party in dense jungle to learn the wholly unfamiliar but highly ingenious techniques which the Survey Department had worked out for surveying, in effect, in the dark. For, since it was rarely possible to see more than twenty yards ahead in the rain forest, we often had to take bearings by sound instead of sight, the man at the other end indicating his presence by singing out, preferably in a deep bass voice which was not likely to be mistaken for birdsong, though perhaps it might have been confused with the trumpeting of a young elephant.

Although there were elephants, as well as tigers, in the jungle, I soon discovered that the degree of trouble we encountered from the local fauna was inversely proportionate to their size. While the elephants and tigers kept their distance, snakes of many kinds were everywhere—above, below and beside us—but much the most unpleasant were the leeches which managed to get through puttees and even boots, to fasten themselves into our legs and feet and then suck away to their hearts' content. Meanwhile insects of every size and shape abounded, and at times we seemed to live in a haze of ravenous mosquitoes, as well as being simultaneously scratched by sharp-spined vegetation. Although I was under the supervision of a most congenial young Australian, who had explored extensively in even worse conditions in New Guinea, I cannot pretend that I became an enthusiastic jungle surveyor, but it was certainly a fascinating experience.

Moreover the visit to Kedah also provided my first opportunity to see the Malayan countryside, and like all newcomers I was enchanted by the beauty of the flooded ricefields, reflecting the rich colours of the sky, changing from pink through carmine to crimson as the day advanced from dawn to sunset, while great piles of towering snow-white cumulus clouds prepared the scene for the grand spectacular of the late-afternoon or evening thunderstorm. Most captivating of all, however, were the people, especially the diminutive and soulful little brown boys astride ferocious-looking water buffaloes, caked in grey mud from wallowing in the ricefields to cool themselves down. Everyone from toddlers to greybeards instinctively seemed to realize what so many of us in the West have forgotten—that life is for living, that loveliness is to be loved, and that a stranger is to be befriended.

After this idyllic interlude my next task was to spend three weeks in the Survey Department's headquarters in Kuala Lumpur, first in the Computing Department, where my training at Fort Widley stood me in good stead, secondly in the Drawing Office, under the direction of a most whimsically entertaining Scot, John Moir, and finally in the Reproduction Department or, in other words, the map-printing works. Apart from the most senior two or three people in each department, who were British or Australians, virtually the entire staff were local people, that is Malays, Indians (mostly Tamils) or Chinese. Significantly each of these three communities clearly preponderated in one of the three main departments. Yet this was in no sense an organized segregation into racial groups, but represented a quite spontaneous recognition on the part of the people themselves of the particular respects in which each culture excelled. Thus Indians dominated the computational work because they had been brought up in an awareness of the great mathematical tradition of India; the Chinese gravitated automatically to the drawing office because they had known since childhood that skilled calligraphy, the hall-mark of civilized man, is based on excellence in brush-work; and the Malays, whose traditions were more rural than urban, and who therefore were more interested in practical matters than in book learning, took to machinery, whether printing or vehicular, like ducks to water.

So the Federated Malay States and Straits Settlements Survey Department was a veritable microcosm of Malaya and as such was the most colourful, cheerful and friendly place I have ever worked in, which was not really surprising to anyone who knew Noel Bridges, a moral and intellectual giant of a man, who towered above the great majority of the expatriates in what was then the rather pretentious little white-man's-capital of the Federated Malay States.

It was shortly after my arrival in Kuala Lumpur that it suddenly occurred to me that although there were then more than two million Chinese in Malaya (including Singapore) I had not, so far as I knew, seen a single Japanese there, though on checking the figures I discovered that there was in fact a small Japanese community of rather fewer than ten thousand. Most of these fell clearly within one of three occupational groups, namely barbers, photographers and commercial representatives. While the last category seemed obvious enough, the other two were generally assumed by the British to be disguises for spying activities, the barber's shop providing the collecting centre for gossip and other surreptitious information, while photographers took apparently innocuous pictures which usually however also managed to include some place or object of military significance in the background.

What brought this to my attention was a chance encounter in the street with yet another of my old *Capetown Castle* colleagues, a Captain Lister of the Intelligence Corps who, much to my surprise, was not in army uniform but in 'civvies'—or what the army in its curious way used to call 'undress uniform'. Seeing him thus undressed, I asked facetiously if he'd been unfrocked or dismissed from service. With a broad smile he disclaimed this distinction, and went on to explain that, as the army wanted him to improve his knowledge of Japanese, they had arranged for him to receive instruction from a Japanese teacher resident in Kuala Lumpur. This man was known to be the Number One Japanese spy in the Federal capital, a fact which Lister had already been informed of, and meanwhile the spy knew that Lister knew that that was what he was.

A face-saving formula was therefore worked out. Whenever Lister went for his Japanese lesson he went in civilian clothes and if, by any mishap, he met his teacher in the street neither recognized the other. If, however, Lister was in uniform and met his teacher in the street, common courtesy between Lister as the pupil and the spy as his teacher required that the former should pay his respects to the latter, so both recognized each other in the appropriate order of deference. So face was preserved, the Orient remained inscrutable, and the Japanese conquered Malaya a few weeks later.

Another small incident which also occurred during my few weeks in Kuala Lumpur also left a sharp but very different kind of impression on my consciousness. Being rather late for a lunch appointment one day, when the sun—virtually overhead—was scorchingly hot, and I was rapidly beginning to liquefy, I decided to stop walking and hailed a rickshaw. Feeling very satisfied with my decision, I lay back and relaxed, relishing the slight breeze which was produced as the Chinese rickshaw coolie began to trot at a steady seven or eight miles an hour along the shadeless road. And then suddenly he was racked with the most appalling cough I'd ever heard, and he began to spit blood. I yelled to him to stop trotting but, no doubt because he was counting on getting the price we'd already agreed on for the longish journey, he didn't want to stop. As he turned round to expostulate with me I realized that this pathetically emaciated wreck of a man was more than old enough to be my father. I jumped out, paid him two or three times the agreed fare, and told him to sit down and rest for a bit. He looked at me in total amazement, as if I was out of my mind. And then it dawned on me that he was quite right: for no society that permits a tubercular old man to be treated as a beast of burden by a healthy well-fed twenty-five-year-old can seriously be regarded as sane. But how else could he earn enough to live on?

Although my stay in Kuala Lumpur proved to be both useful and interesting I could never understand why most of the pre-war British community preferred K.L., as they always called it, to Singapore which, by any standards, was an impressive, well-ordered and stimulating city, with a magnificent frontage on to the open sea whose invigorating breezes seemed to infuse the whole community with a zest which was conspicuously absent from K.L. Indeed, both climatically and socially K.L. struck me as an exceptionally stuffy little place, whose expatriates kept themselves largely to themselves. Everybody within that circumscribed little 'in-group' knew everyone else, which was boring, or if he didn't he knew somebody else's wife, which was worse.

Fundamentally, however, the trouble was that K.L. was a sham, thought up by Frank Swettenham, a much inferior man to his great predecessor, Stamford Raffles, whom he apparently aspired to outshine in the history books of the future. Thus, whereas Singapore and indeed all the Straits Settlements were unashamedly cosmopolitan, the Federated Malay States and especially K.L. pretended to be 'the real Malaya' though in fact their population was more Chinese and Indian than Malay, and their wealth came overwhelmingly from the tin and rubber produced mainly by the labour of these two immigrant communities.

Alongside the harsh reality that the Malays were thus being pushed into the background in their own country by the influx of more immigrant labour from China and India, the excessively spectacular government buildings and railway station, complete with minarets and other frenzied fancies 'in the modern Moorish style' as the official handbook put it, were inexcusable extravagances which had fooled nobody—except perhaps Swettenham himself—into believing that this was still a predominantly Muslim, Malay country. Nor indeed was it recognizably any other kind of country, for in Western terms it remained a cultural desert, while its attractive indigenous traditions still awaited the call of *merdeka* (independence) to give them the kiss of life.

Not surprisingly, therefore, I was glad to return to Singapore where I had already made many friends, particularly among the local Chinese and other Asian communities. Time passed quickly during my first two weeks back in this dynamic and fascinatingly cosmopolitan metropolis, as I was invited to innumerable bathing parties on Siglap beach, followed by a seemingly unending sequence of Chinese dinner parties. So, surrounded by bevies of local beauties in tantalizingly slit cheongsams, I consumed suckling pig with chopsticks and shouted *yam seng!* as I downed my *samsu*, before finishing up at midnight Malay *ronggengs* and *makans* in secluded *kampongs* that looked so realistic that I almost expected to find Dorothy Lamour reclining on the nearest tiger-skin.

Much less enjoyable, however, were the occasional dinner parties to which some of our senior officers invited us newcomers, for I was not good at concealing my prejudices about their prejudices. At my first such encounter I blotted my copybook irrevocably when our excessively languid hostess began by asking me if I wasn't frightfully bored with Singapore. When I replied that, on the contrary, it seemed to be one of the most fascinating cities I'd ever been in, she was totally nonplussed. 'What on earth's fascinating about Singapore? It's got no history—the only place with any history in Malaya is Malacca and that's too much of a sleepy hollow to interest anyone.' I explained that what I found most interesting about Singapore was its people. 'Its *people*? *What* people?' she asked. I battled on to add that I found the great diversity of racial and cultural groups, living and working cheerfully side by side in Singapore, utterly fascinating. 'Good God, you mean the natives! What on earth's fascinating about them? The Chinese are only interested in making money; the Malays are bone idle; and the Tamils smell.' I have never ceased to regret that I didn't tell her that both she and I also smelt, but that the Asians, among whom she'd lived much longer than I had—though apparently without making any attempt to comprehend them—found our smell more pungent than theirs. More specifically our greater consumption of animal fat and protein led them to think that we smelt like cheese. They were, of course, quite right in this assumption; we did, and we still do, especially when we perspire heavily in hot and humid weather.

Much the most distasteful aspect of such people's behaviour was the despicably disparaging way in which some of them would talk about their servants in the latters' presence. To me this subtle but deliberate attempt to destroy another—and far less secure—human being's self-respect was the most contemptible form of petty cruelty I had ever witnessed, and not least so because most—if not all—of the servants concerned were decent, hard-working and—incredible though it may seem—thoroughly loyal people, trying to do the best they could to please these inscrutable Occidentals lording it in self-imposed authority over them.

Fortunately colour prejudice of the kind I have described was far from being universal among the expatriates, though it was depressingly common among the upper strata of the military, particularly the 'county' regiments and other supposedly 'heaven-born' groups who apparently still believed, against all the evidence, that they were born to command. Indeed, ever since my early days as a private in the Suffolk Regiment, I have always felt that the upper crust of the army laboured under the delusion that a verse had been inadvertently omitted from the second chapter of Genesis (between verses 27 and 28) which should have read approximately: 'Officers and men created he them, each after his kind; and the officers shall have dominion over the men; and never the twain shall meet.'

By contrast, the many members of the Malayan Civil Service whom I got to know, and in particular those at the District Officer level, were almost without exception genuinely and impartially concerned for the well-being of all the communities within their respective districts, and while their attitudes were unashamedly paternalistic, they were not lacking in wisdom, idealism or down-to-earth common sense. Moreover, among the expatriate commercial element, in the widest sense of that term, racial prejudice was not conspicuous, if only for the obvious and essentially pragmatic reason that business took precedence over sentiment.

For my own part, however, by far the most congenial group of people I encountered was the Singapore Orchestral Society, which must surely have constituted the most multi-coloured and polyglot bunch of musicians—nearly all amateurs—who ever played together. The cellos, for example, included one French lady, two Australians, an Indian medical student, a young Chinese, and myself, more or less, I regret to say, in that order of proficiency. The violins, understandably in view of their greater number, were even more variously assorted, while the smallest member of the orchestra—a diminutive little Chinese girl—played the largest instrument of all, the double-bass—though she had to stand on a wooden box to do so. But the most delightful juxtaposition of all was presented by our two flautists, the one a handsome grey-haired lieutenant-commander, R.N., invariably in spotless white ducks with lashings of gold braid, and the other a soulful-looking little Malay boy in his early teens. These two shared a desk, and could frequently be seen during intervals engaged in earnest man-to-man discussions on fingering and allied problems, each treating the other with the utmost courtesy and deference.

For large public concerts we needed to reinforce ourselves with an assortment of trumpeters, trombonists and other brass performers from the band of whatever British regiment happened to be temporarily stationed in Singapore. The combined effect had to be heard to be believed, but we all enjoyed ourselves immensely, and for my part I have never since had any doubt that music is the most satisfying of all the arts, for its language knows no frontiers and its message transcends all creeds.

Of all the three main Asian communities in Malaya the British tended to get along best with the Chinese, quite simply because both were so completely convinced of their own innate superiority over all other forms of human life that neither ever entertained the possibility that this might not be so. Admittedly there were times when the British were distinctly suspicious of Chinese intentions towards Malaya, notably during the early 1930s when, under the Kuomintang regime, there was much talk of Malaya as 'China's nineteenth province'. But, especially after Japanese aggression in Manchuria was followed in 1937 by much deeper and more sinister inroads into China proper, many of the Malayan Chinese began to draw closer to the British. For both were deeply alarmed by Japanese expansionist ambitions which became more and more strident and increasingly focused on Malaya, and especially on Singapore as the supposedly impregnable fortress guarding the seaways to both India and Australia. It was in this context that Brigadier Simson, with a foresight unequalled by any of the other leading figures, military or civilian, in Singapore, urged the need for taking the Singapore Chinese leaders into the confidence of the British administration, in order to prepare more effectively to meet the growing threat which the Japanese posed. But again, despite all his efforts, which were welcomed by many of the more far-sighted Chinese, he received little or no support from the mostly unimpressive group of blinkered expatriates who controlled the levers of power, with the result that the battle for the survival of Singapore was lost before it began.

Thus, notwithstanding my pleasure at returning to Singapore at the beginning of December 1941, it was already clear that time was fast running out, and I felt a sense of foreboding when, a few days later, my second tour as night duty officer came round. However, being by now much more familiar with the local situation, I felt far more self-possessed than on the first occasion. It was as well that I did, for shortly before midnight the telephone rang and I received a message that the Japanese navy had been sighted moving southwards into the South China Sea, and appeared to be heading for Singapore. After taking the necessary action I remained on duty until my relief arrived next morning and, after a shower and some breakfast, I spent the following day in the office, returning to my digs in the evening. But although I felt tired enough to sleep through anything, I awoke with a start in the small hours to the chatter of anti-aircraft guns and the swish of a descending bomb which landed less than fifty yards from my bedroom.

Back on duty at Confusion Castle that morning we were given a fatuous briefing to the effect that a few Japanese soldiers had been landed on a beach in south-eastern Thailand (a short distance north of the border with Malaya) but, when last seen, 'the little men' appeared to be running back to their landing craft! Yet so thoroughly accustomed had we become to facile optimism of this kind that, when I got back to Morningside in the late afternoon of 10 December I found my Dental Corps friends helpless with laughter at the supposed naïveté of the Japanese in thinking that anyone would believe their latest news flash, which claimed that they had just sunk both the battleship *Prince of Wales* and the battle cruiser *Repulse*. But two hours later all such laughter likewise sank without trace as the evening bulletin from New Delhi confirmed that these two great warships, totally bereft of fighter cover, had indeed been sunk by Japanese torpedo bombers.

Reactions to this appalling news obviously differed widely in different parts of the world, but I doubt whether any were quite so ridiculously inappropriate as those of our little group at Morningside. Within a few minutes a violent argument had broken out between those who were still in favour of going to the Cathay Cinema—as we had all planned to do—and those who rallied to the stirring words of one of the dentists that *he* was not prepared to fiddle while Singapore fell. I, on the other hand, adhered to the opposing group which remained irrevocably committed to Madeleine Carroll (which clearly dates us rather badly) and weren't going to miss her even if Singapore was facing annihilation. So we split into two warring factions, though I was the only one in either group who possessed any form of armament—specifically my service revolver with six rounds of ammunition. The totally disarmed dentists remained at Morningside and were miserable, while the other more romantic lot went to the Cathay and were equally miserable, Madeleine Carroll notwithstanding.

However, as we romantics returned very disgruntled, very late, and in almost total darkness, we were met at the driveway by the non-fiddling dentist who whispered, 'There's someone up that tree signalling to the Japanese planes. He keeps flashing a light at them—Look——' and, sure enough, there was a flash, though not a very brilliant one. 'Have you got your revolver, Fisher?'

'Sure,' I said, 'and it's got six rounds in it.'

'Well then, challenge him, and if he doesn't reply, shoot.' So, when the next flicker of light appeared up the tree I challenged, without getting any reply, and repeated this performance five times, until I had used up all my ammunition and, like the boy on the burning deck, I finally stood shorn of any means of either attack or defence. Nevertheless, all was not lost, for at this juncture it slowly began to dawn on us that the lights, which were now much more frequent, were coming from all over the garden, which was alive and positively lit-up with glow-worms.

Psychologically the simultaneous sinking of the two great warships, *Prince of Wales* and *Repulse*, on 10 December 1941, produced Malaya's long overdue moment of truth, but it had come too late to be of any avail. From the day I first arrived in Singapore, in mid-August 1941, I had never ceased to marvel at the all-pervading atmosphere of 'business as usual'. Virtually every significant organization—not excluding Fort Canning itself—took a leisurely week-end as if this were a normal peacetime situation. Shops, hotels and restaurants were doing a roaring trade in luxuries, most of which were far beyond my range as a mere army officer on Malaya Command Headquarters staff. To us, coming direct from a grimly embattled Britain, the contrast between our own long-accustomed austerity and the overflowing opulence of this city of sandy-headed ostriches, seemed a positive affront. But woe betide any service man who dared to say so. 'Everyone', we were told *ad nauseam*, 'knows that Malaya is making a magnificent contribution to the war effort.' Her task, she was being told daily, was to produce all the tin and rubber she possibly could, and what better way could there be of serving one's country than by spending the war years in making handsome profits by producing goods which were so urgently needed?

But that was not all. While all over Britain the hoardings were exhorting everyone to 'Lend to defend the right to be free', Malaya seemed surreptitiously to have replaced the word 'lend' by the more seductive 'spend'. Whenever I was moved to expostulate at the sight of crates of luxury goods, like chocolates or silk underwear, long since unobtainable at home, bearing the proud motto 'Britain delivers the goods', I was treated to lengthy lectures from ardent local expatriates on the necessity of buying as many British goods as possible, and so putting money into the mother country.

If I persisted with my minority view that it would be even better to pay British rates of income tax, I was usually told to go and study the local Chinese problem, which in fact I had been doing for quite a time. Not unnaturally the Malayan Chinese disliked the idea of paying income tax to the British, when they were saving all they could to send home to help China in its even more desperate struggle against the common Japanese enemy.

But surely that was no reason why the expatriate British, who were now doing even better than usual in Malaya, should not pay British rates of income tax, though presumably that would have been opposed on the grounds of racial inequality, which the Governor had assured everyone would in no circumstances be tolerated. Nevertheless it struck me as very strange that the much maligned 'heathen Chinese' should have had so superior a grasp of their country's plight than did so many of their far more affluent British counterparts in Malaya.

However, by the time the Japanese had landed on Singapore Island, I had no time to spare for such thoughts, as my main preoccupation was to get copies and printing plates, plus relevant information of all maps out of the country by whatever means, and at all costs. It entailed days and nights of blood, tears, toil, and sweat in the docks, which were none too healthy at the time; and, when that was finished, there remained the dreary job of burning all the maps that were left, maps which had been produced with such difficulty and efficiency, in some cases only a few days previously. That brought us to Friday 13 February, when I helped my remaining civilian friends aboard the last ships that were leaving. Some of the sights of those last days at the docks will never be forgotten. Sick and dying being carried aboard overcrowded ships; civilians and certain selected military people, who were leaving, trying hard not to feel embarrassed; and those who were staying pretending not to be sick with envy; and far and away the worst of all, the partings between husbands who had to stay, and wives who didn't want to go. One civilian friend of mine, who was afraid he wouldn't be able to get a passage, drove into the docks in one of the smartest sportscars in Singapore, got out and blacked himself and his clothes with grease and dirt and, after joining a crowd of sailors shovelling coal into a ship, stowed away on her in the engine-room later in the afternoon. Meanwhile I was offered a berth on the same ship by the skipper! I have sometimes wondered why I didn't take it, though of course it would have been against orders to do so.

Having finished everything I had to do, I spent the last night before the end helping the F.M.S. Volunteer Forces Field Survey Coy. who were flash spotting from the top of the Cathay building, Singapore's largest cinema-cum-block-of-flats. Throughout the last week a thickening pall of oily smoke hung over the city. It looked gloomy and sinister enough by day, but at night, lit up by the lurid flames of burning buildings and dumps, and the wild flashes streaking from the big guns, its gaudy hideousness transcended anything I had ever imagined. The whole, tightly packed sky seemed to be pressing down on top of one, while the contracting circle of enemy artillery, lit up in an almost continuous blaze round the long, ragged skyline, completed the feeling of claustrophobia. It was pretty hot on the roof of the Cathay that night. Mortar bombs whistled by far too frequently for my liking, but the flash spotting was able to continue, and made possible the silencing of several guns before daybreak.

Late the following afternoon, news came through that at five p.m. the Union Jack would be hauled down from Government House, and all resistance would then cease. There followed an orgy of destruction. Papers and records were burned, revolvers, cameras and theodolites hacked to pieces. As the frenzy subsided, we collected what personal kit we could carry and, in accordance with instructions, improvised a white flag which we stuck on the pole outside the door; then we waited. Five o'clock passed, but the firing continued, sporadically at first, and then more heavily as the light began to fade. Just before dark, the sound of a motorbike approaching along the drive made us sit up. But instead of the Japanese, as we expected, it turned out to be our adjutant looking pale and harassed, bearing a message which he handed to the commanding officer. The latter uttered one unprintable remark and then read out: 'From III Corps H.Q. To all units. There is no truth whatever in the rumours that are circulating concerning a cease-fire order. No such thoughts must be considered by any troops in the area. Fighting continues to the last.' We hitched up our lower jaws and tried to take it in. Was it treachery, or a mistake, or just the usual incompetence? Somebody remarked bitterly that, having messed up the campaign from start to finish, we couldn't expect to start capitulating with any greater efficiency.

Meanwhile we had neither arms nor equipment; it was getting late, and we were hungry. But firing had almost ceased now, and we decided to make for the Survey Headquarters in Fullerton Buildings, a mile or so away. As we passed the Government offices we saw a large crowd listening to something being announced from the steps. It was the official notification of surrender being made by the Governor. So that was that. We climbed the five flights of stairs to the Survey Department, the lifts having been out of action for some days. We swallowed a few whiskys and, after exchanging a few pointless platitudes, settled down for the night on the more comfortable-looking parts of the floor.

Contrary to expectation, no Japanese fighting troops entered the city, and Singapore was thus at least spared the horror of a raging mob of battle-drunk hooligans. But the little hero gods—as their press so disarmingly described them—were not deprived of their just deserts. Lorryloads of terrified young Chinese women could be seen next morning being driven out to the waiting warriors in the suburbs. Co-prosperity was on its way. Grinning, bowing, little officers, fawning upon the disgusted populace, were strutting through the streets, so puffed up in their own conceit that one expected to hear them pop at any moment. But the people of Singapore were not amused, and the only expression visible on the faces of the Chinese crowds was one of unqualified contempt. British troops wandered unmolested about the city during the whole of Monday, but early on Tuesday morning orders were published that all must be within the Changi perimeter by nightfall.

Changi was a vast military cantonment situated at the eastern end of the Island, some fifteen miles from the city centre. A certain amount of transport was provided for essential stores and wounded; the rest of us marched, carrying whatever we could. I decided to report back to Command Headquarters in order to keep with my friends so, having said goodbye to the Survey Company, I made my way to Fort Canning and tacked myself on to the tail-end of one of the last parties to march off.

The time was a few minutes past midday and it was sizzlingly hot. At the first main crossroads an Indian truck driver, presumably of strong political opinions, tried to run us down—and nearly succeeded—and, a little later, another Indian sepoy passed us, studiously omitting to salute the commanding officer, who was marching in front. The officer in question was a large, red and rotund colonel, with a face like a pork butcher. He halted the whole column, stormed up to the terrified Indian, and in a voice like the last trump, only more so, gave him the most violent dressing-down I have ever witnessed. By the time it was over the sepoy was quivering with fright; he saluted about fifty times in all directions, and then bolted like a rabbit. But the incident had served a useful purpose. I had spotted a new pair of shoes, a few socks, and a pullover that some overladen predecessor had discarded, and while the fun was at its height I managed to nip out of the ranks and grab them, thereby practically doubling my wardrobe.

As the march proceeded the road became more and more choked with troops and transport; each successive crossroads saw fresh contingents of men, all converging on the Changi road. Innumerable forced stops soon brought our average rate of advance down to little over a mile an hour, and at that miserable pace we crawled the remaining ten miles of the journey. Sleek Japanese staff cars screamed by in unending streams, sometimes driving us into the ditch, while others slowed down to enable the cocky little press photographers on the running boards to snap us as they passed. In many places the streets were littered with débris, or blocked by unexploded bombs; and blackened corpses, one with a long string of charred entrails dangling from its middle, were almost trodden underfoot in the crush.

Outside the town itself, sometimes for a mile at a stretch, Asians, mainly Chinese, lined the road, staring in silent amazement at us as we trudged by. There was no trace of exultation or contempt in their expressions; the Chinese knew too well what they were in for to indulge in any such cheap feelings at our expense. Most were obviously ill at ease, and many actually in tears, as they watched our endless procession winding along the dusty road. As the afternoon wore on, the heat and stench became almost unbearable; several people collapsed and had to be hoisted on to passing trucks, and the demand for water grew ever more acute. At one point, where we halted for a few moments, stood a small squatter's hovel, nearly hidden under the rubber. The occupant, an ordinary low-class Chinese, dripping with sweat, was working like mad at the windlass of his little well, and all his family were rushing round carrying out water to the troops as fast as they fell out. Many of the latter, in their gratitude, offered him money, in one case a ten-dollar bill, which meant a good deal more to a Chinese peasant than ten pounds would mean to an English farm labourer. But he refused to take a cent, and merely carried on with his job, regardless of anything else. And there were many others like him. The superbly dignified behaviour of the humblest Chinese on that unforgettable day, and indeed throughout the terrible bombings of Singapore before, and under the studied insolence and cruelty of the Imperial Japanese Army personnel, was the one redeeming feature of the decline and fall of Singapore.

Per contra, the most contemptible aspect of this whole disgraceful episode, which made inevitable what Churchill described as 'the worst disaster and largest capitulation in British history', was the way in which expatriate British colour prejudice had been allowed to blind the Singapore administration to the true character of its Chinese population. For, as the events described in the preceding paragraphs show, the sympathies of the vast majority of the Chinese community, comprising over two-thirds of the island's total population, could readily and loyally have been harnessed in support of the Allies, most obviously because China, their ancestral homeland to which they remained deeply attached, was itself fighting for survival against the same Japanese enemy.

Though less spectacular in scale than the infamous Bataan 'Death March' in the Philippines, our march into Changi bore obvious traces of the same basic orchestration. By the time I myself—now wholly separated from any of my friends—hobbled into Changi close on midnight, the pandemonium of horrors which had filled the preceding twenty-four hours had subsided, and I was left with a total numbness of body and spirit. Without even a sheet to cover me I lay down on the polished stone floor of the crowded cubicle into which I had stumbled in the dark. Only as I was finally slipping over the threshold of consciousness into fitful sleep did I remember that I had not had a bite of food during the entire day.

3. MYSTERIOUS FRIENDS

You and I met on the battlefield as enemy each other. But it was the collision between the two countries. This fact does not mean that there were private enmity and hate between you and us. Now we shaking hands are not enemy already. We are mysterious friends that have met here by mysterious Providence.

Extract from Message to the Transport Company by L. Fukuda.

In trying to recall our state of mind when, at dawn on 17 February 1942, our first day in captivity, we stumbled slowly out of troubled sleep into painfully stiff semi-consciousness, I am instantly reminded of the unintentionally comic words of the Old Testament: '. . . and when they arose early in the morning, behold they were all dead corpses' (2 Kings 19:35).

Yet although that was exactly how we did feel at first, it was not long before the early morning sunshine flooding over the magnificent Straits of Johore, immediately outside our barrack block, began to warm our chilled bodies and gave a lift to our dejected spirits. Nevertheless, although few of us at this stage expected any serious brutality at the hands of our Japanese captors, none of us pretended that the prospect of at least three years of captivity was anything other than profoundly dispiriting. Since events had moved so quickly during the preceding few weeks we had scarcely had time to consider what captivity might entail, but as we now began to think about it, the outlook assumed an increasingly gloomy aspect.

For, virtually overnight, we had descended from the top of the priority list, as British military personnel in Malaya, to the bottom level among our Japanese captors' non-essentials. To put it bluntly, the prisoner of war is merely an unwanted addition to the victor country's burden, merely another body to feed and clothe, and while it may be possible to get some work out of him, this is likely to be only reluctant and unskilled labour, and in South-east Asia there were millions of local people who could do this more efficiently and even more cheaply than European prisoners.

Not surprisingly, many of our older members found it much harder to adjust to our new situation than the rest of us did, and one of them spent several days in apparently total bewilderment, endlessly reiterating 'I can't take it in.' More significant was the reaction of our old Japan hand, the oldest man in Changi. At the sight of several hundreds of our well-tanned troops, clad only in a pair of shorts, I had commented to him that most of them looked remarkably fit. 'Oh yes,' he replied, 'they're fit enough now, but only a remnant will ever come out alive.' Little did I realize how near the truth he was. Meanwhile, however, our immediate problem was that for two days the Japanese hadn't given us any food at all. In a few days, so it was said, they would start issuing us with some sort of rations, but until then we were to feed ourselves. Our British quartermaster at Farey Point, Changi, took stock of the little pile of tinned food which he had been able to scrounge, and announced that, until further notice, there would be two 'light meals' a day, one at ten in the morning and the other at six in the evening. I was so ravenous from the previous day's exhaustion and privation that the single slice of bacon and two army biscuits which constituted breakfast made no impression at all, and I spent the afternoon in a vain attempt to forget my hunger in sleep. Next day we decided that from ten until six was too long a stretch to survive on such a breakfast, so 'dinner' was put forward to five p.m. The result was, if anything, worse, for we were so sickeningly empty by the time it got dark that most of us lay awake all night.

Not all units were as short of food as we were; some who had managed to get hold of a truck brought in substantial supplies which tided them over this initial lean time. During these early days an interesting and instructive incident occurred. One afternoon, as I was trying to doze, the noise of a dog yapping in the next building proved so irritating that I went out to see if anything could be done to shut it up. I arrived at the verandah just in time to see a well-fed-looking officer presenting the young mongrel with the full contents of a tin of salmon, which represented as much food as I had seen in the last three days. I learned more about the psychology of Communism in that instant than I had ever suspected before. However, a useful little trick, taught me by our old Japan hand, helped me through the remaining stretch on starvation diet. A teaspoonful of salt, and the same quantity of pepper, swallowed fairly slowly at about hourly intervals, can relieve hunger surprisingly effectively, at least for a time. So I scrounged a small quantity of both commodities, and consumed them in secret in the manner prescribed.

Towards the end of the week the Japanese, faithful to their promise, began to issue us with daily rations and the immediate worry, that of gnawing hunger, ceased for the time being. The food—almost entirely rice—was unbelievably insipid, and for a long time, until the army cooks could be persuaded not to cook it like a rice pudding minus milk, sugar and salt, it was appalling in its gluey consistency. But at least it filled up the stomach and quieted the rumblings within. The average B.O.R. (British Other Ranks) proved very pig-headed in his refusal to 'go native', as he termed cooking rice in the Oriental fashion, and indeed any culinary innovation suggested by more far-seeing members of the community usually met with stiff and protracted opposition. For example, in order to overcome the very serious salt deficiency, caused by heavy perspiration, we decided in our building to boil our rice in sea water, and to this end laid on a fatigue party of officers to collect half a dozen buckets full of brine from the beach every day before breakfast. After this had been going on for weeks, someone discovered that our troops had invariably chucked the whole lot of brine down the drain as soon as the officers' backs were turned, because they 'didn't like their rice salty'.

Beri-beri, the most common of the vitamin B1 deficiency diseases, began to show itself almost at once, striking first, oddly enough, at quartermasters and other heavy drinkers, and thereby causing terrible panic in high places. Clearly some addition had to be found to the diet, or the whole lot of us would certainly succumb. Two suggestions went a long way towards saving the situation. The first, yeast culture, was rapidly taken up throughout the whole area, and soon we were all drinking a new version of our once familiar little nightcap at sundown again. Still more efficacious, however, was the consumption of fertilizer and cattle-cake. Supplies of these highly unpalatable commodities were provided by our hosts, and we consumed them, raw or baked into horrid little biscuits, according to taste. So, for the moment, the crisis passed and the beri-beri incidence fell off to some extent. Meanwhile other avenues were being explored, gardens planted in the first few days came into early fruition, thanks to the equatorial climate, and some more adventurous spirits began experimenting with the cooking of various birds, monkeys and snails, and the brewing of sinister concoctions from suspicious-looking herbs. A black market in tinned goods also started up, but its prices rocketed so swiftly that only a few plutocrats were able to keep pace with them. A group of us patronized it once, for the most expensive birthday party I've ever participated in. We had a tin of sausages, and another of fruit among four, and it seemed to be the grandest moment of our lives.

A happier solution came later on with the institution, under Japanese authorization, of a limited amount of local purchase. In this way small quantities of such things as raisins, dates, bananas, and coconuts, as well as cigarettes, and, by far the most important, peanuts and red palm-oil, came into the camp. But for these last the death toll would have been immeasurably higher, particularly in the later years, among those of our number who remained behind in Changi. Red palm-oil is far from being a delicacy, but its vitamin content earns it a noble place among the world's foodstuffs. God knows what we should have done without it.

Apart from the food shortage, life in Changi during the early days was far more comfortable than we had dared to expect, for the simple reason that the Japanese, preoccupied with more urgent matters in Singapore, left us entirely to ourselves. A British interpreter maintained contact with the Japanese liaison officer, living outside the military cantonment, in Changi Jail, and within the perimeter we managed our own affairs free from interference. With the exception of one or two victory parades which we were forced to attend, and a very occasional tour of inspection by some 'high-ranking Japanese officer', we saw nothing of our hosts, and for a time lived a life that must have been almost unique in prisoner of war history.

Certainly there could be few more attractive military stations than Changi, with its clean and spacious bungalows and barracks dotted among the trees, on the hills overlooking the eastern end of the Johore Straits. Strong sea-breezes tempered the equatorial heat to something relatively bearable, and several large shark-proof enclosures—or *pagars*—provided ample facilities for safe bathing. Accommodation was admittedly a little cramped, with some fifty or sixty inhabitants to the normal one-family bungalow, but at any rate there was a sound roof over one's head, and enough space to eat and sleep without suffering acute discomfort.

Only in the complete absence of news did these early days of captivity appear to conform with our preconceived ideas. Not a breath of authentic information penetrated through to us, and although various parties went out of the camp to start cleaning up Singapore, and another to build a shrine (a leading Japanese industry, this) nobody seemed to come in. However, since mankind apparently has an insatiable thirst for news, it soon became clear that if we couldn't get any from outside, there were plenty of willing and disinterested workers in the camp ready to experiment in producing synthetic substitutes from whatever materials were available.

And so the first great spate of rumours began. The Russians, who had been rumbling heavily forwards during the previous few weeks, now shot ahead, as though on wings, before sweeping like a tornado through Eastern Europe, while simultaneously two-, three-, and sometimes even four-point naval landings were made by the British in almost every European country, including some which had hitherto possessed no known coastline. A faint air of reality was given to these dazzling Allied successes by a detailed statement delivered by one of our generals to his staff, in a fatuous attempt to raise morale, as he later admitted, though anyone with a glimmering of gumption would have realized that such nonsense would produce precisely the opposite effect once its falsity was revealed. According to this statement, the Russian 16th Army, having swept through the Baltic states, had advanced along the coast and captured Stettin, thereby linking up with the new British line which, starting somewhere in central Holland, passed through Hamburg and along the south bank of the Kiel Canal, ultimately terminating on the Baltic coast. Approximate Russian casualties were tentatively assessed at a million and a half, but the corresponding British figures were fortunately believed to be considerably lighter.

After that there was no holding our well-informed circles. Hitler had been assassinated; Queen Mary was variously reported as dead, or sinking rapidly, though an alternative source assured us that it was not Queen Mary herself who was sinking, but the R.M.S. *Queen Mary*, after a dastardly hit by a German torpedo. But to compensate for this, the Americans sank the Japanese fleet even more frequently than the Japanese press could sink the American fleet, and towards the end of March Germany was capitulating with unfailing regularity every other Friday.

The classic case of trailing a rumour was performed by a friend of mine, Evan Jones, who one night received the somewhat improbable but supposedly encouraging news from one of his non-commissioned officers that 'the Russians are in Greece'. Since this sounded rather curious, Evan decided to trace the story back to its source. After a whole day's strenuous chase, during which the rumour had not varied by a hair's breadth from its original form, he felt himself hot on the trail, when he found the corporal who had heard it himself from the sergeant arriving on the quartermaster's lorry from Singapore the previous evening. 'Yes sir, he shouted it out as plain as a bloody pikestaff as he rode past me. Good news, he says, the Russians are in Greece.' So, still mystified as ever, Evan pursued his researches right to the fountain-head, and eventually succeeded in finding the quartermaster's sergeant. The latter at first denied all knowledge of the rumour but, after he had been confronted with the corporal's story, a faint sign of recognition slowly lit up his rugged features. 'No sir, that's not what I said,' replied the honest fellow, 'Corporal Tomkinson, he looked a bit unhappy, so I shouted out to him, "Good news, corporal," I says, "the rations are increased."'

Rather similar, and certainly no less diverting, was the great wave of prophecy which, true to Biblical tradition, sprang from a period of chastening and spiritual darkness among the people, perhaps as a divine punishment for our fighting the Japanese. Soothsaying and necromancy flourished most prolifically among the Australians, who despite their hard-bitten countenances, and their even more ruthlessly masticated monosyllables, were a warm-hearted crowd. So much so, indeed, that on one occasion when a draft which eventually found its way to Burma, was about to leave Singapore, it was revealed in a vision to one of the Aussies that they were going to Timor to be repatriated, and so firmly was this believed that several of the prospective travellers generously visited the British lines and offered to deliver any mail we cared to give them.

But we also had our own astrologers and clairvoyants, mostly mysterious young privates who had previously foretold with unfailing accuracy staggering series of events, and had now begun to prophesy the precise date of our release. This, for some wholly inexplicable reason, they invariably wrote down and placed in a sealed envelope, which they deposited with their sergeant-major, presumably, though it is perhaps difficult to believe, for want of anyone better. The celebrated prophet of the Beds. and Herts. who, like the poor, was always with us, performed this mystic rite at least a dozen times with unflagging optimism during the course of our captivity, and indeed never ceased to say sooth until a few days before the end, when the growing cynicism of his neighbours eventually silenced the spirit voices.

Another case which gained much notoriety at the time was the forecast of a certain signalman that, within a specified number of weeks, his unit would be on its way home, but he would not be with them. Great excitement was occasioned when, shortly afterwards, he was suddenly taken ill, and died in hospital. But—alas—the day of liberation passed unnoticed by the Japanese, and hopes faded slowly away.

I personally knew only one of the many persons reputedly gifted with second sight and he, curiously enough, was a Malayan planter, though far removed from any available sources of whisky. From time to time, at very rare intervals, he had strangely vivid dreams, and in the last of these, some eighteen months previously, he had seen the war come to

Malaya and himself taken prisoner and incarcerated in Changi. Every morning as he came in to breakfast, his neighbours could be seen eyeing him suspiciously to see if he looked as if he'd been dreaming again. But for months his sleep seemed to exhibit the unruffled calm of a young infant, and not even the most fleeting thought disturbed his peaceful slumbers. And then one night the vision came. We were to be free in November. The precise year in question, unfortunately, was not stated, but he assured us there was good reason for assuming it to be 1942. In November 1942 we moved up to Thailand on a railway construction party. Probably that was what the vision meant after all for, on mature consideration, the seer admitted that it had only referred to our being out of Changi at the appointed time.

It was during these early days in Changi that most of us got our first close-up view of the Imperial Japanese Army *en masse*, on the occasion of their first victory parade through our area. Viewed against the background of their well-deserved reputation as an excellent fighting force, their appearance came as a profound shock to us all. To begin with, the vast majority were so small that they seemed to us to be mere boys rather than grown men, and the extreme shortness of their legs had the effect of turning their marching style into a strut which to us appeared both insufferably arrogant and excruciatingly comic. But it was above all the elation and consequent bombast of these callow rubber-necking youths—many of whom had never been more than a day's journey from their home villages in rural Japan before they had been posted overseas—which were most galling to us.

These characteristics, coupled with their complete lack of 'spit and polish', and their inability—even on a victory parade—to march (or strut) in step, created among our own well-drilled troops a sense of contempt which served only to intensify our feeling of humiliation at having been defeated by what appeared to us as a rabble rather than an army. Roman citizens in the days of the barbarian invasions must have felt much as we did in February 1942.

Moreover, and likewise related to their rural background, most of the Japanese troops appeared to be almost totally ignorant of modern machinery and equipment, and very few had any practical experience of driving cars or trucks. And, as we later discovered in Thailand, only a handful of the engineers in charge of 'railway construction wardom' knew how to construct a medium-sized bridge.

Finally—and relatedly—the Japanese tended to get extremely worked up over relatively trivial difficulties, and often became almost berserk when anything went seriously wrong. And, since they were so pathologically prone to panics and flaps, they became all the more enraged by the condescending unflappability of the British. Significantly the Japanese greatly resented any sign, real or imagined (mostly, in fact, the latter) of what they called 'proudness' (that is, pride, supposedly synonymous with an assumption of white supremacy) on our part, and at least one of our officers was made to stand to attention for hours, merely for 'looking proud' (though he was totally unaware of this crime) as he passed the Japanese guard house. Nevertheless, in the early days in Changi such incidents were very rare, if only because contact between 'us' and 'them' was still on a very small scale.

Here it is perhaps appropriate to mention that, although officially all Imperial Japanese Army personnel were referred to as Japanese, many of those involved merely in guarding prisoners and other similarly menial and humiliating tasks were Koreans, who before the war were low-paid, and mostly ill-educated immigrant labourers in Japan. In fact, though not in theory, these Koreans were treated by the Japanese distinctly as inferiors.

The more the tide of war turned against Japan and living standards in consequence deteriorated still further during 1944–5, the more miserable became the lot of the unfortunate Koreans, on whom the increasingly disillusioned and embittered Japanese troops—themselves bullied and pushed around by their own officers—vented their spleen. And, in their turn, the Koreans took it out on us, for the simple reason that we were at the bottom of the refuse dump and there was nobody else to kick.

Occasionally individual Japanese officers might peep inside a garden or bungalow in the course of a stroll round the area. At such times their politeness would be effusive and embarrassing, and, like the grin of the Cheshire cat, their gold-toothed smiles seemed to linger in the doorway long after their ungainly little figures had waddled away out of sight. And once we were privileged to hear a speech, complete with translation, from the new officer commanding all P.O.W. camps in the Southern Region, Major-General Shimpei Fukuye, the correct pronunciation of whose somewhat disconcerting name all ranks were officially instructed to learn as a matter of the highest priority. Formed up in a hollow square facing the little man, we were then treated to a blood-curdling display of Japanese sword drill, accompanied by a shattering series of staccato *banzais* ('Long live the Emperor'). Whereupon the General informed us that Japan, carefully having avoided to sign any conventions, was bound by none, but, he added as an afterthought, 'I think I shall treat you in accordance with international law.' Various threats followed about what might happen if we didn't wash behind our ears, but nobody seemed to be particularly worried, and the performance ended with a renewed burst of *banzais*.

It was at this stage, immediately after the fall of Singapore, when the course of the war was going unexpectedly well from their point of view, that the Japanese first began, little by little, to fraternize with us in Changi. Characteristically they would laugh themselves into hysterics at the sight of prisoners of war digging their vegetable gardens, assuring us, between their spasms of mirth, that the war would be over long before we got any return from our labour. One fanatical Japanese subaltern went farther, and told Brigadier Simson that any day now they would land a division on the Californian coast. Since America was entirely unprepared, nothing would be able to stop the division's triumphant march across the continent, and New York would be captured within a month. America would sue for peace and Britain would follow suit as a matter of course.

Though a certain similarity existed here to the attitude of the Germans after Dunkirk, they at least had a good deal of reason on their side, and their only serious miscalculation lay in their under-estimation of British morale. The gullibility of the Japanese on the other hand appeared to know no limits, and this was not simply a matter of education. Dr Erwin Baelz, in his fascinating diary of life in Japan, *Awakening Japan*, perhaps the most revealing study of the evolution of the modern Japanese mind, described an encounter with an official at the Japanese War Ministry shortly after their victory over the Russians at Sha-ho in southern Manchuria had been announced on 20 October 1904. 'What now?' asked the German representative of Krupps, after offering his congratulations to the official in question. Without relaxing a muscle of his face, the little man uttered the single word: 'Moscow.'

As fraternization proceeded a curious new *lingua franca*—which I called Japanglo—gradually emerged more or less spontaneously to provide at least some means of communication between the Japanese and ourselves. Although many Japanese had a smattering of English, most of it was virtually incomprehensible, at least until we had been exposed to its subtleties for some time. We picked up many Japanese words in everyday use by our captors, such as *tenko* (roll call), *suijiba* (cookhouse), *byoki* (sick), *benjo* (lavatory). From 'speedo', Japanglo for quickly or hurry up, came in turn 'speedo-benjo' for dysentery or diarrhoea—which had meanwhile become an almost universal complaint.

The Japanese themselves tacked on all kinds of excrescences to their sentences, such as *ano* (well . . .), *ano-ne* (well? . . .), *ka* (interrogatory), *danna* (I think), etc. In the process of being taken over into Japanglo, the pronunciations of English words often changed. Both Japanese and Koreans had difficulty in pronouncing F, the Japanese substituting Wh, and the Koreans P. Thus my name became Whisha to a Japanese and Pisha to a Korean. L also gave rise to difficulties, both Japanese and Koreans changing it to R (while conversely the Chinese pronounced R as L). Thus the Hall Islands in the Pacific became 'Horu' in Japanese—though Guadalcanal, which became 'Gudarukanaru', gave them the most trouble, both phonetically and militarily.

One of the most characteristic features of Japanese is that clusters of consonants are avoided, apparently on the principle that every little consonant needs his own little vowel for companionship. Hence Christmas—a very popular festival in Japan—became 'Kurisumasu', and a beefsteak a 'biputeki'.

For the most part vowels presented no problem, with the notable exception that most Japanese seemed totally unable to distinguish between 'ar' and 'er', and interchanged these sounds in the most incomprehensible way.

As an example of Japanese attempts to speak English, a few of my renderings of Co-prosperous conversations follow.

SELECTED CO-PROSPEROUS CONVERSATIONS

Vocabulary

Pinto = a slap
suijiba = cookhouse
sukoshi = little
ushi = cow
shoko = officer
meshi = food
bakayero = stupid fool
no-good-house = guard-room

GREATER EAST ASIAN (JAPANGLO)	ENGLISH
1 Thiso morning, one-o come-rooku-see-go-backo-speako-aeroprano ober my house, prying-prying.	1 A reconnaissance plane flew over my hut this morning.
2 Japan soja, he bery smoru man, he bery big worko. Engrish soja he bery big man, he bery smoru worko. No good dakarane.	2 The Japanese soldier, though small in stature, does much work. The reverse is true of the British who should try to do better.

3 Bery good, no gooddana; no gooddana O.K. (Instructions given to a Dutch officer in charge of a working party, who decoded them in 30 seconds, thereby gaining Full Marks.)

3 There is no need to work painstakingly; I shall be quite satisfied with rough results.

4 You speako my speako this man why he no speako.

4 Tell this man I want to know why he doesn't answer.

5 Tomorrow number one riso O.K.; number two riso O.K.; number three riso, suijiba riso-boxo.

5 Breakfast and lunch tomorrow will be as usual. For supper draw haversack rations from the cook-house.

6 Sukoshi-ushi-meshi-make-shoko no-good-house go.

6 The officer who prepares fodder for the calves has been sent to the guard room.

7 My pather, he number one Kurisitian man Japan. He bery goodo man—no whissaki, no kissing.

7 My father is a non-conformist minister in Tokyo. He is a total abstainer and does not indulge in womanizing.

On this basis we managed, within certain limits, to sustain some interchange of ideas and even to acquire a few scraps of news about the outside world, though most of such information remained within narrowly defined grooves. An early example of this occurred when a Japanese officer, with a tolerably good command of English, harangued a large group of us on the subject of the imminent defeat of Britain. The climax came when he informed us that German submarines had sunk virtually the entire British merchant navy and so 'there is now no more rice left in London', whereupon, to his total mystification, several hundreds of British soldiers burst into an ear-splitting orgy of cheering.

In similar vein, though at a somewhat less exalted level, one little Japanese corporal entertained us with his version of the news, approximately as follows: 'Ano, New York bomb bomb bomb, oru [all] pinish! Ano, Sydney [specially for the Aussies' benefit] bomb bomb bomb, oru pinish! Ano, Rondon, bomb bomb bomb, oru pinish!' With typical British *sang froid* his audience yelled back: 'Never mind, they'll rebuild it.' But the corporal stuck to his guns. 'No, no; Rondon no rebuild. No bamboo!'

However, one intricate linguistic problem took rather longer to resolve. Almost from the beginning of our mutual contact, certain of the more seriously minded Japanese officers, who were seizing the opportunity to improve their knowledge of English, became increasingly puzzled by a certain word which, although extensively used by the British troops, could not be found in any of their Anglo-Japanese dictionaries. Lengthy discussions followed with one of our British interpreters, as the Japanese explained laboriously that the word in question usually seemed to be a monosyllable, though on certain occasions it appeared to be lengthened by the addition of a second syllable. What puzzled them most of all, however, was that the word in question seemed at different times to be used as different parts of speech. One minute it was a noun, then it turned up as a verb, or an adverb, or even an adjective. Obviously, such a multi-purpose word was of more than ordinary utility, and accordingly our embarrassed interpreter was constantly being plagued with requests for enlightenment as to what its proper grammatical role really was.

With what can only be described as a flash of genius, however, the interpreter explained that it was in fact an honorific—a word which in itself had no precise meaning but, when juxtaposed with another word, conveyed a sense of special dignity and distinction upon the latter. For a time all went well, and the new honorific was used with ever growing frequency by all the senior Japanese officers. But, alas, the inevitable happened, when one of our troops hit his own big toe with a pickaxe and, in the course of the unorthodox but much admired war dance which followed, the honorific suddenly acquired a whole new range of meanings, none of which bore any recognizable resemblance to those with which it had previously been credited.

*

During this remarkable interlude in early-mid 1942 conditions in Changi were more or less up to the international standards prescribed by the Geneva Convention for the treatment of prisoners of war. Within a few hours of being taken prisoner scores of people had taken stock of the situation from various angles, and were drawing up plans to cope with it. Since prior attention had obviously to be given to essential services, the sappers got to work immediately on restoring the water supply and repairing such buildings and installations as required it, and no time was lost in organizing volunteer sanitation and anti-malarial squads. Even the few days of disrupted services caused by the fighting on Singapore Island had already left their mark, for nature never stands still, least of all in the tropics.

Nevertheless, much the most important side of the medical work was the running of Roberts Hospital. Hospitals of one kind or another were to loom large in P.O.W. life, but only in Changi did they bear any recognizable resemblance to those of normal times. That, however, is in no sense a reflection on the medical staff who subsequently ran those in the other camps. Although the most distinguished team, under Colonel Julian Taylor, remained for obvious reasons at the Changi base, many fine physicians and surgeons accompanied the up-country parties. If their skill was exceeded by anything it was only by their devotion to their work. But Roberts was the solitary pre-captivity hospital; elsewhere everything had to be improvised, usually with insignificant assistance from the Japanese.

Meanwhile some excellent productions were presented by the 18th Division theatrical company, notably of *Dover Road* and *I Killed the Count*, and 18th Division also led the way in the presentation of serious music, in which we possessed a real galaxy of talent. This included two pianists, Eric Cliffe and Reginald Rennison; Denis East, a violinist from the London Philharmonic Orchestra; and two singers, Padre Foster Haigh ('John Foster') tenor, and George Wall (bass), whose regular concerts invariably drew packed audiences which greatly appreciated the richness of the musical fare they were offered.

Nevertheless perhaps the most remarkable achievement of all was the founding in Changi of two P.O.W. universities which enabled many talented young men to continue their education, at least for three successive terms, during their captivity. These two institutions differed considerably in character, 18th Division University concentrating on the sort of instruction given by senior school teachers to adult pupils attending evening classes, while Southern Area University provided genuine university-level courses. This was made possible by two fortunate coincidences. First, several professors and other senior staff members of Raffles College—which was later to become the University of Malaya in Singapore (now University of Singapore)—had already joined the local defence forces, just in time to become prisoners of war with the rest of us who belonged to the regular British armed forces. Having already met some of these Raffles College staff members, I, as a captain—though as yet only a very junior part-time university teacher—was able to introduce this most congenial group of academics—now temporarily privates, corporals and lance-bombardiers—to my commanding officer, Brigadier Simson, who I knew could be relied upon to cut through all the red tape in South-east Asia in order to put into practice the suggestion which some of us had made to establish a real P.O.W. university in Changi.

The second, and in some ways even more surprising, coincidence was that there was a remarkably helpful Japanese Officer, Lieutenant Okazaki, in Changi at that time, who agreed to provide a truck to take a party of us to Raffles College in order to 'borrow'—or loot—several hundred books from its library for use in Changi University. Thus sustained bibliographically, we were able to give courses of a standard at least comparable to that of a typical British redbrick university, a claim which may seem less surprising when it is realized that our staff included such now internationally renowned scholars as Dato Sir Alexander Oppenheim (Mathematics), Professor T. H. Silcock (Economics), Professor Graham Hough (English), Dr Charles Webb (Physics); and last, but potentially one of the greatest, Professor Donald Purdie (Chemistry).

Inevitably this idyllic interlude could not be expected to last for ever, and by the middle of 1942, when the truth gradually dawned on the Japanese that the tide of war had already turned decisively against them, the whole atmosphere began to change. The first intimation of this came with the promulgation of new orders rigidly segregating the various subdivisions of the Changi area from one another, and the stationing of Sikh guards—former British Indian Army troops—along all roads to prevent our crossing them. For good measure the guards were ordered to slap our faces if we didn't salute them.

Not surprisingly this piece of typically Imperial Japanese Army behaviour caused great resentment, particularly among our Indian Army officers. However, although one or two of the Sikhs appeared to be enjoying the situation and took advantage of it to give expression to long-suppressed feelings of racial resentment, it was obvious that most of them were acutely embarrassed and found their new role extremely distasteful. We soon discovered that the great majority had been tortured before finally complying with the Japanese demands, and several of them secretly sent pitiful apologies to their officers in the Changi area.

More serious in its implications, however, was the order received by the British camp commander, Lieutenant-Colonel Holmes, on 1 September 1942, that all British officers and other ranks were to be asked to sign a declaration that they would not attempt to escape. Since British military law expressly forbade the giving of any such parole, Colonel Holmes firmly refused to order anyone to sign it. Infuriated by this resistance on our part, the Japanese next day ordered all of us to move to the barrack blocks at Selarang, inside the Australian P.O.W. area, by dusk. In effect this necessitated virtually everyone's marching a total distance of sixteen miles on a scorchingly hot afternoon, at the end of which some 17,000 men had been crowded into accommodation designed for 600, or in other words more than twenty-four times its normal capacity, a density which forced some hundreds to ooze out onto the barrack square or overflow onto the roofs, in both cases with no protection whatsoever against either rain or sun.

In the middle of all this chaos, one man suddenly developed appendicitis and was operated on in the middle of the barrack square, and another lost his nerve and tried to throw himself over the edge of the roof of a six-storey barrack block. When night descended those who could find a space lay down and tried to sleep, and those who couldn't didn't.

Next day, by standing in a queue for half an hour, one obtained some breakfast; the queue then formed up again, in a different direction leading to a latrine; about half an hour later it slewed round towards a water-point, and by midday it had completely boxed the compass and was once more facing the improvised cookhouse where lunch eventually materialized. This process more or less repeated itself during the afternoon, and after supper we washed in half a teacup of dirty water and prepared once again for the night.

Since neither the Japanese nor ourselves would climb down it seemed to be a case of the irresistible force meeting the immovable mass. But the resemblance was only superficial for, as the rapidly rising dysentery figures showed, the mass was anything but immovable. Reluctantly, our doctors insisted that if we didn't call off our resistance the situation would soon be completely out of control and widespread deaths would then be inevitable. So, regretfully, but without further hesitation, Colonel Holmes told the Japanese that he would ask everyone to sign under duress, adding in an impressively worded message to us all that such a forced signature could not and would not be regarded as morally binding. Although the Japanese obviously thought that we had lost a frightful amount of face, we in turn were convinced that we were more than one up on them. Everyone had pulled together superbly and morale was probably higher then than at any other time during our entire captivity.

*

By contrast, Japanese confidence was already beginning to sag under the impact of the news now percolating effectively into the camp from the world outside, and accordingly the Japanese began to devise more and more fantastic propaganda in an increasingly vain attempt to boost their troops' morale.

Rarely a week passed without the *Syonan Times* (the *Straits Times*, temporarily under Japanese control but still published in English; Syonan was the new Japanese name for Singapore) announcing that the American navy had been 'decisively annihilated', and another local paper achieved distinction with the arresting headline 'U.S. Navy Sunk Again'. Throughout 1942 the dazzling successes of their opening campaigns had completely blinded all but the shrewdest to the possibility of defeat and, in the absence of any trained critical faculty, their optimism remained unbounded. After all, they had only recently defeated China, and a generation earlier had similarly beaten Russia, the two largest states in the world. And who had ever defeated them in any comparable encounter? Thus, so long as they remained flushed with victory, everything seemed possible, but once it had become clear that the Japanese were losing faith in the prospect of an early and victorious termination of the war, their arrogance and cocksureness soon appeared in their true colours as mere outward trappings, rather ineffectively cloaking an acute sense of fear and weakness.

Although this sense was soon shown by subsequent events to have been amply justified, it was based not so much on sound reasoning as on intuitive feeling. Nohara, in his book *The True Face of Japan*, maintained that the processes of logical argument were anathema to his fellow countrymen, who preferred to trust their instinctive reactions. Whether that be true or not—though in general our experience confirmed it—there could be no doubt whatever that the key to the behaviour of the Japanese throughout the remainder of our captivity lay in their all-pervading sense of inferiority, whether real or imagined.

One obvious manifestation of this was their almost pathological suspiciousness, which in more normal times gave rise to the celebrated 'spy mania', and within our camps assumed the not very dissimilar form of repeated searches (referred to by a characteristic Japanese euphemism as 'domestic affairs examinations') and the consequent purloining of anything which they could not understand. All written documents were destroyed, presumably on the assumption that they might be plans for some counter-offensive on our part, and once several Bibles were removed from individual prisoners because they contained maps (of Palestine in the time of Christ) which they assumed might assist us in attempts to escape. Indeed one Welsh prisoner was much annoyed at losing his copy of H. V. Morton's *In Search of Wales*, not I think because he was believed to have been actually looking for Wales—though that would certainly have necessitated an escape—but because this book also contained a map (of Wales, presumably in the time of H. V. Morton).

Similarly, in addition to outgoing mail—even though it consisted merely of brief and purely formal postcards—all incoming letters were subjected to the most rigorous censorship, notwithstanding their advanced age, which was rarely less than a year, and their having been previously censored both in England and Japan before eventually being sent on to P.O.W. camps in Thailand. Yet I know of only one instance in which the local Japanese censor found anything to object to. A mother had written—admittedly rather tactlessly—to her son: 'Isn't it cruel of the Japs not to allow you to write to us?' Surprisingly, the trouble in this case arose not from the sentiments expressed, but solely on account of the use of the humiliating word 'Japs', which the censor had encircled in red ink, before adding the blood-curdling comment 'Take care' in the same lurid colour.

One of the least excusable aspects of Japanese behaviour towards us was their extreme dilatoriness in passing on mail from relatives at home to prisoners in their camps. From my own experience I can still recall the shock of receiving a letter informing me that my father was dying, but although my family wrote regularly throughout the entire period of my captivity, I received no further mail for well over a year.

Among the most extraordinary problems arising out of such delays (which were caused exclusively by the Japanese insistence on re-censoring already doubly censored mail) was that of a young and apparently not over sensitive soldier who received a very tender letter from his parents, breaking as gently as they could the news that he had been mistakenly reported dead, and after an interval of a year or so his wife had remarried, and sold their home, together with most of his personal belongings. His parents had gone out of their way to stress that there had been no question of infidelity on the part of his wife; that she still loved him deeply; and that as soon as he returned to England everything possible would be done to sort out this tragic situation. The prisoner himself read out aloud, very slowly and hesitatingly, the entire contents of the letter in the presence of a few close friends, who then waited with bated breath, before he eventually made his sole comment: 'I 'ope she 'asn't sold me bloody radiogram.'

To me, one of the most fascinating aspects of P.O.W. camp psychology was the way in which the behaviour patterns respectively of prisoners and captors often seemed unconsciously to mirror each other. For example, just as we, having been humiliated by defeat, kept up our morale very largely by whatever devices we could think of to make us feel superior to the Japanese, so they in turn, especially as they began to lose the war, were deliberately reminded—by the Japanese press and doubtless also by pep talks—of their innate supremacy as descendants (if somewhat remote) of the Sun Goddess. This found its most obvious expression in such practices as referring to Japanese pilots (the most admired and honoured members of the Japanese armed forces) as 'hero gods', and, in greater detail, by extraordinary accounts of the exploits of these and other members of their forces.

Among the more fantastic of these accounts, all of which I obtained during captivity from my perusal of the *Nippon Times*, the *Bangkok Chronicle* (an important English-language daily, temporarily under Japanese control) or the *Voice of Nippon*, which mysteriously found their way into our camp, was the following inspiring story.

Apparently one day a Japanese 'war-eagle' (bomber), having run out of ammunition, was returning to base when the pilot spotted an enemy Flying Fortress a few thousand feet below. The crew of the bomber were just finishing their lunch at the time, so, 'rolling the remaining rice into a ball', the gunner threw it overboard at the Fortress. The rice-ball hit the Fortress's propeller which thereupon disintegrated in mid-air, and the aircraft crashed into the jungle.

During the Philippine campaign even more wonderful things happened. A veteran warrior swam for forty-eight hours carrying, in a sealed wallet tied round his waist, a box containing his son's ashes and 'a message too important to be conveyed by wireless'. Moreover, a pilot of a dive-bomber, swooping down across the bows of an American battleship, caught sight of the miserable captain cowering behind the bridge, so, with great presence of mind, he whipped out his sword (all pilots and many other unlikely Japanese officers carried swords) and cut off the captain's head as he flew past. Nevertheless the prize must surely go to the author—alas unknown—of the story of another hero-god who, just as he was approaching his base, suddenly realized, from signs made to him by his comrades on the ground, that his undercarriage had been shot away. Nothing daunted, he zoomed up again and, while circling around for a few brief moments, drew his trusty blade, cut two holes in the bottom of the fuselage, stuck his little legs through, and—presumably while supporting the aircraft on his shoulders—'landed running on the aerodrome'.

Not all manifestations of such linguistic legerdemain were so amusing, however. During a serious outbreak of diphtheria, soon after we arrived in Thailand our captors felt they were losing a great deal of face through their inability to supply serum, which was believed to have been available in Bangkok. Diphtheria was therefore forbidden, and a burial certificate for those who died from it had to bear the legend 'heart failure' or 'suffocation' as the cause of death.

Such a psychology provided a strange setting for Western material culture and technology, but what else could one expect from a people who had been indoctrinated to believe in the literal divinity of their manifestly very human little emperor? In the end, perhaps it was easiest to take refuge in such seductive sentiments as those expessed to us by Colonel Nagatomo: 'The Imperial thoughts are inestimable, and the Imperial favours are infinite, and as such you should weep with gratitude at the greatness of them, and should mend or correct the misleading anti-Japanese ideas.'

Perhaps it would have been easiest to do just that. But my own rather strict upbringing rebelled against such slaughter of language and prostitution of logic, and I found it significant when, later on, I learned that Sir J. G. Frazer had pointed out in *The Golden Bough* that the Japanese were one of the few peoples in the world with no apparent consciousness of sin, though I had meanwhile become well aware that they were almost obsessively concerned with what was, and what was not, considered formally correct behaviour in any given circumstances.

However, not all the unintentional humour which appeared in the pages of the *Bangkok Chronicle* was concerned with Japanese deeds of daring. Indeed one of the two best misprints (or Freudian slips?) that I ever read appeared in that newspaper *à propos* of Mahatma Gandhi's prolonged fast in 1943 when, clearly in an extremely frail condition, he began to suffer acute discomfort from a surfeit of saliva. The Japanese, who at that time controlled the newspaper, seemed scarcely able to conceal their delight at what appeared to be an increasing probability that Gandhi would die, and that the great revulsion of feeling which would then sweep through Asia would play right into their hands. In the event, however, their headline next day backfired. It read simply 'Gandhi Suffering from Excessive Salvation', and although that was certainly true, fortunately neither it nor his salivation proved fatal. (The only other slip of comparable quality which I ever remember reading was contained in a Ph.D. thesis for which I was external examiner. After a rigorous analysis of demographic and economic data in the part of Asia in question, the candidate—now an internationally renowned scholar—concluded that he had proved beyond any possible doubt that, in the area studied, there was a direct and unmistakable correlation between the density of population and the standard of loving. I have little doubt that he was right, and I informed the university concerned that, on these grounds alone, he deserved the Ph.D., though fortunately there was other evidence to support my recommendation. He got his doctorate.)

*

It was in the summer of 1942 that, for the only time in my life, I made a successful prophecy. One day when I was lecturing on Thailand at Changi University, I made a passing reference to a scheme dating from the 1880s for building a railway to link Thailand to Burma, and facetiously suggested that the Japanese might now find such a railway useful and decide to send some of us to build it. I gave the matter no further thought until suddenly in October apparently official Japanese news began to circulate to the effect that most of us were shortly going to be sent to a large new rest camp, somewhere 'up country'. In no time at all our unofficial rumour-mongers had added some encouraging titbits: the new camp had been built under the supervision of Swiss Red Cross officials; it was on the outskirts of Bangkok and, among other things, was fully equipped with running water and electric light. It sounded pretty good.

On 27 October we were driven to Singapore railway station and were all tremendously excited at being outside Changi again, for Singapore looked very much as usual, and, to our delight, a surprisingly large number of local people seemed quite willing to risk a slap or a bash from the Japanese by encouraging us with friendly grins and surreptitious 'V' signs. We found it very heartening to see them all bearing up so well in spite of their liberation.

Eventually, in the late afternoon, having been counted and recounted umpteen times, we were herded into standard Federated Malay States Railways four-wheel box-cars, 30 feet long by 9 feet wide, which, being constructed of sheet steel, were excellent conductors of heat, and during the afternoons the inside temperatures probably topped 150° F. In normal times cattle or horses were not allowed to travel in such vehicles, but it seems only fair to point out that these were not normal times, nor for that matter were we cattle or horses. The original load per box-car had been put at thirty persons, along with odds and ends of Japanese and P.O.W. junk, but, as we were officers, the number per vehicle was graciously reduced to twenty-eight. Just before the train moved off at 5.30 p.m. a Japanese officer popped his head inside each truck in turn and, with the inevitable smile, said: 'You are going to Thailand where you will be treated like English gentlemen.' It really was rather nice of him, though the Aussies among us expressed it differently.

In the course of this excruciatingly uncomfortable three-and-a-half-day excursion, during which we had nothing to sit or sleep on except the floor, we were alternately frozen and broiled, rather like a pre-cooked meal (though nobody attempted to eat us) and natural functions had to be performed somewhat blatantly over the passing countryside. With our naked backsides facing the audience outside, and ourselves clutching the arms of our comrades inside, we did the best we could through the open door to add a little more fertility to the adjacent ricefields.

To relative newcomers like myself, the trip at least enabled us to see something of both Malaya and southern Thailand, and those of us with a philosophical turn of mind found much to interest us in our new worm's eye view of a situation which hitherto we had merely looked down upon from our privileged position above. But to some of the older British Malayans the situation was unbearably poignant, and at least one of them burst into tears as, from the inside of his box-car, he peered out to catch a fleeting glimpse of the once beautiful bungalow, a mere hundred yards away, where he and his wife had lived happily for the past twenty-odd years.

Eventually, in the early hours of 31 October, the train rumbled into Ban Pong station and, cramped and aching, we stumbled down on to the track. One of the optimists in our party yelled to a scruffy but friendly British soldier 'Where's the rest camp?' and received the cheerful reply: ''Oo the 'ell d'you think you are? You're going to build a bloody railway.'

4. LATS, RICE AND GEOGRAPHY

Infectious disease is one of the great tragedies of living things—the struggle for existence between different forms of life. . . . Incessantly, the pitiless war goes on, without quarter or armistice—a nationalism of species against species. Usually, however, among the so-called 'lower' forms of life, there is a solidarity of class relationship which prevents them from preying upon their own kind by that excess of ferocity which appears to prevail only among human beings, rats, and some of the more savage varieties of fish.

Hans Zinsser, *Rats, Lice and History*

Ban Pong, a station on the main line from Singapore to Bangkok, was the jumping-off point for the new railway which the Japanese, with P.O.W. labour, were beginning to build via the Three Pagodas Pass, through the mountain ranges which separate Thailand from Burma. But in coming here we had crossed another watershed of a different kind. For whereas hitherto our captivity had been in territory which was efficiently organized and where modern technology had achieved a high degree of control over the characteristic problems of the humid tropics—such as floods, typhoons, seriously polluted water, and the whole range of related diseases like malaria, dysentery and cholera—here on the remote western periphery of Thailand we were, in terms of such environmental control, almost at the back of beyond.

This fact forced itself upon our consciousness the moment we entered Ban Pong camp after a short march from the railway station. To us, coming as we did, straight from Changi, the impression created by this first prison camp built according to Japanese principles was something never to be forgotten. A series of long rickety bamboo huts with weather-beaten *atap* roofs (roofs thatched with the dried leaves of the *nipah* palm), dominated the landscape, rising like a tangle of battered wrecks out of a sea of billowing mud. Built to a standard pattern, these Co-prosperous-looking residences, which superficially resembled traditional Borneo long-houses, had a uniform length of a hundred metres and a breadth of seven. They were open from end to end, and their sole furnishing consisted of a raised platform of split bamboo slats, two metres wide down each side, which served as bedding space. The allotment per person of this far from luxurious *Lebensraum* (or *Liebestraum*, as one of our colonels persisted in calling it) was at that time relatively generous, being somewhere in the neighbourhood of two-thirds of a metre, or about two-foot-six.

To make matters worse, the Japanese, in sublime disregard of local advice, had erected the camp in a shallow clay-lined depression. In due course the rains had come as everyone knew they would—though the Japanese thought they knew better—and the camp flooded. In several of the huts even the bed platforms were awash, and getting in and out was vaguely like travelling down the Grand Canal in Venice without a gondola. In such flood conditions, which seasonally affected most of our camps, it was quite common for large and poisonous snakes to be swimming about beneath one's bed space, and an occasional frog might even leap out of the water and land with a chilling wet thud on the bare chest of a sleeping prisoner. Meanwhile, it was an everyday fact of life for rats to be scurrying hither and thither along the bamboo beams and supports, while the slats on which we slept were alive with bugs, until our weekly debugging sessions temporarily reduced their numbers.

A neighbour of mine, formerly an inspector under the Ministry of Agriculture, stated that he would unhesitatingly have condemned the Ban Pong huts even for pigs, and it was not meant as a figure of speech. Elsewhere the camp stood knee-deep in mud, and the only way of making any reasonable progress about the place was to follow behind someone larger and more energetic than oneself, placing one's feet carefully in his footsteps. A short distance from the main residential area a shimmering cloud of buzzing bluebottles marked the site of the latrines—or 'lats' as they were invariably called—vast open pits at the bottom of which was a seething, squirming mass of white maggots. The stench beggared description; no wonder the place was called Ban Pong.

And yet life went on. Shortly after our arrival cries of 'Come and get it!' rent the air; tins of greasy stew and dirty rice were plonked down outside the huts, and their occupants rushed out, apparently eager to consume the stuff. We stared at each other sadly, and I dare say with a wild surmise, silent in a swamp in Siam.

Yet Ban Pong provided a final surprise in the course of our one-day stay there. On our arrival we had noticed a bunch of about a dozen scared-looking Thais lined up outside the guard room, as we trooped in. It now appeared that they had been caught carrying on a highly illicit trade in bananas and other equally dangerous goods with the prisoners, and were to be punished accordingly. One by one they were dragged forward, and thrown to a waiting gang of Japanese toughs who alternately pummelled, punched, and slapped them, or kicked them in unmentionable but proportionately painful places. Then each of four guards seized a leg or an arm of each of the victims in turn and swung the wretched men wildly to and fro in the air for a few minutes to gain momentum, before flinging them into a stinking puddle. For most of us this was the first sight of naked brutality on the part of the Japanese, and it was horrible. As I watched this revolting spectacle I could feel my gorge rising and my fists tingling with excitement and rage, and, to judge from the wild looks on their faces, all the other newcomers seemed to be experiencing the same feeling. I remember thinking that any moment some of our chaps are going to teach these Japanese something they won't forget. But we didn't. The wisdom bred of experience, exhaustion and apathy among the earlier arrivals here suddenly made itself felt, and mysteriously the fever passed, leaving behind only a sickening realization of our useless, unspeakably hopeless, impotence. There was absolutely nothing we could do.

We were to have many opportunities in the ensuing months and years to plumb these emotions to the depths, had we so desired, but the experience was too shattering to bear unnecessary repetition. Instead, defence mechanisms got to work, and, superficially at least, we became callous and the boiling point of our blood rose to unheard-of heights. In time we could even watch our friends receiving such treatment without going to their rescue, and correspondingly we could, if necessary, take it ourselves, without hitting back. It was just as well that we could. Some couldn't, and it cost them their lives.

Fortunately we stayed only twenty-four hours in Ban Pong before moving on. Next day a fleet of dilapidated trucks took us, over some very lousy roads through some very lovely country, to the attractive little town of Kanchanaburi (usually shortened to Kanburi) some sixty miles west of Bangkok. At Kanburi we were met by a little Japanese, himself abbreviated to a mere four-foot-six, who welcomed us, in painstaking but passable English, to a small water-logged camp built, in typically Japanese fashion, in the middle of a swamp. The familiar bamboo huts appeared to be the standard accommodation here, too, but fortunately they were not so dilapidated, and we passed the night in comparative comfort.

The following morning we crossed the river (the Mekhlong Khwae Yai) in barges, and marched along its bank to Chungkai, one of the big base camps then being built for the railway construction gangs. We noticed plenty more bamboo huts a hundred metres by seven, and early in the afternoon we received a speech of welcome by a pompous but affable little Japanese officer, Lieutenant-Colonel Yanagida. Little four-foot-six, who had meanwhile arrived by motor launch, translated fairly fluently.

Everyone was in high spirits on account of an unexpected *yasumi* (holiday) which had been granted in honour of one of our British prisoners who had rescued a Japanese guard from drowning, a most unusual deed. A further cause for rejoicing was the discovery of a Chinese canteen in the camp where, if one waited long enough, it was possible to get quite a decent omelette for twenty-five cents. And then to my delight, a few minutes later I bumped into David Arkush, the camp dentist who had travelled out with me on the *Capetown Castle*, and later lodged with me in Singapore, where we had become close friends. I hadn't seen him for six months, and it was great to meet again. He assured me that, despite appearances to the contrary, Chungkai wasn't a bad camp, and promised to show me round the next morning. With him in the camp, at least it wouldn't be as bad as Ban Pong.

Except in the final stages of our captivity the various prisoner of war camps established in Thailand by the Imperial Japanese Army fell into one of two categories, namely base camps, and railway construction camps. The former were mostly situated close to stations, on the existing railway system of south-western Thailand, while the construction camps were set up, as needed, at intervals along the route to be followed by the new Japanese railway which we prisoners of war were building to the north-west of Ban Pong. For the most part it ran through rugged, densely forested, intensely malarious, and very sparsely inhabited country, along the eastern bank of the Mekhlong Khwae Noi, though to reach the latter it was necessary first to build a bridge across the Khwae Yai, a short distance above Kanburi.

In general character, though not strictly in geographical location, the dreary and depressing Ban Pong was the first of the construction camps, while Kanburi, a few miles to the north-west, was the last—in other words the remotest from Bangkok—of the base camps, though at the time of our arrival the new Chungkai was already about to overtake Kanburi in that capacity.

Situated as they were in the fertile lowlands, where rations, though not luxurious, were reasonably reliable, malaria less virulent, and the climate pleasanter than up-river, the base camps were distinctly preferable to the construction camps. Moreover, while all prisoners in both kinds of camp were liable for railway construction and maintenance work as well as for routine jobs in the camps themselves, the average work load was usually much heavier up-river, partly because this was where the real pioneering was being done, but also because, virtually from the outset, numbers there were much more seriously depleted by sickness than in the more effectively administered lowlands.

For all these reasons, therefore, and also because in the early days our Japanese camp commander at Chungkai was none other than

Lieutenant-Colonel Yanagida, who belonged to the generation which approved of the Anglo-Japanese Alliance of 1902 and even displayed a solitary British medal ribbon among the several Japanese ones decorating his tunic, Chungkai more than lived up to David Arkush's reassuring description. Indeed during the time I spent there in late 1942 and early 1943, it was almost certainly the best camp on the river. Not only did we begin to receive a small but regular amount of pay, roughly comparable to a schoolboy's pocket-money in pre-war days, but Thai vendors of soap, cigarettes, tobacco, and such supplementary foods as bananas, oranges, duck eggs and local fish—raw or cooked—were allowed to ply their trade in a corner of the camp, which quickly became known as Bond Street, presumably because many prisoners of war sold their watches and odd bits of jewellery in order to buy these delicacies.

Beyond any doubt Yanagida was really concerned about our well-being, and particularly about our health in these unfamiliar circumstances. So much so indeed that, notwithstanding his age, he used to give public demonstrations of callisthenics and urge us to practise them ourselves. Moreover, from time to time he would assemble the whole camp on what passed for the parade ground, and deliver well-intentioned pep talks, at the top of his voice, completely drenching the first few rows of his audience in the spray which his efforts unintentionally produced. Most memorable of all, however, was the occasion when, on some festive day in the Japanese calendar, he delivered an oration to the assembled camp, and ended by calling his British opposite number, our senior officer, Lieutenant-Colonel Williamson, on to the rostrum, where, as a token of gratitude for his co-operation, he presented him with fifty cents in the local 'bamboo'—virtually worthless—currency! Later in the day one of our even more decrepit colonels, who had missed this remarkable ceremony, commented in doom-laden tones, 'How humiliating: a British field officah presented with fifty cents by a Japanese. How uttahly humiliating. It ought to have been at least a dollah.'

However, diversions of a different kind were soon to follow. Precisely one week before Christmas Day, 1942, while Lieutenant-Colonel Yanagida had staged a temporary strategic withdrawal, the British camp commandant was informed in writing that the Japanese would henceforth expect officers to work on the railway. In reply a letter was sent, stating that such a request did not accord with international law, and further, since British military law expressly forbade officers to work for the enemy, we could not comply with their requirements. The

Japanese thereupon played their trump card, one that was always produced whenever any form of resistance or obstruction was even hinted at by us. They would take it out on the B.O.R.s and, more particularly on the sick. If the officers would not work, the sick would have to take their place. So far from showing any sense of shame over the disgraceful state of sickness to which their treatment had already brought large numbers of our men, they never ceased to use it as a lever to extract the last ounce from us, whenever the occasion was considered to demand it.

However, this was the first time these particular tactics had been applied, and many of us doubted that the threat would be carried out. Accordingly, the officers as a group decided that, as a matter of principle, it would be quite unjustifiable for us to climb down, at least until the matter had been put to the test. So, after prolonged discussions in which all officers participated, we reiterated our inability to comply with the orders.

The Japanese retaliated by ordering every officer, other than the bedded-down sick, to parade at 10 a.m. on 20 December. Although I had only just recovered from three weeks' malaria and enteritis I was able to attend the parade, though I felt somewhat shaky and muddle-headed. The Japanese began by ordering us to work, and we, in accordance with a pre-arranged plan, stood fast while our senior officer, Lieutenant-Colonel Williamson, once again stated our position.

Then, said the Japanese, we will force you to work. Japanese sentries with fixed bayonets were posted all round us and ordered to charge magazines with ten rounds. We watched them load, without being much impressed by their proficiency in weapon training, after which the senior British and Japanese officers disappeared into the Japanese hut. After a tense and prolonged interval, they emerged again, and I seem to remember one of our less impressive colonels flapping around and telling us all: 'They're going to shoot—beginning with the colonels. Do you want to change your minds?' Whereupon the rest of us assured him that we had no intention whatever of going back on our decision. Presumably we thought we'd wait and see what happened to the colonels; but if they got polished off and the process was then extended to the majors we might perhaps consider that honour had been satisfied and we'd call the thing off—'we' in this context being the captains and subalterns.

However, after another brief discussion Colonel Williamson announced that, in view of further threats by the Japanese to resort to any form of violence necessary to make us work, it had been decided to comply so as to avoid bloodshed and unnecessary danger to the sick. Eventually we were all dismissed and told to parade for work in the afternoon. So the Chungkai officers' working party was born, and came as a nice little Christmas present to all concerned.

The programme opened with a speech from Tarimoto, who was a weedy but ferocious-looking little fellow, with the sort of roughage on his chin that in a European indicates an unsuccessful shave, but in a Japanese more commonly represents months of painstaking effort. He tried hard to look like a villain in an old-fashioned melodrama, and was fond of leaning on his stick and snarling: 'How I hate all Anglo-Saxons.' On this occasion he limited himself to telling us that the railway was not being built for Japan alone, but for the 'warld' in general. When Japan had brought peace to the 'warld', presumably by annihilating everybody else, we could all travel on the railway in the 'era of warld peace' that would follow. Meanwhile our treatment would depend on our behaviour. However, as befitted officers, our work was to be of a more highly skilled order than that performed by the other ranks. Our task was not to lay the track, but to build bridges and, in retrospect, I think that the officers were selected for this task because very few of the Japanese railway engineers seemed capable of understanding a blueprint, though several of us could get the hang of one even if we knew no Japanese.

In fact, however, most of our time was spent on primitive pile-driving, powered exclusively by human muscles. Long lines of almost naked officers pulled on ropes until the weight reached the top of the rickety structure, and then let it drop with a wallop on the pile. Usually it worked well enough, though once when the pile in question struck bed rock only two feet down, we were ordered to pull it out and cut an appropriate length off the other end.

As in a tug-of-war team, co-ordination was the main difficulty, and to solve this Tarimoto suggested the singing in unison of a little Japanese coolie ditty, '*Ichi-Ni-No-San-Na*' which can be approximately rendered into English as 'One, two, and three, oh'. However, popular opinion felt that this was going a little too far. We might have to work like coolies, and even have to live like coolies, but we weren't going to behave like them if we could help it. So we appointed our own cheer-leader instead, and the work went on fairly successfully.

In another officers' bridge-building party—under the supervision of a celebrated Indian Army colonel of the old school, the officers objected even more strongly to singing a Japanese song, and the colonel made a gallant attempt to get the Japanese sergeant to agree to a change of tune. After a prolonged absence the colonel returned from the parley with a glowing countenance to announce, 'We've won a great moral victory. From now on we shall sing an English song.' Whereupon, in a quavering baritone he led the way with the opening, 'Yo-ho, heave-ho' of the Volga Boat Song.

Viewed retrospectively, the early months in Chungkai were the most carefree period of our entire captivity. The summer monsoon was over, and what we later discovered was the pleasantest season of the year—the cooler and much drier period from November to February—set in. The scenery was beautiful, and as work on the railway was only in its earliest stages, our daily task was not excessive, though pile-driving—especially during the peak heat of the afternoon—could be extremely exhausting. But already by January it was clear that a change was on the way. The engineers were now coming under pressure from Tokyo to get the railway through to Burma as quickly as possible, and thereafter workloads rose steadily, and those for the other ranks became outrageously heavy. Moreover, as the cool season drew to a close in February, the increasing heat, accompanied by intensifying dryness and dustiness, and the inability of the dwindling streams and rivers to flush away the garbage, excreta and other filth for which they provided the only means of disposal, began to produce a sharp deterioration in sanitation and hence a mounting proliferation of disease.

This was bad enough in the down-river areas which had already experienced one severe epidemic of diphtheria, while both malaria and dysentery had become routine facts of life, all too often degenerating into statistics of death. But at least in these down-river base camps there were hospitals with some excellent army doctors, though their wards consisted merely of bamboo huts, virtually identical to those occupied by the rest of us, and the supply of drugs and hospital equipment which we received from the Japanese was little more than nominal.

Nevertheless, conditions up-river were infinitely worse, owing to the combination of starvation rations, the virulence and ubiquity of malaria which, together with grossly excessive workloads, so lowered the resistance of an ever growing proportion of our men that they became sitting targets for major epidemics—particularly of diphtheria or cholera—which periodically swept through the area. Yet perhaps the most dreaded of all were tropical ulcers, most commonly caused, in the everyday process of jungle clearing, by a scratch or bruise, which would fester into a steadily widening circle of suppuration that might reach six inches or more in diameter. Since a sore such as this, besides being excruciatingly painful, produced an increasing drain on the rapidly declining vitality of the unfortunate sufferer, some of our medical officers concluded that it was worth amputating a leg or an arm so affected, in order to give the patient some chance of survival. In many cases this grim treatment paid off, and many 'amputs', as they called themselves, were more than grateful for it, not least because it also eliminated them from being sent back up-river to probable death.

Towards the end of April 1943 the first large-scale evacuation of sick from up-river to the base-camp hospitals began and, having only recently been discharged from the one at Chungkai, I was among those who witnessed the arrival there of the first barge-loads of what the Imperial Japanese Army officially termed 'the heavy sick', a tragically ironic name for these indescribably frail human cargoes, contemptuously dismissed by one Japanese colonel as 'a few remaining skeletons'.

Having already described the sickening impact made on us by our first experiences of Japanese brutality at Ban Pong, I can only say that what we saw there was like a Sunday School treat by comparison with the nightmare, that alas was not a nightmare, which we now experienced at Chungkai.

Like refugees from Dante's Inferno, in every stage from dangerously ill to dying (and many of them were dead before they reached dry land) they came in their hundreds, huddled under filthy scraps of blanket or tattered rice-sacks, for it could be really cold at night on the river. And still more followed, covered from head to foot with sores, emaciated, sunken-eyed, and trembling, with the outline of every bone in their wretched bodies showing through their skins, till their chests looked like wall bars and their limbs like Chippendale. At a rough guess, the average weight of these mostly young men was barely half what it had been when they had arrived fresh from home between one and two years previously.

And with the sick came casualty lists which included friends of almost everybody in Chungkai. Donald Purdie, one of our Raffles College colleagues and a brilliant chemist, was dead; and Alexander Oppenheim, the most senior and most distinguished of them all, was said to be too ill to move, a superlative which made the mind reel when one looked at some of those who had managed to survive the long, arduous and dangerous journey down the Khwae Noi. Yet only three months earlier, Colonel Nakamura, in a speech curiously entitled 'Railway Construction Wardom', had expressed regret over 'seriousness in health matters' before going on to say that this was 'due mainly to absence of firm belief as Japanese Health Follows Will'.

Nevertheless, in retrospect, one must admit that there was an element of truth in this Japanese variant of Coué-cum-Christian Science. As Hospital Welfare Officer, I had asked one of our most senior medical officers about the survival prospects of two of my personal friends, who had both arrived in the dysentery ward, from up country, on the same day. Apart from suffering almost equally acutely from the same complaint, they were totally unlike each other; the younger (probably about twenty-eight) being a complete extrovert outdoor type who, when I had last seen him barely a year before, had been in magnificent shape, while the other, a professional mathematician, was some years older and not outstanding in physique.

Yet although those best qualified to judge considered the former to have the better chance of survival, and although both received all of such treatment as it was possible to give, I watched the young extrovert, demoralized by his own physical deterioration, slowly but irrevocably abandon the struggle to survive; while the mathematician, lying prone on his bug-ridden bamboo slats, took the opportunity of this highly unorthodox long vacation to continue his research. And that is why Dato Sir Alexander Oppenheim, formerly Professor of Mathematics at Raffles College, Singapore, and subsequently Vice-Chancellor of the University of Malaya (in Singapore) still seems to be as mentally and physically active in his retirement as he was when I first met him as a lance bombardier in the Local Defence Volunteers during the early days of our captivity in Changi, before both of us were sent to Thailand.

However, to return from Changi to Chungkai, there can be little doubt that it was the traumatic experiences of 1943, when the callous and outrageous treatment meted out to those involved in the immense Japanese drive to get the railway built led directly or indirectly to tens of thousands of deaths, which more than anything else determined what, for want of a better term, one may call 'the ethos of the River Kwai'. Moreover, it seems probable that at least some influential person or persons in Tokyo may by that stage have become concerned to try to forestall possible foreign condemnation, if news of these outrages should leak—most easily via the European (largely Danish) community in Bangkok—to the outside world which had not forgotten the appalling atrocities committed by the Japanese forces during the so-called 'China incident', or more accurately the Sino-Japanese War, which began in 1937 and merged with the Pacific War after the attack on Pearl Harbor on 7 December 1941.

Such an interpretation might well explain why it was that, on 30 March 1943, the *Nippon Times* outlined the policy which the Japanese claimed to be pursuing in their treatment of Allied prisoners:

> No one would think that our humanism in war is confined to the activities of the Japanese Red Cross Society. This organization has its own functions to perform in wartime. . . . But the scope of our humanism is bigger and broader than the objective of the Red Cross organization. That is why we usually accord more generous treatment to our enemies than those provided in the Red Cross Regulations. The fact is that our humane instincts propel us to regard defeated foes as our guests, and so we treat them accordingly.

In the event this information did not percolate through to us in Chungkai immediately but eventually arrived at roughly the same time as the first barge-loads of 'heavy sick' from up-river. Funerals now became an almost daily occurrence. The pathetically dignified little cortèges, headed by the comic and incongruous figure of Lieutenant-Colonel Yanagida, used to file slowly past our hut, usually at midday, and served even further to diminish our appetite for rice. On 19 April the use of coffins was forbidden since the number of funerals was beginning to exceed the supply of available boxwood; henceforward the corpses were to be buried in rice-sacks. About the same time Yanagida's attendances slackened off—after all, the daily total of burials now regularly ran into double figures. And soon the funeral custom itself conformed to the spirit of the times and died a natural death.

Within a few weeks, against this background of galloping deterioration in almost every aspect of our existence, a deepening sense of alarm, at times reaching a crescendo of desperation, began to spread through the camp, as the truth finally dawned upon everybody that we were up against something far more terrible than most of us had ever suspected at the time of our surrender. In short, we were face to face with the most fundamental of all human conflicts, the struggle for the survival of 'us'—our own 'kith and kin'—against 'them'—the Japanese—who, so far from being 'our little yellow brothers' were now instantaneously transmogrified into—and thereafter remained—'the little yellow bastards'.

Thus, by means of a swift and intuitive descent to the level of our lowest common denominator, an intensely powerful group solidarity, compounded of hatred and contempt for our captors, emerged to provide what was probably the most important single factor conducing to the ultimate survival, some three years later, of rather more than half of the original total of Allied prisoners of war in Thailand.

Nevertheless to think in terms of such 'gut-reactions' is grossly to over-simplify the situation. Certainly the vast majority of British prisoners of war in Thailand felt their first loyalty to be to their fellows within this same 'in-group', and the recent revulsion against the enemy had made it much less likely that any other British P.O.W. would attempt to rescue a drowning Japanese guard, if only because to do so might automatically result in him making himself an outcast. On the other hand, within so large—and in a sense so fortuitously based—an in-group as this, there were many of us who, while fundamentally loyal to the solidarity of that group, had no desire to indulge in indiscriminate hatred and/or contempt towards the Japanese *per se*. Thus I found myself in something of a quandary when, as an indirect result of my earlier activities as a supposed comic and mimic in the *Capetown Castle*'s concert party, I was asked to take over as Welfare Officer (the Japanese for some incomprehensible reason called it Number One Music Man) at an early stage during my sojourn in Chungkai Camp.

In the end, in characteristic British fashion, I worked out a compromise which at least was acceptable to me. Clearly, we prisoners needed at all costs to keep up our morale, both individual and collective, *vis à vis* the Japanese, who had recently outfought us and were now doing all they could to humiliate us, though at that time we had no idea that they regarded humiliation as the deepest of all degradation. However, since hatred is essentially negative and corrosive, to the donor as well as to the recipient, while almost anything that could be done to raise a laugh was helpful for morale, I opted for laughing at the Imperial Japanese Army and for using such opportunities as I could find in my capacity as Welfare Officer to encourage others to do likewise. Since, moreover, so much about the Japanese appeared to be so intrinsically comic, this course of action seemed to appeal to everyone, except of course the Japanese themselves, on the few occasions when they suspected that we were making fun of them.

To begin with, I introduced a practice of writing and surreptitiously distributing occasional snide verses debunking the bombast and hypocrisy of their speeches, which we had to listen to, in Japanese, after which 'English' translations were circulated—initially with specific instructions to all British officers to 'make sure that this document gets to the bottom of your soldiers'. This it invariably did, and was generally considered to be more trustworthy than banana leaves.

Otherwise the supreme moment of glory in my short-lived role as Number One Music Man came about in a curious way when, one day, after several warnings had been issued against the illicit purchase of local liquor from Thai traders, three of our men were caught red-handed. It was then announced that they would receive 'the worst punishment known to the Imperial Japanese Army', which shook us considerably since the latter had already shot some of our men for trying to escape.

At that stage the Japanese H.Q. sent for me and ordered me to get together a band of instrumentalists. The purpose of this was to lead a procession of the three guilty men, each carrying a placard proclaiming the enormity of his crime, in a march all round the camp, while everyone else was called on parade in a huge circle facing inwards. We were then told that the criminals would be paraded round the entire area, while everyone was supposed to laugh and jeer at them.

Doing my best to be co-operative I told the band to begin with 'Roll out the Barrel', followed by 'Drink to me only', 'In Cellar Cool', 'There is a Tavern in the Town', and sundry similar ditties, ending with a rousing version of the 'Colonel Bogey' march (the famous march by Alford which was used as the theme tune of *The Bridge on the River Kwai*), accentuating the blaring brass notes accompanying the obscenities of the unofficial words ('bollocks and the same to you') associated with this march, which all our troops knew, as the procession finally passed the Japanese guard-room. The laughter was loud and prolonged, and the Japanese, though somewhat mystified, were particularly pleased with our efforts.

This extraordinary affair, which was taken extremely seriously by the Japanese and even more hilariously by our troops—particularly the three 'criminals' once they realized that they were not after all going to suffer the worst of all possible fates—clearly confirmed the importance which the Japanese attached to humiliation as a punishment. But equally significantly, the fact that the British were laughing, not at the 'criminals'—with whom at heart we all sympathized—but at the Japanese, whose behaviour we regarded as intrinsically absurd, served to demonstrate that the most effective way of boosting our own morale was to have some ready excuse for looking down on the Japanese as silly little men, self-evidently inferior to ourselves.

In this context, the celebrated film *The Bridge on the River Kwai*, although brilliantly effective in its portrayal of the details of P.O.W. life in Thailand, was not only factually untrue but also false psychologically. For since in the last analysis the solidarity of the P.O.W. in-group was based on our regarding ourselves as completely antithetical to the Japanese, the one unforgivable crime in our calendar was to be 'Jap-happy'—that is, to be willing to co-operate, except under the most extreme duress, with our captors in any matter, however trivial. Indeed, on several occasions when, rightly or wrongly, the majority of officers considered our current British camp commandant to be too accommodating towards the Japanese, the pressure of opinion in effect forced him to make way for someone willing to take a tougher line. In short, if any British officer had suggested positive co-operation with the Japanese in building a really magnificent bridge, as depicted in the film, he would automatically have been regarded as either a traitor, or insane, or more probably both; and indeed the prevailing attitude of our Officers Bridge Building Party was that it was our duty to do the shoddiest work we could get away with, so that the bridges might collapse while trainloads of Japanese reinforcements were being transported over them to Burma.

Ironically, however, the only 'accident' of this kind which ever occurred came shortly after the war, when a group of senior Thai railway engineers and other officials was making a preliminary inspection of the line, and one of our shoddily built bridges did collapse, killing several members of the party. Such sabotage on our part, though obviously unethical by normal peace-time standards, contributed strongly to the solidarity of our own in-groups, which theoretically comprised all the English prisoners of war in the camps.

However, as time went on, a growing proportion of the P.O.W.s in the Thailand camps were not from England, and moreover not all the prisoners were loyal to their fellows. Among the former category were considerable numbers of Australians, and Dutch, most of whom had initially been sent to work on the Burma end of the railway. Later, however, owing to the constant need for evacuating sick men down-river to the base hospitals in Thailand which, in due course, sent 'recovered' patients back up-river, virtually all camps came to contain a mixture—though in widely differing proportions—of Australian, English, and Dutch prisoners of war, while there was also a much smaller group of Americans, in the predominantly Australian and Dutch camp at Tha Makan, where the bridge was built over the Khwae Noi—the 'Bridge on the River Kwai'—a few miles from Chungkai.

For obvious reasons, the normal practice was that a senior officer of the largest national group in any particular camp was made responsible, under the Japanese camp commander, for the day-to-day running of that camp. In general this worked out reasonably well, and from personal experience in several camps in various parts of Thailand I would say that relations between British, Australian and American prisoners were surprisingly good, given the hardships and frustrations which all of us in greater or lesser degree shared.

Indeed, the presence of one or two 'minority' national groups in a camp often contributed greatly to its morale by bringing in new and hitherto unfamiliar expertise and interests, as was well illustrated by the small group of Americans at the Tha Makan camp. The nucleus of this group consisted of some fifty Texas gunners, under the command of a real southern gentleman, Lieutenant-Colonel Blucher S. Tharpe who, with all his men, had suddenly been cut off and left isolated in the middle of thousands of Japanese soldiers in central Java in 1942, and on realizing his predicament had instantly but unavailingly cabled his Senator back home: 'You got me into this. Now get me out.'

The Australians, always referred to as the Aussies, were outstanding for their skill in improvising almost anything—after a fashion—almost anywhere, and as such they were invaluable in the more remote up-river camps. They also maintained an unending but basically friendly rivalry with the Americans, which reached its peak at breakfast time on 4 July 1944, when a small—and unusually smartly dressed—delegation of Aussies entered the American hut and with great solemnity expressed their condolences to the American nation for its tragic mistake in withdrawing from the British Empire in 1776. The point was well taken.

By comparison with the three Anglophone groups—Americans, Australians and British—between whom there was rarely any significant friction, the Dutch tended to be the odd men out. Superficially it might seem that the obvious differences between the first three and the last one was that of language, but in fact nearly all the Dutch understood English and many spoke it far better than a high proportion of B.O.R.s (British Other Ranks). To most of the latter, the most surprising thing about the Dutch was their curiously unmilitary-looking jungle-green uniforms, with billowing breeches and tight-waisted tunics, topped with similarly green straw hats. For a few weeks our other ranks continued to regard the Dutch as a hitherto unsuspected species, to be stared at suspiciously from as safe a distance as possible. However, this isolation began to break down when, within a few weeks of the arrival of the Dutch in Chungkai, a minor economic revolution swept through the camp. Cigarette factories, peanut-toffee factories, bake-houses and cookhouses sprang up overnight; elaborately organized advertising agencies canvassed their wares; and hordes of pedestrian salesmen unloaded them on an astonished public. One gentleman, with a longish jacket but—so far as one could see—no trousers, used to patrol the camp, offering, in a suitably metallic voice, to 'sharpen your razor blades in my new and improved machine, for one cent a blade only'.

Although some of the more erudite among us were quick to recall Canning's quip that—

> In matters of commerce the fault of the Dutch
> Is offering too little and asking too much

—most prisoners of war readily availed themselves of these unexpected and remarkably good services. Accordingly money changed hands at a fantastic rate, and before long the whole camp began to resemble the orthodox desert island community that has just hit on the ingenious notion of the division of labour.

Of more fundamental importance were the residual barriers to mutual understanding, arising from folk memories of former bitter enmities between the British and Dutch as naval and commercial rivals for the political and economic mastery of the Indies, both East and West. And, associated with these, there was the still deeper divergence over the colour question. For, to the great surprise of many British prisoners in Thailand, the majority of the Dutch prisoners of war looked far more Asian than European, though they varied in skin colour from almost platinum blond to pure ebony. This was the result of over three centuries of miscegenation, deliberately encouraged by the Dutch administration which, until well into the nineteenth century, had considered the East Indies as too unhealthy for European women to live in, but was anxious to keep its European staff reasonably content.

The Dutch attitude to the colour question was curiously ambivalent. Any Eurasian whose surname was Dutch—which applied to the great majority—was treated exactly as a European-born Dutchman, but any other was treated as an *Indische jongen*—that is, 'Indian [which meant Indonesian] boy', regardless of age. In other words a colour bar was maintained, but the line ran through the middle of the Eurasian community. In my own personal experience all but one of the most able and likeable members of the Dutch forces whom I got to know in captivity were Eurasians 'above the line', and they were among the most artistic, intelligent and cosmopolitan people I have ever known. Several were in the topmost ranks of the Netherlands Indies administrative service, and were outstanding people by any standards. But later I also had a remarkable opportunity to get to know many *Indische jongens*, when, because I spoke Dutch, I was put in charge of a small up-river camp, nearly half of whose members were *Indische jongens*. The fact that I, as an Englishman, had troubled to learn Dutch had an extraordinary effect, and they welcomed me as one of themselves. The evenings I spent in their company, round a jungle fire, learning of their life back home and what it meant to them, were among the happiest of my life.

I do not pretend to know what this teaches about the colour question, or about Dutch colonial policy which baffled me. But I do know that my behaviour in associating with the 'Indos', as the British called them, was considered extremely odd by most of our officers, though I do not recall losing any sleep over this supposed misdemeanour on my part.

Yet of all the diverse attitudes which we encountered towards the colour question in South-east Asia, none was quite so crude as that of the Japanese themselves. This became apparent when, owing to the increasingly serious shortage of skilled labour in Japan, the authorities began in 1944 to recruit prisoners of war from the Thailand camps. Large numbers of appropriately qualified technicians, both British and Dutch, were selected in Chungkai on the basis of data obtained by means of a questionnaire[1], and were then subjected to a 'sick parade' to weed out the unwanted. Everyone on the list was made to file past the Japanese medical officer who politely passed all the Europeans, with the phrase 'White man O.K.', and rejected all the Eurasians with a not exactly tactful 'Black man no good.' Obviously the arrival of large numbers of Asian-looking prisoners in Tokyo would have required considerable explaining away to the great mass of ordinary Japanese who had been brought up from childhood on the doctrine of Asia for the Asiatics (the term Asiatics was not changed to Asians until after the Second World War).

What most of us found almost impossible to understand, however, was the behaviour of a small minority—a self-created out-group within our own much larger in-group—who capitalized on the miseries of their comrades as they lay dying in our camp hospital. Most of these pathetically sick individuals possessed virtually nothing beyond a blanket, but in so far as they had any other belongings which they valued—such as a few cigarettes, some scraps of Japanese 'bamboo' currency, perhaps a watch which they had hoped to sell in order to buy food, or, most treasured of all, some personal photograph or other

[1] In my own answers to the question on employment and experience I stated I was a university teacher with two years' experience, and was accordingly classified as Second Class Professor. When called upon to list my hobbies (as a further clue to latent talent) I opted for wine-tasting and foreign travel. Neither was of any avail, and I remained soberly in Chungkai.

keepsake which reminded them of home—they would wrap them in a bundle and place it for safety under their pillow. But our thieves outsmarted them. They operated in pairs, deep in the night when the only light came from an occasional flickering coconut-oil lamp, easily blown out. The inside man tiptoed along from bed to bed tickling the bare feet of the patients who would then sit up suddenly, whereupon the outside man, creeping under the eaves, whipped away whatever was under the now unprotected pillow. Any items of value thus obtained, such as watches, rings or other jewellery were immediately sold to Thai 'dealers' outside the camp fence. After all, the British also are a nation of shopkeepers.

With the exception of the very small minority referred to in the preceding paragraph, the general level of morale among all the main groups of prisoners—whether American, Australian, British or Dutch —was, all things considered, remarkably high. Unquestionably the superb courage and dedication to duty displayed, above all by our medical officers, notwithstanding the appalling difficulties under which they worked, set a standard which commanded the admiration of virtually everyone in the camp and, though less outwardly spectacular, all the various denominational chaplains tended their respective flocks with genuine devotion, religious services were well attended, and hymn singing—especially when led by Captain Inglefield's choir—was invariably a real source of uplift both to participants and to others who listened from afar.

Nevertheless, the most universal of all in their appeal were the shows—usually weekly—staged in our open-air theatre. These varied widely in character, from typical more or less bawdy concert parties, to some very skilled production of professional quality, *inter alia* of Emlyn Williams' *Night Must Fall* and Katscher's *Wonder Bar*, both of which managed fleetingly to recapture for us something of the atmosphere of the West End. Obviously in such an exclusively male community as ours inevitably was, we had to rely heavily on female impersonators, and it was astonishing to see how so many of the least impressive-looking prisoners managed to transform themselves into remarkably glamorous creatures with the aid of locally improvised theatrical make-up and elegant dresses which many of them, who had previously been active in army concert parties, had brought with them into captivity. Clearly some of our leading ladies seemed to be as intensely sought after by their respective fans as were their real-life counterparts in London's theatre-land, and more than a few wells of loneliness apparently changed overnight into fountains of desire.

For obvious reasons, it was the succession of Christmas pantomimes which were looked forward to with the keenest anticipation, though on one memorable occasion the title landed us in trouble. This was the notorious *Thai Diddle Diddle*, devised and produced by Dudley Gotla, one of our most respected doctors, and myself. Dudley worked on the essentially sound principle that 'the troops don't want all this arty stuff; all they want is to see their officers get up on the stage and make bloody fools of themselves.' Many of us certainly did this to perfection, until the Japanese, ever suspicious, consulted a dictionary from which they concluded that our innocuous little review was meant to imply that under the Greater East Asia Co-prosperity Sphere the Japanese were diddling—or cheating—the Thai population! All stage shows were thereupon banned for several weeks, and life thereafter became very dreary until fortunately Eric Cliffe was allowed to fill the gap with some very successful orchestral concerts.

However, as the Japanese officers were reluctant to go without our regular entertainments, Number One Music Man was called back from retirement to organize a purely private concert, in effect a command performance, for their exclusive benefit.

So I suddenly found myself summoned to the Japanese H.Q. hut, to lead a party of assorted entertainers and an even more ill assorted group of instrumentalists. Since we had had no opportunity whatsoever of rehearsing as a group, I began by asking who knew what tunes, and the only item which everyone seemed capable of performing turned out to be 'In the Shade of the Old Apple Tree', which, after the fourth or fifth time round was clearly recognizable.

By this stage the Camp Commander and his staff were all well saturated with *sake*, the Commander himself well in the lead. After telling me that in Tokyo he had many 'babies' (children) he requested that 'Number One Violin Man' should play a 'baby go to sleepo song'.

Fortunately our violinist—there was only one, though the Japanese insisted on calling him Number One Violin Man—produced a passable rendering of Brahms's *Wiegenlied*, which—for good or ill—led to copious weeping on the part of the Japanese Commander. However, his appetite having thus been whetted, he now aspired to higher things, and peremptorily demanded the Mendelssohn Violin Concerto in full. Number One Violin Man shot an anguished glance in my direction, and I tentatively interjected that the concerto required 'a much bigger band' and also that the musicians would need some regular rehearsal time before we could do justice to so eminent a work. However, if the Commander would allow me to go into Kanburi and buy some more instruments, strings and related equipment, I assured him that, after a few rehearsals the concerto could be performed next week. This clearly was going too far, so he answered brusquely: 'I understand. Instead he play St Louis Blues,' after which he lined up the entire group and solemnly presented each of us with a bar of soap and a roll of toilet paper.

Probably the most memorable performances of our camp theatre were those associated with two pieces of brilliant staging on our bamboo and matting set. The first, preceded by a B.B.C.-style announcement that 'We are now taking you over to King's College Cambridge for the annual festival of carols and lessons', showed our choir, appropriately clad in surplices and cassocks, in an interior setting illuminated only by candlelight, just beginning the opening carol.

In an instant the shuffles and chatter of some thousands of soldiers suddenly ceased and the entire performance was listened to in complete silence. The second, and perhaps even more impressive, was the work of some of our Dutch fellow prisoners. Before the curtain was raised we heard the opening bars of the glorious tenor and baritone duet 'In the depths of the temple' from Bizet's *Pearl Fishers*, sung really superbly; and then the curtain slowly rose to display a breath-taking and almost life-size view of the Grand Canal in Venice, superbly painted on doctored coconut matting. This time the response was the opposite—but equally apposite—one of prolonged and thunderous applause. What made it even more impressive, to those of us in the know, was that all the paints had been made in the camp, the red out of powdered bricks, and the beautiful greens, yellows and browns from assorted specimens of bullock and buffalo dung (the army, of course, has its own name for this but for once it was completely forgotten)!

What these two spectacles had in common was the ability instantly to make an entire, and very diverse, audience suddenly feel transported from its surrounding squalor, filth, and drearily monotonous diet of rice and watery stew, into a totally different—and yet more real—world of beauty and sanity. Even those who had come only for their weekly ration of bawdy jokes went back to their huts almost in a trance. It was the most powerful demonstration of the uplifting powers of genuine art and sheer artistry that I have ever witnessed.

Yet, in the final analysis, the morale of the camp was something which had to come from each of us individually. Certainly the fact that we were all in the bag together contributed a great deal, if only for no other reason than that to betray the dispiritedness—to which everyone at some time or other succumbed—only intensified one's own dejection. So, instinctively, everyone strove to put the best face on it, whatever the feelings behind that face might be, and in so doing we kept up one another's morale.

Perhaps I can best illustrate this process by recounting an incident which I still recall as vividly as if it had happened only yesterday. One of the most popular and respected men in Chungkai camp was an elderly Scottish planter, Jim Maclean. Having worked all his adult life in Malaya, he had just reached retirement age and was all set to go home to Scotland. But then the sudden extension of the war into South-east Asia prevented his departure, and so instead he became a P.O.W. with the rest of us, the second-oldest man in Chungkai. Some two years later, when things were at their most depressing and when, if the truth be told, few of us seriously believed we would ever see home again, I was walking gloomily across the camp to fall in for the daily working party, when I caught sight of old Jim, whose shambling gait was unmistakable even at several hundred yards' range. Immediately I felt myself breaking into a grin as I tried to think of something facetious by way of a greeting to the old boy. And then I saw that he was grinning too, and as he came up to me he grabbed my arm and blurted out: 'How the hell d'ye do it, Charruls?'

'Do what?' I asked, completely mystified.

'How on earth d'ye keep so cheerful? I'm an old bastard and I've had a good life and I've no regrets, but here are you, wasting the best years of your life in this Godforsaken place, and yet you've always got a twinkle in your eye. I don't know how the hell ye do it.'

In fact I am sure he knew, just as I knew how he and hundreds of others of us did it. We did it because it was the only way of concealing the real feelings which lurked only skin deep beneath the surface and were too painfully embarrassing to reveal. But it worked because, unlike the Japanese, we could—and did—laugh at ourselves, and so were not vulnerable to their attempts to humiliate us.

One of the largely unforeseen problems which emerged, as our captivity wore on and our clothing wore out, was the virtual impossibility of obtaining replacements for the latter. While most officers still had one or possibly two pairs of shorts, and perhaps a shirt as well, even as late as 1944, the other ranks were rarely so well off, mainly because many of them had sold clothing, usually in order to buy cigarettes. So the 'G-string', or 'Jap-happy' as it was also known as, a sort of utility cloth fig-leaf, soon became the prevailing costume among all ranks, at any rate during working hours, and to this was added, if available, a pair of wooden clogs or *klompen* as the Dutch called them, and some species of headgear as protection against the sun. I myself favoured a rather smart but uncomfortable line in shorts made of sackcloth advertising a local brand of flour, and was regarded as being very snooty on that account.

Not the least interesting result of this almost complete nudity was the number of surprising disclosures and startling revelations in the form of tattoos that soon began to come to light. We had long been accustomed to the 'hot' and 'cold', or alternatively 'sweet' and 'sour', that adorned the space beneath the left and right breast of certain troops, and there was nothing new about the wonderful assortment of dragons sprawling over the bare forearms of the older generation of Malayan planters.

But now we were treated to whole galleries full of crucifixes, tombstones, and bleeding hearts, punctured from various angles. 'In memory of my dear mother [or father]' was also popular, and one husky sergeant carried a picture of what appeared to be a somewhat battered-looking boxer wearing a fluffy yellow wig, with the inscription 'True Love' underneath.

Other people of a more classical turn of mind, however, went in for the great masters, the most celebrated example of all these being a striking version of Leonardo da Vinci's *Last Supper*, on one fellow's chest. It was quite a good reproduction in many respects, but lacked some of the finer points of the original, and I often wondered whether, if sunburn ever caused him to shed his top layer, we might have found a portrait of Mussolini by some more modern master underneath.

Curiously enough the most famous bit of tattooing was to be found, not on a B.O.R. but on one of the officers. The gentleman in question appeared to believe that variety is the spice of life, for, in addition to sundry butterflies and bowls of flowers on his arms, he sported an enormous windjammer in full sail on his chest. But the real *pièce de résistance* was only revealed when he turned round to display a spirited version of the recognized masterpiece of the tattooer's art, The Hunt. Situated about north-centre is a huntsman, complete with top-hat and all the other associated regalia, seated astride his horse, while from north, south, east and west, a pack of hounds in full cry converges upon the retreating fox, which has just succeeded in disappearing (south-centre) into the only really safe cover available, his fast retreating brush cheekily pointing the way. Of course the whole of this work of art was not immediately visible at the outset, but the gradual striptease forced upon him, as on the rest of us, by the slow disintegration of our clothing, served greatly to heighten the fun of the chase.

Despite all the miseries of P.O.W. life, however, one fundamental difference between our Japanese P.O.W. camps and the better-known ones in Germany and other parts of Europe, namely the absence of any surrounding barbed wire and watch towers, may well have played an invaluable role in preventing the development of a sense of claustrophobia, though I doubt whether the Japanese ever thought of that.

In fact our camps were delimited by flimsy bamboo fences, unpatrolled by guards, and their purpose was not so much to keep us inside as simply to indicate to the local people precisely where the perimeter was. The reason for this apparent laxity was essentially a matter of geography, for even if we got out of our camps, we couldn't possibly get out of the country. During the earliest days in captivity when everything was in a rudimentary stage, a Malayan Government geologist and I crawled through the fence and spent a day outside, climbing the highest peak in the district to try to see whether there was any possibility of escaping west across the mountains to the coast of Burma. As we gazed across the unending series of serrated parallel ridges, each covered to the top with dense and sharp-spined vegetation, of the kind which had scratched our clothing to shreds during our climb, we agreed at once that there wasn't a hope in hell of getting away. On our descent we summed up the position by saying that only if the situation in camp became totally hopeless—in other words if we were being actively or passively exterminated—would it be worth trying to escape.

But the obstacles were not limited to the geography. The mere facts of our colour and physiognomy meant that we were instantly recognizable as escapees, and since the Japanese had subsequently demonstrated that attempted escape could carry the death penalty, and also announced that a very large sum—by local standards—would be paid to any Thai who caught and turned in an escaping prisoner, it was clear to all but the most wishful of wishful thinkers that escape simply wasn't on. Only a handful of rather silly people ever tried seriously, and none, so far as I know, succeeded.

However, at least one highly original variation was played on this subdominant theme, by a most enterprising Dutch Eurasian. Since both in features and colour he closely resembled the local Thai people, he managed for close on three years to lead a double life, passing his days working punctiliously in Chungkai camp, and—after slipping quietly through the bamboo fence at dusk—spending his nights with one of the local village ladies, who is alleged to have borne him three children during the extended period of what may not inappropriately be called their joint confinement.

*

Throughout the period described in this chapter work on railway- and related bridge-construction continued with fluctuating degrees of intensity related primarily to seasonal conditions. But the worst was to come.

Whether a bad miscalculation was made in this connection, or whether Tokyo decided to rush the line through more quickly than had originally been intended, we never found out, but, for one reason or the other, the last few months of its construction saw the crowning atrocity of all, with the arrival on the Thai–Burma railway of the so-called Forces H. and F. from Changi. These ten thousand officers and men, of whom close on half died within three or four months, were drafted up as reinforcements to put the finishing touches to the railway. Naturally, with the disarming politeness for which the Japanese are so justly famed, this was not mentioned to them before they left Changi, and instead they were told that their destination was yet another new rest camp, where food and living conditions would be immeasurably superior to those in Changi. (We, of course, were not in contact with them at the time, and could not warn them of their impending fate.) Accordingly, the doctors in Changi decided to send up large numbers of malnutrition cases, many of whom were specially discharged from hospital in order to join the party bound for the land flowing with milk and honey.

Naturally, a rest camp would be provided with all luxuries, but it was deemed advisable to take up a piano just in case that had been overlooked. So, cheerful and optimistic, the boys were driven into Singapore, where they got into standard Federated Malay States Railway box-cars, thirty at a time, an inconvenience they were prepared to overlook in view of the sumptuous conditions awaiting them at the end of the journey. Three and a half days later, when the train stopped at Ban Pong, they were blandly told that the programme started with a two-hundred-mile march through the jungle.

Despite all protests, heavy kit had to be dumped, and the march began. I will spare you the horrors of that march, as I, thank God, was spared them myself. Suffice it to say, that as they trudged on through the sodden jungle, perpetually soaked, outwardly from the rain and inwardly from sweat, and bitten to distraction by mosquitoes, their feet shredded into ribbons, and their legs swollen with beri-beri, they presented such a picture of complete despair and degradation that even now one's blood runs cold at the recollection. Most of them seemed utterly dazed and incapable of taking in what had happened; others still believed, even now, that the rest camp would mysteriously materialize somewhere beyond the blue horizon, and we hadn't the heart to disillusion them.

So, beaten before they started, already more reminiscent of the evacuated sick parties than a crowd of reinforcements, H. and F. Forces came to Thailand, only to melt away like snow before the sirocco. Among the casualties were scores of old friends including the whole 18th Division classical concert group except Denis East, and Eric Cliffe who was not in H. or F. Forces. George Wall, Reginald Rennison and Foster Hague were all dead, and heaven only knew who else. How many of my old friends perished in this particular episode I shall never know. Nearly fifty per cent of 10,000 in under four months was pretty good going even for the Imperial Japanese Army.

5. HOPING AGAINST HOPE

Hope springs eternal in the human breast. Pope, *An Essay on Man*

Hope deferred maketh the heart sick. Proverbs 13:12

With the completion of the railway link between Thailand and Burma in the 'winter' of 1943, our basic task was accomplished, and from 1944 onwards such further working parties as were called for up-river were needed mainly for maintenance work. Already by the latter part of that year Allied bombing and low-level machine gunning of the upper portions of the line had begun in earnest, and further depredations occurred as a result of very heavy rains during the last few weeks of the monsoon. As these working parties consisted of relatively small groups of men, dispersed at wide intervals along the line, the Japanese decided to establish near Kai Sayok an up-river headquarters—to be known as *Dai Ichi Bun Kensho*—for the distribution of pay and supplies to these remote centres. The Japanese had stated that the officer in charge of this new outfit would also act as British liaison officer between it and the down-river base camps, and for this reason they had at first intended that the person appointed must be able to speak Japanese. However, as no spare Japanese interpreters were available they eventually appointed me, apparently because I spoke four other languages! What use French, German and a smattering of Russian might be in the remote reaches of the Thai jungle was never made clear, but my Dutch was certainly relevant and I welcomed the chance of improving it and putting it to use.

Meanwhile an even more interesting prospect seemed to be emerging when, just before I was due to be sent up-river, a pamphlet, printed in English and presumably dropped by one of our planes, found its way into Chungkai camp. Although most of the factual information it contained had already reached us via our radio, what really excited us was the arresting headline: 'Hold on boys, we're coming'.

With these exhilarating words sizzling inside my head I cheerfully complied with a Japanese order to board a barge to Kanburi landing stage, where a truck would take me to the railway station to catch the next train up to Kai Sayok. At the landing stage three Dutch Eurasians and two Australian non-commissioned officers were also waiting for the same truck, and told me that they, too, were destined for 'a new liaison office' up-river. Being the only officer present, I assumed command of this little party, and meanwhile two Korean guards mysteriously materialized and gave me to understand that they were supposed to be taking us to Kai Sayok.

So far, everything seemed to be fitting together like a well-constructed jigsaw puzzle, and the only remaining snag appeared to be the complete absence of any trains. However, a prolonged search eventually led to the discovery of an inoffensive-looking locomotive performing its morning ablutions in a siding. We waited while it pottered to and fro, hesitantly collecting a few odd box-cars, and then, gaining courage, it blew off a lot of steam and announced its intention of starting immediately.

Amid tremendous excitement the Koreans shepherded us into an empty truck, spread a few coconut mats on the floor, and told us we could sit on them. Apparently I was not sufficiently scraping in my thanks, for I soon found myself, so to speak, on the mat. Did I keep my boots on in England when I was offered a clean mat to sit on? Yes, I replied, invariably; it was an old English custom. However, if the Koreans preferred my bare and sweaty feet it didn't worry me, so off came the offending footwear, whereupon they suddenly changed their minds and ordered me to put my boots back on again.

In due course the train started. The weather was pleasant, we had adequate haversack rations, and altogether it looked like being a reasonably comfortable trip. We chugged along at a good steady fifteen miles per hour across the Tha Makan bridge, past Chungkai, and so up into the jungle. Late in the afternoon speed was reduced to a merely nominal figure as we crawled round the creaking sinuosities of the Whampoa viaduct, a precariously poised piece of bamboo bridge-building, clinging to a limestone cliff, like a spider suspended from a ceiling.

Every now and then we stopped for an hour or two in a siding to wait for a passing train, and by the time darkness descended we still had about thirty miles of switchback gradients and spindly viaducts to negotiate before reaching Kai Sayok. A fountain of sparks poured forth from the funnel of the locomotive as if from a huge Roman candle, and it was all remarkably reminiscent of the Marx Brothers film *Go West*.

Meanwhile, the Koreans had grown a trifle restive, like tired children who had been on the journey too long. Fed up with their own company—and who, after all, could blame them for that?—they started on us. Did I like dancing? No. Could I teach them how to do a tango? No. Bakayero. Bruddy pooru. Finally, what was my name? Fisher. Pisha-ka? No, Fisher. Ppphhhisha? (this time with a noise like escaping steam and astonishing facial contortions). Ppphhhisha. F, ka? All right then, have it your own way, Pisha. Ha, ha, I think bery punny name. Ha, ha, so do I.

Eventually we reach Kai Sayok, a largish looking station, so far as could be seen in the dark. 'Out! speedo! *speedo*!' Pintos (slaps) for the last three men to get out, and then a long stumbling trek behind an elusive lantern, to a half-finished hut with no bed slats. 'Here sleepo', and away goes the lantern, and here we are in Kai Sayok, tired, but with nowhere to sleep; and hungry, but without any food. But there are always ways and means. We grope around in the jungle for a bit, and succeed in finding a Japanese cookhouse manned by B.O.R.s. We switch on the charm, and in due course are rewarded with a bucket of stew and another of rice. After that we doss down on the floor, and go to sleep. All in all, it had been a much more tolerable journey than we'd had any right to expect.

After breakfast next morning I was summoned to meet my new boss, a severely pock-marked and completely unshaven Korean, who spoke a fair amount of English, and appeared to understand a good deal more. His name, he said, was Konoye and he had studied at Waseda University in Tokyo. That was fine, I replied, my name was Fisher and I had been at Cambridge which was almost as good. This remark seemed to please him, and he offered me a cigarette, before going on to explain that Dai Ichi Bun Kensho was his office and I was to be his stooge.

After pestering Konoye for about a week, we managed to get permission to visit the neighbouring working camp at Kai Sayok, whenever we wanted, and that widened our social circle appreciably. Several old friends were there, including Dudley Gotla, who had been sent up country immediately after the production of our notorious *Thai Diddle Diddle* at Chungkai, though not necessarily on that account. He was in cracking form, and busy at work on a new and better revue, to be called *Hi-Tiddly-Hi-Thai*.

Life at Kai Sayok was not at all bad. We were able to purchase a certain amount of eggs, bananas and tobacco at not more than double the Chungkai prices, and after I had put a couple of Dutch Eurasians into our little cookhouse we fed extremely well, particularly as far as *sambals* (spicy side-dishes) were concerned. Our numbers remained quite small, around the thirty mark, until just before we left, but we had an almost continual stream of visitors from surrounding camps, mostly officers, who had been sent to collect the pay which periodically I brought up from Tha Makan. During the 'winter' months it could be quite chilly at night, and we used to light large fires in the middle of the huts, while the roar of an occasional tiger somewhere in the jungle served to provide enough local colour to make us feel that we were really being rather tough.

Our Aussies here were an excellent little group, mostly middle-aged men who had held quite good jobs before the war, and were conspicuously lacking in the exaggerated boisterousness which characterizes some of their countrymen. Indeed, they gave the impression of being on their best behaviour towards us Pommy officers, and punctiliously stressed their 'Sirs' and 'Captains', though on parade they were as democratic as Soviets. 'Come on, boys,' the sergeant-major would say a few minutes before eight o'clock every morning, 'Let's fall in for *tenko*' (roll call—the Aussies had a predilection for Japanese terms). One by one they would troop out, yawning sleepily and rubbing their eyes in a dazed sort of fashion. 'Would you mind getting in the rear rank, Harry?'—'Righto, Tom'—'Goodo. Well how many have we got? Twenty-three, twenty-four, twenty-five. That makes only three short. That's not at all bad.' Voice from the rear: 'Tom, I think one of the other bastards is just coming out of the hut now.'—'Come on, George, we're waiting.'—'O.K.'—'Well, we're only two short. I'll go and report all present and correct to the skipper [that is, the captain —me].'

As I very quickly found out, so long as you ask but never order, an Aussie will do anything under the sun for you, and probably do it very well. But if you try pulling rank on him you'll be faced with a passive resistance movement that Gandhi himself would have envied. On one memorable morning, immediately after an unexpected crowd of visitors had made an overnight stop in one of our huts, our Australian sergeant-major came to me in a tremendous rage to say that the visitors—themselves Aussies, who incidentally were just having breakfast from our cookhouse—had stolen a considerable amount of kit of various kinds from our regular inhabitants. I extracted from him a complete list of what was alleged to be missing and then went along to where the visitors were breakfasting.

For about five minutes I talked to them all like a Pommy bastard version of a Dutch uncle—saying that I would never have believed that Aussies would have treated their cobbers like that. I read out the list of what was missing: blankets, haversacks, boots, etc. And then I added, 'I'm not asking any questions but I'm going to leave you all alone for five minutes, and when I come back I expect to find all this missing kit laid out in the hut.' Sure enough, when I returned there it was, but instead of the six blankets, eight haversacks and two pairs of boots on the company sergeant-major's list there were eight blankets, ten haversacks and three pairs of boots.

Konoye, our 'Number One', turned out to be a great character, though not exactly an attractive one, and provided a continuous source of amusement, when he wasn't too bad tempered. He belonged to the very large group of Koreans who had begun by behaving atrociously to us, but had now succeeded in deciphering the writing on the wall, and were desperately making hurried attempts to live down their former reputations. Thus he offered to supply us with 'whissaki', and even with women if we so desired, and was greatly puzzled by our refusal of the latter, especially since, as he charmingly put it, 'in jungle no man see'.

Despite strict orders to the contrary, Konoye and many other Koreans in the camp went out of their way to tell us the news. Kunihara, our quartermaster, for example, was both garrulous and disillusioned. 'Big navy battle in Pirripines,' he announced one day. 'America pipty ships lose—Japan two ships lose.' We greeted this with loud laughter and Kunihara joined in. 'Yes,' he added, 'I think paper make mistake. I think Japan a hundred and two ships lose.' Towards the end of 1944 Konoye told me, in a little heart-to-heart talk, that Germany was nearly 'pinished', and six months would see its end. I professed surprise, which I later allowed slowly and surreptitiously to change to agreement, before asking what would happen to Japan when Germany was finished. He put on his inscrutable Oriental act for a few minutes, before replying, with much head-shaking: 'Bery dippicurt, bery dippicurt. I think Japan pinish too.' On the whole it was a pretty sound assessment, but after all he did claim to be a graduate of Waseda University.

Our monthly visits to Tha Makan made very welcome breaks in the monotony of jungle life. We usually went in pairs, accompanied by a Korean guard, and spent at least a week at the base trying to sort out pay claims, which were in an unbelievable muddle. With a good guard like young Arai, a trip could be really enjoyable. Arai was a genial and enormously husky fellow, with a face like a rather lecherous lizard. He had a tremendous (and entirely unfounded) respect for me as a hard-drinking man, which arose in a curious way.

From the beginning of our captivity we had been bombarded by Japanese propaganda about the wickedness of 'red-faced, meat-eating, whisky-swilling Anglo-Americans'. As it happened, I was in pretty good health even at this late stage in captivity, and my cheeks still retained a good deal of colour. So, on our first trip to Tha Makan together, Arai seized the opportunity to discuss the problem which had obviously been causing him much deep thought. He opened the bowling as follows: 'You—Pisher—you bery red pace. I think you bery much whissaki drinking.'

'No,' I replied, 'I Thailand whissaki not very much liking—very sukoshi drinking.'

He agreed that Thai whissaki (strictly known as *lao rong*) left much to be desired, but then went on: 'When you in England, how much whissaki you drink, ka?'

Acting on the principle that if you ask a silly question you get a silly answer, I replied, 'Oh, very sukoshi—perhaps one bottle a day—not more.'

His eyes popped right out at this. 'One botteru ebery day, ka?'

'Well,' I conceded, 'on big days, Number One days—like birthday or Kurisumasu—perhaps two or three bottles, but ordinary days usually only one bottle.'

From this moment he ate out of my hand, and behaved more like a brother than a guard. Every time we encountered any of his friends on the journey he would point out my red 'pace', and boast admiringly of my exploits, which would be followed by roars of laughter and usually a close inspection of my person by all concerned. Moreover, Arai seemed to be so deeply distressed by the thought of such a premature alcoholic as myself being deprived of the one remaining solace in life that on one memorable occasion, and entirely at his own expense, he bootlegged a supply of the whissaki upon which I was so pathetically dependent, and I had no option but to drink this awful stuff, on an empty stomach, before breakfast.

However, times were beginning to change, and these relatively comfortable and relaxed days were clearly drawing to a close. On Japanese Navy Day (which celebrates their naval victory over the Russians at Tsushima in May 1905) in 1943 we had all received a full day's holiday accompanied by one can of pineapple per six men, as well as a considerable lubrication in the form of whissaki for everybody. By evening most of the guards were incapable of guarding anything, even themselves, and I watched with interest as one of them walked straight into a tree and then tried to kick it out of the way before discovering that he had recently removed his boots. But when Navy Day came round again in 1944 there was no pineapple or whissaki, and we received only a half-day's holiday—though, as someone remarked, that was fair enough as by now the Japanese had only half a navy.

More seriously, however, Allied bombing and strafing of the railway were becoming everyday occurrences, and the train journeys to and from Tha Makan were getting too dangerous for comfort. And worse was to come. At about six o'clock one evening, just as I'd arrived at Tha Makàn on my routine visit, a group of us were surreptitiously and excitedly listening to a news bulletin (we didn't receive them up-river) which ended with an account of an Allied attack on a railway bridge near Chiengmai in the far north of Thailand. Somebody made the inevitable remark that it wouldn't be long before they had a crack at our bridge at Tha Makan, and damn it, wasn't that the noise of aircraft in the distance? It was. We rushed outside and, sure enough, there the bombers were, twenty-seven of them, flying at about 10,000 feet and gleaming like great albatrosses in the evening sun.

It was so long since we'd seen anything like it, that we stood there staring at them like a crowd of school kids, until a signalling burst of machine gun fire, followed by the sudden swish of falling bombs, caused us to spring, as though jet-propelled, into the ditches and drains along the edge of the hut. The formation passed, wheeled round and flew back into the sunset without further comment, and we stumbled, more than a little shaken, to our feet, to find clouds of dust and smoke hanging over the south-west corner of the camp. It had been an unlucky effort: they'd missed the bridge completely—though not by very much—but two bombs had landed in the camp, and a number of our men had been killed. A frightful flap ensued among the Japanese, who feared we might try to escape or do something equally impossible. Roll calls were held immediately, and we were kept on parade till nearly midnight, but still they weren't satisfied. Digging for the bodies continued all through the night.

I was due to return to Kai Sayok immediately after breakfast, and was very glad to get away. But I knew perfectly well that yesterday evening's affair was no isolated flash in the pan. We should be seeing those boys again, and not only in Tha Makan; big bridges up the line, and important stations like Kai Sayok wouldn't be forgotten either.

Several times during the next few weeks, in the course of my travels up and down the line, I had the opportunity of witnessing a big attack from the ringside seats, and it wasn't pleasant. The bombers came in at surprisingly low altitudes, for there was no opposition on the ground more serious than a few light machine guns. Then suddenly they would swoop down even lower, like enormous bats, spraying everything within range, cant over on one wing, swing nimbly round and, before you had had time to replace your Adam's apple, start the same process all over again. The din was terrific, with shots, bombs, and splinters of metal ripping through the air in all directions.

Somehow, one felt, this was not in the contract. Coolie work, beatings, disease, and even death from such treatment might be expected, but strafing by one's own planes, hundreds of miles behind the lines, was a bit thick. And it was extremely demoralizing. A tin hat may not be much good against a direct hit, but it's surprising how exposed you can feel without one at times. But the real cause of demoralization lay deeper than mere lack of protecting armour or weapons. When you are being bombed by enemy planes, even if you've only got a rifle, you feel that at least you are playing your part, and anyhow it's war. But when your planes are attacking the enemy, and you happen to be mixed up in it, you feel as uncomfortable as an unexpected intruder at a mass murder. Most of us had been bombed fairly frequently by Germans and Japanese before, and had often wished we could see the sky black with our own planes for a change. Now our prayers had been answered, but hardly in the spirit in which they had been intended. Somehow we had missed the bus once again; it was hard still to be on the losing side after five years of the game. Or as one unofficial regimental motto put it, we were *Semper in excreta*.

*

Early in 1945, the Japanese announced that new policies were to be followed about the employment of prisoners on the railway. Although everything else was shrouded in mystery, two things were clear: all ranks at Kai Sayok and most of the camps in the vicinity were to be returned to Tha Makan or Chungkai in the near future, and all officers would then be collected into one big camp completely separated from their troops. For once the scheme went according to plan. I travelled down to Chungkai without mishap on 10 January and, a month later, was transferred to the aerodrome camp at nearby Kanburi which had been selected as the new officers' abode.

For most officers the transfer to Kanburi involved only a short and relatively painless move. A few, including myself, came down more or less direct from the jungle, and another handful were later sent across from Saigon. But the vast majority came from the big base camps, Chungkai, Tha Makan, Tha Muang, Nom Pladuk and Nakom Patom, all of which were situated within a day's journey of Kanburi. Nevertheless there must have been few who did not feel that the move was one of major significance, for the separation of officers from their men obviously marked an entirely new departure in the Japanese policy towards us. In importance the move recalled the great exodus from Changi in 1942. The first eight months in Changi had formed the initial phase of our imprisonment; the ensuing two and a quarter years up and down the railway comprised the middle period; and now, beyond any doubt, we had entered on the final stage.

Our reactions to this state of affairs were, not unnaturally, somewhat mixed. Ever since 16 February 1942 we had looked forward to the Allied return to our part of the world, and hungrily scanned the horizon for any signs of the approaching end. Of course, we had often said, it will probably be a very sticky time for us. The Japanese may be in such a mood that anything may happen, but it's got to come and when it does, it will mean that either release or death is at hand. And now, after three long years of waiting, we knew that we had entered upon that stage. Quite apart from our radio news, the great increase in air activity, indeed the apparently undisputed Allied mastery of the air over Thailand, could not possibly be interpreted in any other way. Nor, for that matter, could the new Japanese policies, the concentration of officers, the tightening of restrictions, and the strengthening of defences in and around the prison camps. But there were other signs too. The behaviour of both the Japanese and the Koreans was changing unmistakably, and on such a scale as to make obvious its connection with the march of events in the world outside.

That, however, did not mean that they all reacted in the same way. On the whole the attitude of the Korean guards improved. Most of them seemed to have their heads fairly well screwed on and, despite the strenuous attempts by the Japanese to prevent their learning the news, they probably realized far sooner than the average Japanese soldier what the true state of affairs was. To the Koreans, therefore, the problem was simple. They were not Japanese, and though they had apparently made no objections in the foregoing years to swimming with the Japanese tide they were now determined at all costs not to sink with it. Nevertheless many of them began to get very jittery about the reckoning they believed to be coming, on account of their individual treatment of prisoners. Probably at least half of the guards had, at one time or another, struck or beaten officers and men on little or no provocation, and many certainly had far worse crimes on their hands.

So a great wave of repentance began to sweep through our Korean community. Some of the better-behaved ones sought out officers whom they had previously treated well or helped in some way, and tried to obtain from them a 'no pinto' certificate. Others just tried to be pleasant though, to judge from the results obtained, it must have been an uphill struggle in most cases. The essential differences, indeed the diametrically opposed viewpoints between themselves and the Japanese, were the subject of almost daily homilies to us in terribly laboured and painstaking English which, however, we found no difficulty in understanding. Nevertheless not all the Korean guards manifested any visible signs of improvement. Many were such terrors that even six months' hard reformation made no appreciable difference, and at times the strain was too much and they lashed out all the more viciously for their previous unfamiliar abstinence.

By contrast, the reactions of the Japanese showed much more complexity, and at least three quite distinct patterns of behaviour could be recognized among them. There were, first of all, those who had never behaved badly to us. Such people included many who had already had amicable or even cordial business or other relations with Westerners before the war. Most of these had consistently shown little sympathy with the official attitude adopted towards prisoners, and none whatever with its excesses. With the approach of the end their behaviour underwent no change, except that they became understandably worried and exceedingly unhappy. Colonel Yanagida was an example of this group and perhaps Lieutenant Matsushita, our commander at Kai Sayok and subsequently second-in-command at Kanburi, was an even better one. It is impossible to estimate what proportion of the total this group contained. Naturally the more unpleasant of the Japanese were everlastingly obtruding themselves upon our notice, and caused trouble out of all proportion to their numbers, while the reasonable and decent ones deliberately tried to remain in the background and so were apt to be completely unknown to the majority of prisoners. In all probability therefore this group was more numerous than we at first sight supposed.

Almost certainly, however, the largest element comprised the bulk of the ordinary Japanese man-in-the-ricefield, the undistinguished but by no means to be despised little man—who has his counterpart in every nation—who takes no particular interest in politics, and does an honest day's work for a far from adequate day's pay. When the war came he obediently regarded us as the enemies of his emperor and fought us as such; when we became his prisoners he treated us in the way the Japanese army told him to do; and now that Japan was on the verge of defeat, he began to think it would be best to pull his socks up and to watch his step a trifle more carefully, in case any awkward questions might be asked.

And finally there were the fanatics, the overgrown bullies and the psychopaths, who had swallowed hook, line and sinker the insane fantasies—as well as the not inconsiderable element of truth which existed side by side with the latter—in the mish-mash of Japanese propaganda. Among the fanatics were many who, during the first year or two, when they believed Japan to be still riding on the crest of the wave, had often displayed a condescending magnanimity towards us, but who suddenly swung to the opposite extreme when they could no longer conceal from themselves the inevitability of defeat. Perhaps not surprisingly, the two most extreme examples of these ultra-fanatics were two small and very insignificant men, who for the first time in their lives had felt big when Japan appeared to be winning, and then felt smaller than ever when they knew that it was hell-bent for defeat. Specifically these two pathetic individuals were little Adachi—the vest-pocket interpreter in the early days at Chungkai—and Noguchi, who immediately after the capitulation of Japan described himself as 'only a poor chemist', though in the meantime he had for several months made life hell for us while he was group commander at Kanburi.

Unfortunately for himself, and even more so for the rest of us, Noguchi was so consumed by anti-Western hatred that he seemed to spend the greater part of his time provoking us by every conceivable kind of spite, presumably in the hope of making us commit a sufficiently serious misdemeanour to justify violent retribution by him and his two henchmen, Sergeant Shimojo and a Korean guard invariably referred to as 'the undertaker'. Thus, after the first month or so there occurred an unprecedented week of trouble, in which the military police collaborated ably with Noguchi in making life unpleasant. Several officers, who were suspected of having had contacts with the Thais, were carted off and subjected to beatings and torture resulting in a few burst ear-drums, some nasty bruises, and one or two cases of nervous collapse; but from the Japanese point of view the treatment was entirely fruitless, and they learned nothing at all. Next, all written documents were to be handed in. A receipt would be given for these and they would, of course, be placed in safe custody. But if any such documents were found in subsequent searches, the owner would receive extremely severe punishment. Up till then I had carried round, in a fairly well disguised container, what I hoped would become a Ph.D. thesis, written partly before the campaign, and partly in Changi, and I was loath to part with it. But the sight of some of the officers on their return from the military police interrogation decided me, and I handed my papers in. Needless to say, I never got a receipt, and a few weeks later I learned that they, in common with nearly all other documents, had been immediately chucked into the fire. So that was the end of nearly twelve months of hard work.

A fresh wave of purely Noguchian annoyances then ran through the camp. In view of the complete absence of anything to sit on, apart from the bed slats, from which our feet couldn't reach the ground, and without any back to lean against, almost every officer had long since made himself a stool, which he had carried with him to the new camp. All stools must now be handed in for firewood. Then, on some utterly trivial pretext, the canteen was closed, and a few days later all concerts were stopped for a similar reason. Meanwhile, every few days, a search or a beating occurred, or some fresh petty niggling restriction found its way into orders. And so life went on, in a mounting climax of irritation, till after a few months we were reduced to a state of utter exasperation. We could neither lie down, nor read, except during the lunch hour and after six o'clock; there was nowhere to sit properly, nor was there any light after eight-thirty; we couldn't smoke outside, except at certain selected spots, and then only in the evening, nor could we hold lectures or talks inside or outside the huts. Moreover, sufficient guards were now available—another sign of the times—to see that these regulations were obeyed to the letter.

The whole situation was infuriating, the more so because, given a reasonable commandant, this could have been easily the best camp of all; the talent available for theatricals, education, and indeed every form of activity practicable under prison conditions far exceeded anything that had been collected together in one area since Changi days. Nor need there have been more than enough work to occupy everyone for at most three or four hours daily, since the Japanese had definitely decided that officers should no longer be employed on the railway or on anything else of that sort. But the idea of our having the afternoons free positively revolted them, and they were quite prepared to give themselves extra work and trouble in order to prevent it. However, the Japanese—both officers and men—were so depressed by the absence of our shows, that, after a lull of some weeks, it was decided that these could be resumed, though with the strict proviso that there must be no speaking on the stage.

A very clever little revue, relying largely on mime and dumb show, made its appearance shortly afterwards, but that was regarded as quibbling. Henceforth there must be no acting. One has, of course, seen many shows, both in captivity and out of it, in which acting was conspicuously absent, but that was hardly what was meant, and the restriction not unnaturally cramped the style of our producers more than somewhat. Before long, therefore, shows became emasculated in more senses than one, since they contained little more than a number of witty songs written by 'Biggles', and performed by 'Fizzer' Pearson, interspersed with individual appearances by some of the more effeminate members of the camp, suitably dolled up, who shimmered on to the stage looking like dreams and singing like nightmares.

Orchestral music, fortunately, suffered less. Norman Smith had been appointed the new Number One Music Man, and succeeded in maintaining a high standard of entertainment at all performances. But once again the palm went to Eric Cliffe, who produced two really excellent concerts of 'long-haired music', as our Americans called it, including such works as the Egmont Overture, *Finlandia*, three of the Enigma Variations, and the Overture to *The Barber of Seville*. Even the Dutch were impressed, and remained firmly convinced that Eric couldn't possibly be an Englishman.

So, up to a point, life proceeded peacefully for a few weeks, but everybody felt that there was something ominous in the air. The Japanese were putting on their inscrutable Oriental act all the time, and that could ultimately mean only one thing. A precursor of the wrath to come appeared in the form of an intricate series of new ordinances, which were suddenly read out to us one day on parade. Although numbers 1 to 5, 10 to 16, 23 to 27 and a few others were neatly summed up as 'not translated', it was abundantly clear from the remainder that we were not going to be allowed to do anything at all. There was, as yet, no actual proscription on breathing; but even such a relatively harmless activity as visiting the lavatory at night was now hedged in with restrictions. A further proviso of the new regulations was the establishment of an elaborate honorary hierarchy of prisoner officials. Under the British camp commandant, henceforward to be known as the General Assistant, there were to be a series of Assistant Assistants, whose task was neatly summed up as that of assisting the Assistant. The Assistant Assistants having to do so much assisting themselves, were to be assisted in their assisting by a batch of Sub-Assistant Assistants, whose task . . . . It was all very uplifting, and the process of mass-mutual aid soon began in earnest. Everybody was frightfully helpful. But the air remained heavy, and one had the old feeling, well known to cross-channel sufferers, that there was more to come. It did.

A day or two later a nasty little guard demanded that the officers working the cookhouse pump should get him a bucket of water to wash in, and they refused. The spokesman was hauled off to Noguchi, and Captain Drower, the interpreter, was sent for. Bill Drower, whom I'd known since the days of the *Capetown Castle*, was one of the bravest and most respected men in the camp, and he detested even more than most the idea of crawling to the Japanese or indeed to anyone else. Although he spoke better Japanese than most interpreters, he had no time for the face-saving frills of that language, and expressed himself quite unmistakably, in a way that would have been considered straightforward in English but was regarded as distinctly rude in Japanese. Noguchi asked why the officer in question had refused to fill the honourable bucket for the honourable Japanese soldier, and Bill replied that British officers were not batmen.

Whereupon Noguchi and one of his associates, nicknamed the Frog, each seized the nearest piece of available furniture and, letting out a couple of fearsome yells, leapt into the fray and belaboured Bill until, after some three chairs and a stool had been smashed in the process, he finally collapsed. He was dragged unconscious across the ground to the guard-room, and locked in the 'no good house' for an unspecified length of time, on an unspecified charge, but with a strictly specified diet of rice and water. And there he remained, for weeks on end, except that once he was removed from the cell which was urgently required for a few drunken Korean guards, and spent a fortnight in a disused air-raid shelter, half full of water. All appeals to Noguchi for his release proved vain, and eventually Noguchi threatened to shoot the General Assistant if he mentioned the matter again.

Meanwhile the rest of the camp didn't go unpunished. Drower had said that officers were not batmen. Very well, they should not do any more work at all. The hundreds working in the cookhouse, canteen, pumps, sanitation squads, and dozens of other lesser but equally essential services were dismissed, and skeleton staffs recruited from the handful of B.O.R.s, whose original function in the camp had been to act as servants, on the not very liberal scale of one per twenty officers.

At first the whole affair, apart from the savage treatment of Drower, seemed rather ludicrous, and we all laughed a good deal about it. But our hosts soon made it clear that, though we weren't working, they had no intention of letting us do what we wanted all day long. Next day we were confined to the huts until further notice. So, ruffled but hardly daunted, we posted lookouts at the end of each hut, and settled down to reading, card playing, and other forbidden pursuits. Late in the afternoon the Frog spotted the lookouts, and threatened further reprisals. Things were getting bad. However, we hadn't been forbidden to talk yet, though nobody had anything very original to say. Parlour games and quizzes seemed to offer a possible solution, until one officer was marched off to the guard-room for organizing them in his hut. At the end of a fortnight, the incarceration came to a completely unexpected conclusion, and we were allowed back to work on slightly worse terms than before. It was a great relief to get outside the huts again; but Drower still lay in his cell, and a severely strained atmosphere continued to prevail in the camp.

Kanburi was a depressing camp and there was not much comic relief to be had there, except for the goings-on of the *chusa* (field-officers') hut. What we should have done without them I don't know, but an all-wise Providence saw to it that, no matter how bleak the outlook might become, the gossip from that quarter could always be relied on to dispel the gloom.

At an early stage in its career, the *chusa* hut became known unofficially as the Imperial War Museum, and the story is told of one irreverent captain who went in one day and asked to be shown to the Indian Mutiny section. A bright spark among the majors replied that it was two bays further down, 'just past Wellington's officers'. The younger majors there had a grim time so far as one could judge from their accounts. Two of them told us of how they were once grumbling to each other about their neighbour, who had been holding forth uninterruptedly for over an hour on the various stoppages likely to occur on the Bren light machine gun, when another colonel, who had partly overheard the conversation, chipped in with his customary opening, 'When I was on the Somme in '15—' and treated them to another hour and a half on the stoppages liable to affect the corresponding weapon used in the First World War.

Besides the mild entertainment afforded by our respected seniors, there remained one other ray of light amid the gloom of Kanburi. It flickered a good deal more now than before, and soon it was to go out altogether—a fortnight before the end of the captivity, though we didn't know it at the time. Kanburi was the camp in which, before we went there, four officers had been beaten to a pulp for operating a radio receiving set, but nevertheless the Webber brothers—Max and Donald, who had operated our radio at Chungkai, before being moved to Kanburi—were still willing to take the risk, and reception started up again a few weeks after we arrived there. However, very much closer supervision by the guards, together with far more frequent searches, made things almost inhumanly difficult, and the supply of news became correspondingly more meagre and irregular. But what news it was!

This was what we'd been waiting for. Germany was crumbling, Hitler was dead, it was all over in Europe. . . . It called for an almost superhuman effort not to talk about it, but we kept quiet till the Japanese themselves let it out in dribs and drabs, a week or so later. So now we had unquestionably reached the final stage. But how long was it going to be? One thought dominated everyone's mind. Will the Japanese fight to a finish, or will they have the sense to capitulate, and save at least something from the wreckage?

For several weeks nothing else interested us; we thought about it all day long, and dreamed about it as soon as we got to sleep, if we succeeded in doing so. But we couldn't answer it. Our own personal interests, probably our own personal survival, were so inextricably bound up with what happened that we felt utterly incapable of trusting our own judgement on the point. We had been disappointed so bitterly and so often by wishful thinking that we dared not indulge in it again. And yet . . .

That was just it. Logically one couldn't escape the view that Japan would try to get out as quickly as possible. Never again would it have such an opportunity to save some modicum of face, but unless it did so soon there wouldn't be any face left to save. My own estimate, when in a logical mood, was that Japan would survive Germany by three months. But I didn't believe that it would be over as quickly as all that. I didn't believe anything.

It would be very difficult to assess the general attitude of the camp on this matter. The experts on Japan agreed, almost to a man, that the war could not last many more months. Bill Drower, a few days before his incarceration, told me he was betting heavily on the end of July; Gordon Skinner, another interpreter got even closer and, at least three months before the end, gave 15 August as his outside date (which proved to be the exact date of the capitulation). A tremendous burst of optimism, based partly on these opinions, and partly on those of our ebullient soothsayers, suddenly started to surge through the camp, a week or two after the collapse of Germany.

Meanwhile it became apparent that all our necromancers, of whatever type, were now favouring late June or early July 1945 as the final end of the war. One fellow told me of a long and involved story he had received from an Indian fakir, all of which had so far come true; the next item was to be his return to Europe in the summer of 1946. The inevitable Dutch Eurasian who went into trances and saw visions—every camp in Thailand claimed to have one, though the Eurasians themselves never knew who it was—reputedly supported the June thesis, though with certain unstated reservations. Another gentleman convinced himself, from a spate of concentrated palmistry, that early autumn offered better prospects, but all we could get from similar mass observations on the part of an amateur phrenologist was that we were nearly all over-sexed, and unlikely to make much money in the future. Needless to say, none of this information was news to us.

But the weeks passed and nothing happened. Reaction followed inevitably, and pessimism set in with a vengeance. Logically, I reasoned, the situation hadn't changed. The three months were not up; the Russians had not yet had time to transfer adequate reinforcements to the eastern front, and nothing would happen until then. But I couldn't convince any except those who were already convinced; and I was not among them. The gloom deepened with our fortnight's confinement to the huts, during which we got no news at all. A slight break occurred with its sudden resumption, but pessimism returned when we learned that only one more bulletin would be received, as the batteries were practically exhausted. After that we should have to rely on the pamphlets dropped by our planes. These were in Thai or Japanese. We had interpreters who could read them and the local population used to slip them through the fence to us. Some actually fell in the camp on more than one occasion.

And then a terrible thing happened. It was not known to many, but I was one of the few who did get wind of it. News came into the camp, I don't know from what source, that the Thais were planning an insurrection towards the end of August, and furthermore, it was rumoured, the Japanese knew and had plans made for our immediate liquidation if it came off. We had heard disquieting things before, though without any fixed dates being mentioned, and the Koreans had frequently told us that, in the event of local military activity, we shouldn't stand a dog's chance. And, in any case, one always felt that ruthless bombing of Japan, already taking place, might provoke widespread retribution against the prison camps. The temper of the Japanese suggested that this possibility might easily become an actuality.

A sudden negotiated peace seemed to be our only hope, but the chances were rapidly dwindling. Logically, no doubt . . . but the

Japanese weren't logical: that was just the trouble; you never knew where you were with them. My own morale touched its lowest point about this time, and though I did my best to conceal it, and to remain as cheerful as I could, the almost nightly dreams of frustration, now heavily tinged with fear, showed me that it was no use trying to conceal it from myself. Three and a half years was really too much of a good thing. Three I had bargained for, but the prospect of another Christmas in captivity, probably under atrocious conditions, and quite possibly my last one anyway, was a bit hard. We were getting to the end of our tether, and we knew it.

On such occasions, I decided, the only thing to do was to take stock of the situation and face the worst. I did so one weekend, and reached a conclusion which, while not cheerful, would serve as a working basis for the next eight or nine months. By my thirtieth birthday—in April 1946—I should either be free or dead. Probably the issue would be settled several months earlier; it was anyone's guess what the chances were. This was not exactly comforting, but one had to make the best of what consolation was available. I resolved to face the future in that spirit.

How far any such thoughts were entertained by other people, I obviously do not know. Even in my own case I was only partially conscious of them, except at odd moments. But there was a noticeable increase of irritability among people in general during the later days at Kanburi; tempers were becoming more frayed, and conversation seemed very laboured at times. I personally was conscious of a growing intolerance towards the little foibles of my neighbours, and I sometimes got very tired of their faces, in a way that I'd never previously noticed throughout the captivity. No doubt they felt the same about mine, and probably with more justification.

However, at least a temporary diversion lay ahead in the forthcoming move to Nakom Nayok. The Japanese had stated, months previously, that all prisoners were to be moved behind a line well to the east of Bangkok, and the general assumption was that they, with us as their hostages, would make their final suicidal stand in this area.

Later they selected a site for the officers' camp, and in June the advance party had left to clear the jungle and to start building the huts. The rest of us were to follow in batches of four hundred, and my party, the fifth, was due to leave on 10 August. The journey was said to entail a long march—distance unspecified—with no transport for kit, so we should have to dispense with most of such limited material goods as we possessed.

Already the Japanese had stated that the new camp was to be an earthly paradise, so we braced ourselves to expect something pretty ghastly. But at least it would involve a change of scenery and routine, and however lousy it was it could hardly be worse than what we had long become accustomed to. After that God alone knew what would become of us.

6. THE ROAD TO RANGOON

'Does the road wind up-hill all the way?'
'Yes, to the very end.'
'Will the day's journey take the whole long day?'
'From morn to night, my friend.'

Christina Rossetti, *Up-hill*

The move to Nakom Nayok involved a two-day train journey to Bangkok, a river voyage through the city to the dock area, two or three days' wait there for no known reason unless, perhaps, to expose us to any odd bombing that might be coming, another twelve hours of train journey, and finally a twenty-nine-mile march. Less than a week before our party was due to leave, a British plane tried out new tactics over the railway, a few miles from Kanburi, by cutting off its engine some distance short, and swooping down in total silence over a station from behind a line of low hills. It was entirely unexpected, and a train waiting in a siding was virtually annihilated.

A day or two later Captain Noguchi informed one of our party that, for the first time in many months, all the bombed bridges between Kanburi and Bangkok had been repaired, and he hoped we should have a good trip unless, of course, any further bombing occurred. The prospects didn't seem too cheerful to us, and most of us expected a blitz, either before or during the period of the move.

However, we had no choice in the matter. One bright spot on the horizon was that there now seemed to be a chance of getting batteries or accumulators at the other end, so the radio receiver was accompanying us, and the arrangements for its transport appeared to be absolutely foolproof.

The appointed day, 10 August, arrived, and after lunch we paraded in the pouring rain preparatory to departure. Spirits were somewhat damped, but I tried to raise a laugh by saying that it would be just our luck to have to make the whole trip in the pouring rain, and then find on reaching our destination that the war was over after all. Nobody else seemed to find this particularly amusing, so I let the matter drop. At the last moment before we left, some final alterations—in typical Japanese fashion—were made to the party, with the result that our little group of six got split up into three pairs, each travelling in a separate truck. John Beckett and I were attached to a group of rather aged and infirm Dutch officers.

The rain slackened off, and we marched out to the railway, where a long line of open trucks was waiting, later to be joined to a dilapidated locomotive, the whole effect being strongly reminiscent of early prints of the opening of the Stockton and Darlington Railway in 1825.

Thirty-two of us climbed into each truck, and arranged ourselves as best we could, and after tremendous frenzies of shouting, swearing, and general excitement on the part of the Japanese, the train started off in the wrong direction. After due consideration, it changed its mind, and its course, chugged slowly a distance of half a mile, and then stopped for three hours in Kanburi station to recuperate.

Everybody scanned the sky for planes, until dusk brought a temporary relaxation; the train started again, and so did the rain. Some time during the night we stopped at Nom Pladuk, and sat shivering in the open trucks for about two hours, while they slowly filled with water. Then, just as the rain showed signs of stopping, we were allowed to take shelter in some covered wagons in another siding.

The journey continued next morning in somewhat better weather, with consequent heightened anxiety about air attack, but our luck held, and no planes put in an appearance. There was plenty of evidence of extensive and accurate bombing of bridges and sidings, and it was obvious that traffic on the line had been reduced to practically nothing. Towards evening we found ourselves in slightly more civilized-looking country, and shortly afterwards the skyline of Bangkok could be seen in the distance.

It was a city I had always wanted to visit, but hardly in such circumstances. The train drew up just before dusk in a badly shattered station, full of wrecked rolling stock, and we were ordered out, and shepherded to an open space nearby. Hundreds of Thais gazed on, somewhat uninterestedly, eyeing the Japanese with utter contempt and very little of the fear which had hitherto characterized the bearing of virtually all the Asians we had seen under the Japanese occupation.

We scraped together some sort of a meal, and boiled a few buckets of tea, and once more the heavens opened and the rain descended in streams. At about midnight a large party of us had to load hundreds of crates and boxes, belonging to the Japanese, on to the barges in which we were to travel down to the docks. It was a pitch-dark night, and still soaking wet; the ground was a squelching mass of mud and the air hummed with mosquitoes. Dozens of guards yelling conflicting instructions, accompanied by sporadic outbursts of bashing, did little to clarify the situation, and we splashed and slithered about for two or three hours until the job was finished.

After that we were formed up and counted, fallen out and formed up in a different order, and re-counted, *con variazione*, twice more, and eventually were ordered on to the barges. Goodness knows what their normal complement was, but by the time they had got thirty on board they looked pretty full, even by P.O.W. standards. However, it seemed that the local contractors had sent only half the number specified by the Japanese, so thirty more passengers were shoved aboard and, somehow or other, managed to squeeze in. But that was not enough, apparently. A silly little Japanese interpreter then started up in a sing-song voice: 'This barge holds eighty men; you must assist each other';, this monotonous dirge went on, over and over again, for about quarter of an hour.

Unfortunately the glum crowd of Dutch planters, with whom we had somehow got mixed up, showed no signs of assisting each other or anybody else, not even themselves, but just sat there looking tough. This infuriated the guards, and suddenly one of them came to the boil, and started lashing out with a barge pole. A minor stampede occurred, and the Dutchmen retreated further into the interior, while twenty more unfortunates were hustled unceremoniously on board. This was just about the limit. The heat was unbearable and the fug even worse, but the end was not yet. There were still scores of people left ashore and all the barges claimed to be full. We were ordered to number, first in Japanese, standing up, then in Japanese sitting down, and, in succession, in English standing, sitting and standing again. The results obtained were variously 79, 83, 81, 80, and 84. Finally two attempts at numbering, in a medley of Dutch, English and Japanese, agreed on 80 as a compromise figure, and we hoped that honour had been satisfied.

Hurried conferences in Japanese followed, and after frenzied shouting and gesticulation the guards started shoving another batch of about twenty on to our barge. One of them fell in the river (it was still dark, of course) and had to be fished out, to the accompaniment of throaty *bakayeros*, and a moment later two people inside fainted and had to be propelled to the open prow over everyone else's heads. The confusion, screaming, and bashing thereupon hit a new high, when suddenly the tow rope broke, and away lost and pilotless we went, drifting dizzily down the Chao Phrya river, now in spate at the height of the monsoon.

We bumped into dozens of craft and piers during the next few hours, and every time we thought the end had come. I had been on one of these barges before, when it had sunk in a few minutes, and I didn't fancy being one of a milling crowd of a hundred in the middle of the Chao Phrya on a dark night. But somehow we survived, and morning found us far beyond the docks, drifting placidly down towards the sea. A launch eventually collected us and delivered us at the docks, where we staggered out, weary and cramped, and were lined up, counted, and fallen out two or three times, and then told to stay where we were until further notice.

The place in question was a huge new godown (warehouse), built just before the war by a French firm. Part of it housed a large number of British prisoners, who were employed on working parties in Bangkok. We received the strictest orders not to speak to them, but already one of them had managed to slip a note to an officer whom he recognized. It was brief, but to the point. The war was over; five separate Thais and one European, believed to be a Dane, had all shouted this astonishing news to the working party during its trip into Bangkok that very morning.

Of course nobody believed the story. Most of us didn't even bother to listen to the end of it, we'd heard such stories so often before during the past few years that we longed for something a trifle more original. We could see a few Thais from where we were, and they manifested no sign whatsoever of anything out of the ordinary, so the story was dismissed there and then as utter bunkum, and we retired for the night having already forgotten about it.

Next day, however, stories came in thick and fast. A message, pushed through the partition by the doctor looking after the troops next door, said that he had in his possession a copy of the *Bangkok Chronicle* of 12 August, which stated that Japan had 'accepted a Potsdam truce'. Naturally, we had half a dozen people, all of whom knew exactly what a 'Potsdam truce' was, and although all had different ideas, everyone agreed that it was a good thing. I remained sceptical.

But later in the day a Dutch friend, who spoke and read Chinese, came rushing in with the news that his friend had acquired a local (Japanese-controlled) Chinese paper of the 6th, which mentioned a conference in progress at Potsdam, and suggested that one of its aims was to drag Russia into the war against Japan. If this was entirely separate from the doctor's story, then clearly there was something in both of them; but long experience had taught me that the latter was probably merely a fanciful embroidery of the former, and still I refused to believe.

We had to wait one more day in the godowns, and excitement now began to run pretty high. It reached a feverish pitch just before we left, after one of our troops, well known to many of us, succeeded during a moment when a guard was not looking, in conveying the news that a Thai had thrown a packet of cigarettes to him a few minutes before, as he drove past in a truck. On the outside of the packet was written in pencil 'War Over'. Reckless betting now began on an enormous scale, and most of my neighbours seemed convinced that at least something big had happened. So was I, but I wouldn't admit it. I had been disappointed so often before that I wasn't going to be caught again. I offered to bet anyone a thousand to one in anything, that the war was still in progress, and was promptly taken on, fortunately only in cigarettes, by my friend John Beckett.

During the morning we loaded up the train with Japanese belongings and prepared our kit for the next stage of the journey. After a diffident sort of lunch, we were paraded and told to get into the train, thirty-seven to a truck. This time they were covered box-cars, such as we had travelled in when we came up from Singapore nearly three years before. It was a blazingly hot day and the temperature inside appalling. But the journey was to have its compensations.

Crowds of Thais lined the railway at various places in the outskirts of Bangkok, and many of them appeared to be trying to convey some sort of message to us. As we slowed down to a walking pace at one point, the man nearest the door swore he heard a railway official shout: 'The war is over', but nobody else was quite convinced. Then a few moments later, a whole bunch of Thais cheered us vociferously, and one of them, in a burst of inspiration, made signs that shooting had ceased. There was absolutely no doubt about what he meant, but whether he really knew was another matter. Many of us remembered more than one occasion in the past when Thais and Chinese, doubtless in good faith, had given us false news, and we didn't intend to be fooled again. But surely there must be something in it this time. Nothing quite like this had ever happened before.

The train drew into Bangkok Central Station and stopped. The guards assembled for a pep talk, after telling us to stay put. Meanwhile a charming-looking old Thai, in an elaborate uniform with rows of unrecognizable medal ribbons, came tiptoeing down the opposite side of the train from where the Japanese were. He whispered into each truck, perfectly distinctly, 'Only three days more—see you again soon,' and disappeared. Finally, we became nearly delirious with suppressed excitement when, perhaps five minutes after this episode, the Thai driver of a locomotive on a track parallel to ours, started making frantic but utterly incomprehensible signs to us. The old boy was not to be put off, however. He fished out a bit of white asbestos board from somewhere in the cab, and printed on it with a lump of coal:

Newspaper.
England and America
is
V.

Then, calmly and unobtrusively, he started up his loco, and ran her slowly up and down the track for the whole length of our train, with his little placard dangling from the cab window. It was one of the neatest jobs I have ever seen. Even I began to admit there might be some truth in the story now and the tension increased to an astonishing pitch, for the guards were still within earshot and we dared not yet make any audible or visible demonstration.

I have never been slapped in the face with the proverbial wet fish, but I should imagine it feels much as we did on the guards' return from their pow-wow. They were anxiously scanning the sky and told us bluntly that in the event of an air raid, we must remain in the train. So we had allowed ourselves to be fooled after all. The war was still on. We might have known it. The smiles disappeared from thirty-seven faces, as if they had been struck with a whip. John Beckett pulled out a couple of cigarettes, lit one in silence, and handed the other to me. 'I think you've won it after all,' he added with a forced laugh. A long silence followed, broken ultimately by an incurable optimist, who nervously suggested that perhaps it was true all the same, and the Japanese didn't know yet. Nobody even bothered to reply, and gloom settled in for the night.

In due course the train got under way again, but we had lost interest in the outside world now. Rain soon began to pour down and a brisk wind blew it into the truck, soaking many of us to the skin. What a life! Would we ever have any luck? So the 15 August 1945 drew to a close, as we rattled slowly through eastern Thailand, feeling cold, and wet, and very sorry for ourselves.

At about 4 a.m. on the 16th the train stopped, and we were dragged out and ordered to unload it. It was another black night and the rain continued to stream down as fast as ever. The guards were surly and bad-tempered, and one or two minor outbursts of tantrums occurred. Unloading continued until nearly six, and we were then told to lie down until seven, when the march was scheduled to begin.

With the approach of dawn, the rain slackened off to a drizzle, but otherwise the situation showed no improvement. We climbed into our kit, stood hanging about for a quarter of an hour while we were counted, and then started off at a snail's pace, which was all that many of the older ones could manage, along a sodden gravelly road full of potholes and puddles. It was a shocking march. The day turned out to be first muggy, and then scorchingly hot; the guards' tempers grew steadily worse and we were already tired out before we started. We trudged on, with one or two brief halts, until eleven o'clock, when a lorry from the new camp met us with some breakfast, but, owing to a slight mistake, with no tea, the only thing we really wanted. The British officer on the truck was unable to pass on any news, even if he had any, because of the continued presence of a Japanese sergeant, but he didn't look particularly happy. Nor did the behaviour of the scores of Thais we passed during the course of the day give us any cause whatever for believing yesterday's rumours.

We plodded on all through the afternoon, along a shadeless road. Nearly a third of the party collapsed one or more times, but all were bullied back onto their feet before long, if necessary by a little judicious kicking, in appropriately painful places, until, weary and exhausted, we fell out by the roadside for supper round about six o'clock. This time somebody reckoned he had collected a story from the truck driver, namely that Noguchi had stated to Colonel Toosey that morning that he had received a great shock, and refused to discuss even the most pressing camp business with him. A faint glow of optimism began to return, but a sudden downpour soon put it out, and we were once again ordered to start marching.

We stumbled on in blinding rain for another seven hours. Theoretically, we were to spend the night in a disused Buddhist temple, but owing to the extreme darkness the guards had lost their way and their tempers as well, and persisted in forging ahead. (They, of course, had no kit to carry.) But there comes a limit to everything, and at 3 a.m. it was obvious we could go no further. Men were collapsing by the dozen from sheer fatigue and exhaustion, and it was impossible to keep the party together. So, very angrily, the guards ordered us to doss down by the roadside and 'sleepo' till seven. I believe the rain continued all through the night, but fortunately I slept right through it, and awoke, remarkably refreshed, a few minutes before we were due to move off again. We had no more food or tea on the march, and my water-bottle was nearly empty but, after all, it was only another twelve miles, so we ought to be able to make it. After four of them I felt considerably less certain, but continued to hope for the best. Others were not so successful, and before long were collapsing right and left.

By now the guards were acting worse than I'd ever known them at any time in the whole captivity. People who fainted were kicked until they got up, or until the Japanese got tired or urinated on to their faces to speed up the process. So much for the wishful thinking of yesterday's optimists who had claimed to have noticed an improvement in their behaviour, 'as if they knew that the war was over'. We passed more Thais, but they looked sullen and said nothing. It was no good trying to delude oneself any longer. The show was still on. What fools we'd been to let ourselves think otherwise.

We arrived in sight of Nakom Nayok camp, which stood near the top of a rough road winding its way uphill, at 2 p.m. on the 17th, so exhausted that many could barely stand. As of old, Sergeant Shimojo was there to see us in; his ugly figure could be recognized from afar. It needed only this, we felt, to put the finishing touch to a really epic march. So, committing our souls to the Lord, we stumbled into the camp, and drifted slowly towards the barrack square to be counted.

For three and a half years, I had speculated on how—if ever—the news of the end would ultimately reach us, but nothing I had ever conceived of was as dramatic as what happened now. Shimojo waited till we had all staggered onto the square, and then came slowly forward and bowed. Would we please sit down while he counted us; he wouldn't detain us long. And with that we knew, beyond all shadow of doubt, that the wild, crazy, mad rumours of the last three days were true and the long years of waiting had terminated in fulfilment.

There was a little bathing pool in the camp, built by our predecessors who had dammed up a small stream that trickled down from the hillside. We hobbled across to it, chucked off our clothes and splashed about in ecstasy for a few minutes, as the full significance of what had happened slowly registered in our fuddled brains.

We had come through after all. We should be home for Christmas. I should be able to get married. I should have to give John Beckett a thousand and one cigarettes.

Meanwhile sporadic cheering broke out all over the camp, following the official announcement from the office. Shimojo had called on Kampar, the burly Dutch interpreter, and smilingly told him that the war was over. Kampar, poker-faced and diplomatic to the last, bowed politely as he replied: 'Really? Who's won?' It wasn't until next day that we learned that what had ended the war and so almost certainly saved our lives was the dropping of the atomic bomb on Hiroshima. Some of us wondered whether we were worth it.

Nakom Nayok was a lousy camp; it was miles from anywhere, and it rained all the time. Naturally nobody worried much about this on the day of the capitulation. We had held a short victory sing-song that evening, terminating with the British, Dutch and American national anthems, and the appropriate flags mysteriously produced from nowhere now fluttered from three bamboo poles hurriedly erected outside the office. Our choir had managed the British national anthem with great success and had even navigated itself through a somewhat Anglicized and high-pitched version of 'Het Wilhelmus' without serious difficulty. But the 'Star-Spangled Banner' had foxed both us and the Texas Gunners, and had ended up as a baritone solo by a tone-deaf American naval officer. However we were all very happy, and went to bed in a mood that none of us will ever completely forget.

During the next week or so, one excitement followed another. The Japanese disgorged all the mail in their possession—much of which had been in their hands for over a year—and likewise handed over to us similarly accumulated stocks of Red Cross parcels and clothing of various kinds. Then a series of air drops were made by planes from Bangkok which provided us with large quantities of canned food and fruit juice which was particularly welcome, and a day or two later a British Officer arrived at Nakom Nayok with liberal supplies of Thai currency to enable us to purchase whatever local foodstuffs and other necessities we could find.

With this in view, contact was quickly made with the *Nai Amphur*—the provincial governor—and through him with his local subordinates closest to our camp. Everyone we dealt with was extraordinarily friendly and helpful, and all transactions were lavishly lubricated with *lao rong*—we didn't want to offend our new Thai friends by continuing to use the Japanglo 'whissaki'. Vast purchases were made, on a camp basis, of pigs and poultry, and several superannuated water buffaloes were hurriedly extricated from the nearby ricefields to serve as sacrificial victims to the red-faced meat-eating Anglo-Americans.

Inevitably, after more than three years when the only real delicacies were privately purchased duck eggs—concerning which our doctors unanimously advised 'if in doubt, eat: there's no doubt about a really bad duck egg'—our protesting stomachs finally resorted to industrial action, and we in turn adopted a policy of *relâcher pour mieux manger*. The only snag we encountered in the whole of this blissful but brief interlude was one of liquidity, for the Thai banknotes which reached us from Bangkok were of such high denominations as to embarrass our delightful Thais who obviously didn't want to exploit us but never had enough small change to bridge the gap. However, one of our most congenial new friends solved the problem of giving change for a fifty-baht note, tendered by one of our officers in payment for two ducks, by offering in return a small chicken and three eggs, and adding, rather apologetically and euphemistically, that if that wasn't enough, the officer was welcome to accept his daughter as his 'number two wife' for as long as he wished to do so.

Meanwhile a bar was opened where suitably doctored *lao rong* could be obtained every evening, and we began to feel almost as if we were in Malaya once again, as we duly drank our familiar little noggin at sundown. For the first time in years we could now begin to relax and turn our thoughts to the future which, until recently, we had come to regard as a purely hypothetical quantity which had better be left to look after itself. Only at this stage, after the formal Japanese capitulation, did most of us begin to realize the degree of tension under which we had lived for so long and, as it began to relax, we too began to feel a trifle flat. For although contact was maintained with the outside world by radio and camp news bulletins, which could now be read aloud to everyone, outwardly our life had changed but little. The squalor, slush and stench remained as before; we still slept on the rough ground in overcrowded huts, and as the days passed into weeks we began to get restive. One or two senior officers departed to take up staff appointments, for which the main qualification seemed to be the ability to live in a luxury hotel in Bangkok. We were not sorry to see them go, but rather envious none the less. No news whatever had been heard of a move, and rumours began to circulate to the effect that we should remain at Nakom Nayok for at least another six weeks.

Then, on 30 August, entirely out of the blue, we heard that some of us would be leaving for Bangkok airport the same evening, and from there would be flown to Burma. The parties were selected; my name was not on the list, but at the last moment two of us got put on as replacements and, in frenzied excitement, by flickering candlelight, we collected together what few belongings we wanted to retain, and paraded with the others in the pouring rain just after midnight.

To all intents it might have been just another vintage Japanese move. It had been raining hard for most of the past twenty-four hours and the branch road leading up to the camp was absolutely impassable to vehicles. So we had to march the first two miles, sliding and stumbling in the mud through the blinding rain. We averaged nearly a mile an hour. Transport to Bangkok was in the hands of the Japanese, and a line of lorries stood waiting for us on the main road. True to form, there was one missing, so we, along with eighteen others had to force an entrance into someone else's truck. We were lucky enough to get in with a crowd of batmen who preserved excellent humour although they were all soaked to the skin. Strange, unending tuneless songs, such as only soldiers sing, rang out all through the night as we bumped and bounced along the appalling roads of eastern Thailand. Several times we slithered off the road and twice just avoided missing narrow bridges and plunging into the river below.

Shortly after dawn the truck broke down, and a delay of two hours ensued, punctuated only with endless *bakayeros* and 'speedos' from our irrepressible troops, now at long last able to get their own back on the Japanese who remained very subdued. We got moving again after a time, and were now able to see something of the countryside, where to our amazement all the Thais were displaying tremendous exuberance, smiling, shouting, and waving to us, and quite obviously sharing in our enjoyment. The interest and sincerity of these simple but very likeable folk were deeply moving and even today I cannot write of their behaviour on that day without feeling a lump in my throat.

We arrived at the airport just before midday. Nobody knew how long we should have to wait, but it would certainly involve staying at least one or two nights. Everything was still in the improvised stage. Latrines, washing facilities and feeding arrangements were of the most primitive, and after dark the place swarmed with mosquitoes. Everything was still very P.O.W., and all the usual discomforts abounded.

But on the morning of 2 September a few of us received orders to parade at noon for plane number 27. We put on our new shirts and slacks, and threw away most of the rest of our kit. After lounging about in the hangar for a few minutes we marched out to the landing strips where twenty-seven beautiful new Dakotas stood lined up in a row. The navigator of number 27 was the first European from the outside world we had seen for three and a half years, and even as we spoke to him we felt the recent past slipping away from us. He opened the door and told us to hop in.

Everything inside was spick and span. Two rows of comfortable canvas seats piled high with recent papers and magazines lined the sides; the metal work glistened in the sun. The days of makeshift and improvisation were past. This was where we belonged. The pilot, a good-looking young squadron-leader in a trim, well-fitting uniform, popped in to say hello. The lavatory was at the rear, where there was also a basin to be sick in But we needn't worry about that; it was good flying weather today and there should be no bumps worth mentioning.

He promised to tell us what to do if he went up really high. Did we want any lunch? A dozen U.S. Army haversack rations were produced, and handed round. 'Righto, let's go.'

The plane wheeled round, raced swiftly along the runway and slid smoothly into the air. It circled for a few minutes over Bangkok, gaining height, and then headed north-west across the plains towards the mountains and Rangoon.

Nobody spoke. We glanced through the pages of *Picture Post* and the other illustrated papers, looking more at the photographs and the advertisements than at the text, as we tried to piece together some sort of idea of the world to which we were going back. Would it be battle-scarred beyond measure, or still recognizably the same? Would it stand shattered or sublime amid the ruins and rubble of the past? Should we find it embittered or ennobled by the sufferings of six weary years of war?

And ourselves? What had we to bring back? Cynicism and despair, hatred and revenge? Or a new hope and courage, based no longer on the blind optimism of youth, but born out of the very realization of the weakness yet universality of our common humanity, whether we be British, Americans, Dutch—or Japanese? Bitterness is a temptingly cheap sentiment, but it was none the less a luxury that we could ill afford.

There would be few luxuries in the England to which we were returning. But there would be other things that we had learned to value more. An armchair, a pair of slippers, a bed with clean sheets and a pillow; the clammy fog of autumn, the tingling crystal cold of an East Anglian winter, racing winds on a Yorkshire moor, and the surge of the sea round a Cornish headland; bread and cheese with beer in a country pub, the sound of lush layers of strings in an orchestra, and the miracle of our first English spring. And other things, too intimate as yet to express because we had almost forgotten how to behave with gentleness and tenderness. Yet it was true: all these things would be ours again, even though we couldn't believe it yet.

We had crossed far above the ridge of mountains that divided Thailand from Burma, and our ears popped and buzzed as the plane dropped steadily down. It had been a smooth flight, and we should make Rangoon within half an hour, a few minutes under schedule. And away to the west, already dimly discernible beneath the towering ranges of snow-white clouds, lay the coast of the Indian Ocean with its shimmering wave crests scintillating in the afternoon sun.

7. HOME AND BACK EAST AGAIN

Look East, where whole new thousands are.
Robert Browning, *Waring*

My return to England more than exceeded my expectations. In part, no doubt, this was because the latter had been repeatedly discouraged by a succession of briefings, delivered to us mostly by members of the Army Education Corps, who at each port of call on the way home bombarded us with dire warnings not to expect Britain to be what it had been before the war. The devastation caused by German bombs and doodlebugs and the rigours of rationing were reiterated *ad nauseam*, and to make matters worse various medical officers informed us that, after so long a period on starvation diet, it would probably be several years before any of us could hope to achieve paternity. And, just for good measure, our relatives had meanwhile been alerted to the need to regard us as mentally abnormal, comparable in fact to shell-shock cases though, in order to speed our return to normality, wives and girl friends had been advised to put on plenty of make-up and to wear their shortest skirts.

Fortunately this alluring package of recommendations worked wonders for all concerned, and after what in effect had been a glorious two-month cruise spent mainly in sun bathing on the boatdeck of the S.S. *Orduña*, eating and drinking our fill all the way, and fêted to our hearts' content by bevies of Wrens wherever we stopped, we arrived home in fine fettle.

In fact, of course, our first stop was Rangoon, where we were instantly made welcome by ex-Burma campaigners, and were much amused by one enterprising local publisher, who had produced a glossy booklet celebrating the defeat of the Japanese and embellished with a photograph of the Japanese Emperor, described as 'the former Son of Heaven, now in Hell'.

In marked contrast to Rangoon, which was still very down at heel and severely scarred by the recent fighting, Colombo was in good shape and bursting with activity. But the real high spot of our homeward voyage had been the passage through the Suez Canal where, for the first time in our travels, we were entertained by a lively E.N.S.A. Concert Party, and the sight of the Mediterranean at last convinced us that we were now barely a week's journey from home.

Even the German P.O.W.s at Suez, who fitted us out with winter clothing for the last stage of our voyage, had greeted us warmly and had gone out of their way to enquire solicitously about the sufferings—especially the meagre nature of the diet—which we had endured, and then burst into great gusts of uncontrollable laughter as we answered in the affirmative their question: 'Did the Dutch really have to live on the same rations as you did?'

Somewhat unexpectedly the dull, chilly and murky weather which awaited us as the English coast at long last came into view seemed positively delicious after three and a half years of almost continuous tropical heat and humidity. But by far the greatest surprise of all came as the *Orduña* steamed slowly into the Mersey, and suddenly every one of the scores of vessels in sight—from tugs, ferries and dredgers to tramps, oil tankers and ocean-going liners—sounded their sirens in greeting. Certainly it was meant to be a heroes' welcome, but few—if indeed any—of us thought of ourselves in such an exalted capacity. Like the Abbé Sieyès, our only claim to distinction was that we had survived, and with that we were more than content.

Notwithstanding all the warnings we had been given, my own immediate reaction to post-war Britain was that nothing that really mattered had changed, as became only too apparent when the first batch of mail I opened on my return contained an Income Tax demand for the princely sum of £1.12*s*.8*d*., already long overdue on my army pay. Indeed the only fly in the ointment was that everyone in general—and my parents and sister in particular—seemed incapable of accepting the fact that there was manifestly nothing the matter with me other than an all-consuming desire to get back into academic life before such vacant posts as remained in my field had been snapped up by other ex-service men from less remote places than South-east Asia. After all, the Army Medical Board, which had checked us all on our return, passed me A1 on all counts, and the two medical officers involved shook me warmly by the hand and expressed both congratulations and surprise at my fitness. So, in spite of my parents' grave misgivings and dire warnings that I ought to take a long holiday in order to recuperate, I applied forthwith for a newly created post of Assistant Lecturer (salary £250 per annum) at the University College of Leicester, and was appointed there and then to begin my duties immediately after the Christmas vacation.

By an extraordinary coincidence I had meanwhile discovered that Irene, my former teenage sweetheart, who had waited long and patiently for my return, had just been appointed Senior Music Mistress at Wyggeston Girls School, a mere five minutes' walk from the College, and I thereupon succeeded in marrying her with a speed which must have constituted an international record. So began the happiest period of my life, during which I lost no time in doubly disproving the medical prognostications regarding the supposed sterility of ex-P.O.W.s; and meanwhile I began to establish myself professionally as a geographical specialist on the South-east Asian countries which I had come to know during the war, and for whose gracious and warm-hearted people I had already developed a profound and abiding affection. Moreover this specialization led indirectly to my being appointed Professor of Geography at Sheffield in 1959, and one evening during the winter of 1960-61, when I was attending the Annual Dinner of the Geographical Association in London, I discovered that I had been seated next to the guest of honour, Mr Katsumi Ohno, the new Japanese Ambassador to the Court of St James's.

During the conversation which followed, Mr Ohno expressed surprise at the extent of my knowledge of Japan, and asked me when I had been there. I told him that unfortunately I had never been to Japan, and in answer to his further questioning I explained that most of what knowledge I had of things Japanese had been acquired when I was a P.O.W. of his countrymen in Singapore and Thailand. 'And you mean to say that, even after all that, you are still interested in Japan?' he asked incredulously; and then, after a rather embarrassing pause, 'Would you be willing to visit my country?' I assured him that nothing would please me more than to have such an opportunity. Having become acquainted with Japanese people in wholly abnormal circumstances I was particularly anxious to meet them in normal times and more especially in their own country. Such an opportunity of visiting Japan was what I had been hoping for for years. Was it really going to happen?

The conversation drifted to other things and I vaguely hoped that perhaps something might come of it, though I didn't really expect it. But within a couple of weeks, during which the Ambassador had presumably consulted Tokyo, I received a telephone call from the Embassy, inviting me to go to Japan as the guest of the Japanese Foreign Ministry for a month or more, with all travel and hotel expenses paid (first class) and even 'reasonable bar expenses' as well. While the Ministry would be happy to arrange a full programme for me, they would also welcome any suggestions I might care to make as to where to go, what to see, and whom to meet; and they hoped I would feel entirely free to make whatever comments—private or public—I wished to make about their country, however critical my views might be. So, in circumstances about as different as it was possible to imagine from those of my captivity during 1942–5, I again became a guest of the Japanese nation, and unquestionably it was one of the most stimulating and rewarding experiences I have ever known.

Having deliberately chosen to go in late September I was completely captivated by my first view of the Japanese countryside at its most beautiful. For the autumn sun, though still strong, was now relatively low in the sky and so revealed all the delicate nuances of both form and colour, of the coastline, the terraced ricefields, and the innumerable volcanoes which provided the backdrop to virtually every vista. But in another, and perhaps more important sense, I had come at a singularly favourable time, for by the early 1960s, a decade after the ending of the Allied Occupation in 1952, the Japanese people had at last begun to turn the corner in the long and painful struggle to rebuild their devastated country as well as their—in some ways—even more severely shattered sense of national self-respect. Whatever one might previously have felt about the follies, and worse, of the former leadership which had launched Japan on its disastrous road to ruin, one could not be other than profoundly moved by the intensely disciplined, purposeful, and untiring way in which practically everyone, from children to grandparents, seemed to be devoting the whole of his, or her, energies to the supreme tasks of reconstruction and rehabilitation.

Admittedly, having by this time read much about post-war Japan, I was not altogether surprised by the immensity of the effort, and the even more spectacular results, which the Japanese were now beginning to achieve in virtually every part of the country which I was able to visit. But in at least one respect what I experienced was totally at variance with what I had expected. Shortly before I left London for Tokyo a distinguished Oxford don told me that he thought it was very brave of me to be going to Japan! Although I had never for a moment thought I might be in any danger in so doing, it had crossed my mind that, as a Westerner I might occasionally encounter a certain degree of hostility, or even openly expressed resentment, for the memory of Hiroshima, with its racialist overtones, was still very much alive.

Yet nothing could have been further from the truth. Over and over again I was treated with the utmost kindness by complete strangers, who would walk miles to show me the way to my destination, or share their more than half-empty basket of oranges with me while travelling in buses or trains. Never once was I conscious of any hostility, but time without number I, as a former enemy, was warmly accepted as a friend. While pondering over this remarkable graciousness I suddenly felt at home in another sense, as I recalled how, shortly after the outbreak of the Second World War, it had come to the knowledge of the senior members of my old college, St Catharine's, Cambridge, that one long-forgotten name had been omitted from our War Memorial to those who had fallen in its predecessor of 1914–18. So by common consent the name of L. H. Jagenberg, a former German member of St Catharine's, was added to the Memorial, with the inscription *Hostis Amicus*: among the enemy a friend.

Thus, even before I had embarked upon the extraordinarily well planned and wide-ranging itinerary which the Foreign Ministry had organized for me, I had already begun to feel completely at ease in Japan. It seemed a remarkably propitious beginning, and indeed my sense of anticipation rose even higher as I recalled a speech delivered by a particularly likeable Japanese officer, Captain Suzuki, to a large working party of Allied P.O.W.s who were about to leave for Japan in July 1944. This was what he said:

> Looking back on the past year and ten months since Prisoner of War Camps were first established in Thailand you have worked both earnestly and diligently and produced a great achievement in the construction of Thailand-Burma Railway. This work was both energetically proceeded with and successfully completed. For this we wish to express sincere appreciation.
>
> Your work in Thailand having finished you are being transported to the 'Land of the Rising Sun' an island country, choicely situated and rich in beautiful scenery.
>
> From time immemorial our Imperial Nippon has had the honour of respecting justice and morality. The people of Nippon have the nobility and generosity of spirits. They are men and women of determination, generous by nature, despising injustice in accordance with an old Nippon proverb—'The huntsman does not shoot down the wounded bird'. Such is our character.
>
> In spring the cherry blossoms are in full bloom, in summer fresh breezes rustle over the shadow of green trees, in autumn the glorious full moon throws its entrancing light on sea and river, giving the waves an iridescent appearance of gold and silver. Winter brings a

change of appearance, the landscape is covered with a mantle of snow and the scene changes to one of dazzling whiteness; such is the nature of Nippon.

The benevolence of this nature gives us an insight into the Emperor's will and induces us to act firmly together in the discharge of our filial and loyal duties as long as we live in accordance with the example set by nature. Go to glorious Nippon with an easy mind, execute your duty in an efficient manner, then our hundred million people will accept you as you are and you will enjoy our imperial benevolence.

If you have enmity in your minds and oppose our forms of justice thereby marring the Imperial benevolence it will reflect adversely on you for your remaining period as prisoner of war. Think over this and rely on our justice. Bearing in mind the sudden change of climate and customs in which you will shortly find yourselves I advise you to take care.

I pray for your health, your good behaviour, and finally wish you 'Bon voyage'.

PART TWO

GUEST OF GAIMUSHO
THE REBUILDING AND RENEWAL OF JAPAN

Held we fall to rise,
are baffled to fight better,
Sleep to wake.

Browning, *Epilogue to Asolando*

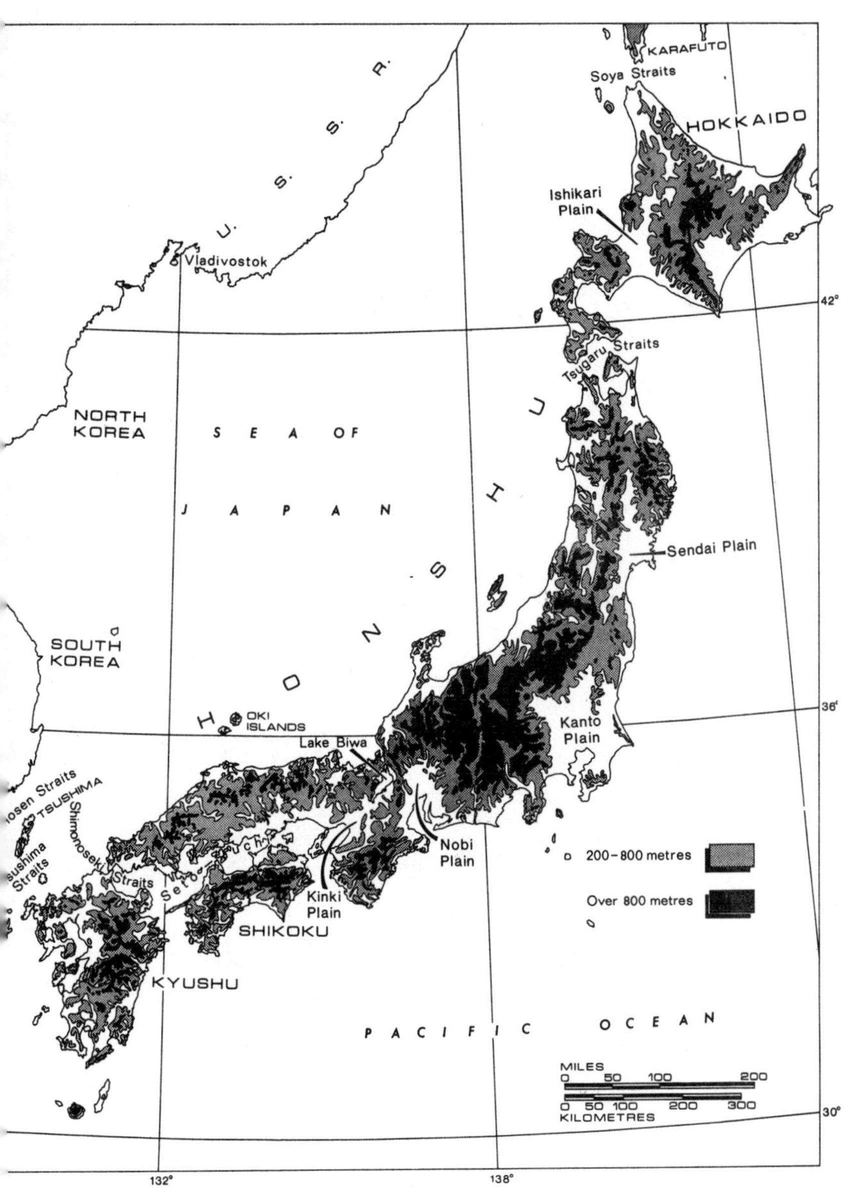

Japan: relief

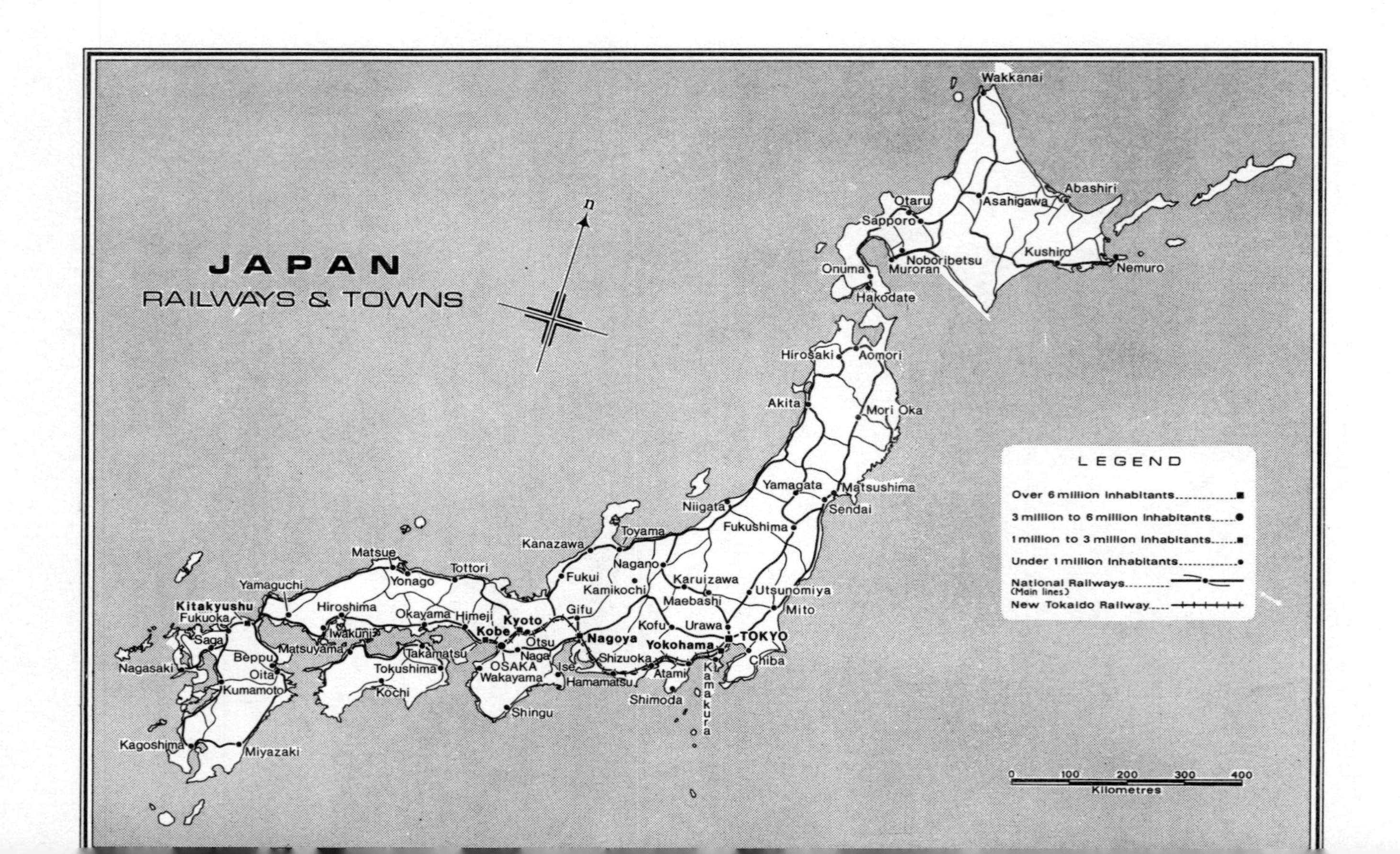

JAPAN
RAILWAYS & TOWNS
n
LEGEND
Over 6 million inhabitants
3 million to 6 million inhabitants
1 million to 3 million inhabitants
Under 1 million inhabitants
National Railways (Main lines)
New Tokaido Railway
0 100 200 300 400
Kilometres
Wakkanai
Abashiri
Otaru
Asahigawa
Sapporo
Kushiro
Nemuro
Onuma
Noboribetsu
Muroran
Hakodate
Hirosaki
Aomori
Akita
Mori Oka
Yamagata
Matsushima
Niigata
Sendai
Fukushima
Toyama
Kanazawa
Nagano
Matsue
Tottori
Fukui
Karuizawa
Yonago
Kamikochi
Utsunomiya
Yamaguchi
Maebashi
Mito
Kitakyushu
Hiroshima
Gifu
Fukuoka
Okayama
Himeji
Kyoto
Kofu
Urawa
Iwakuni
Kobe
Nagoya
TOKYO
Saga
Otsu
Yokohama
Matsuyama
Beppu
Takamatsu
Naga
Shizuoka
Chiba
Nagasaki
OSAKA
Oita
Tokushima
Ise
Atami
Wakayama
Kamakura
Hamamatsu
Kumamoto
Kochi
Shimoda
Shingu
Kagoshima
Miyazaki

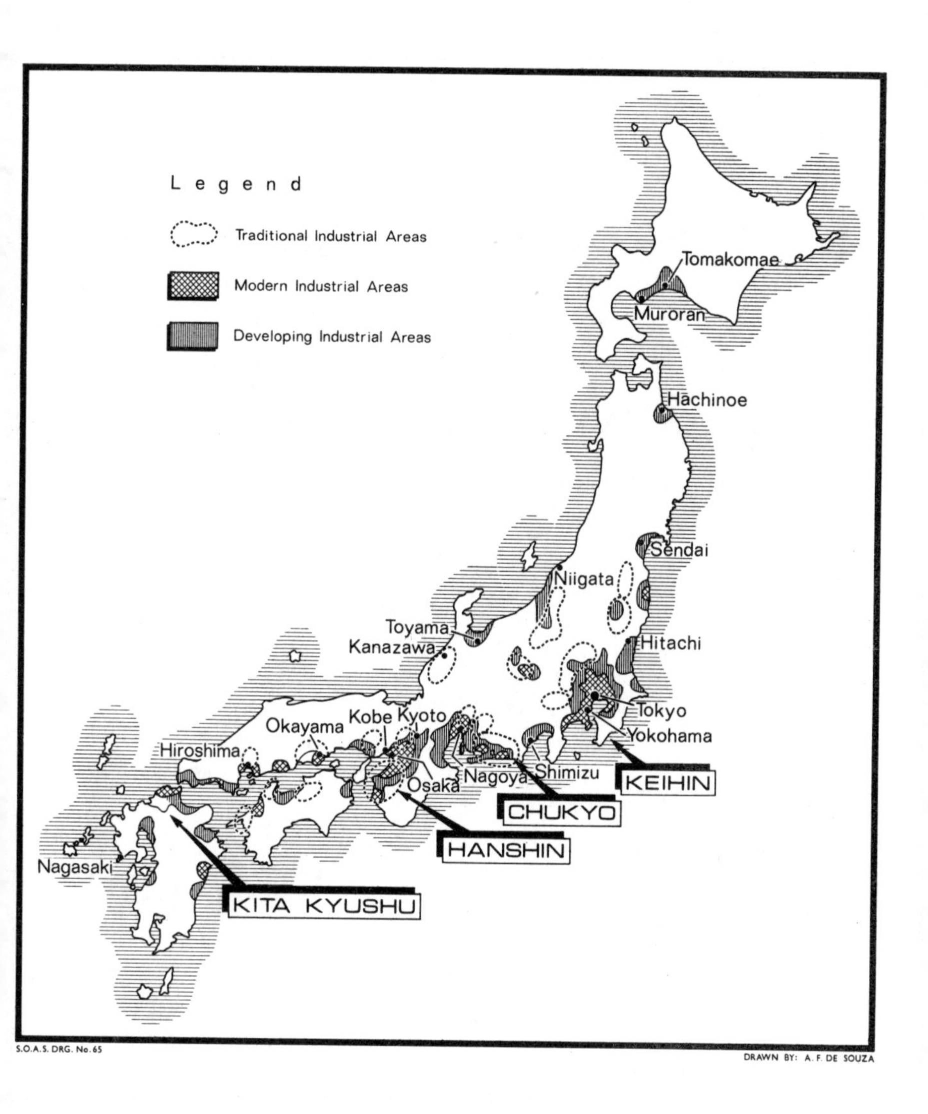
Legend
Traditional Industrial Areas
Modern Industrial Areas
Developing Industrial Areas
Tomakomae
Muroran
Hachinoe
Sendai
Niigata
Hitachi
Toyama
Kanazawa
Tokyo
Yokohama
Kobe
Kyoto
Okayama
Hiroshima
Osaka
Nagoya
Shimizu
KEIHIN
CHUKYO
HANSHIN
KITA KYUSHU
Nagasaki
S.O.A.S. DRG. No. 65
DRAWN BY: A. F. DE SOUZA

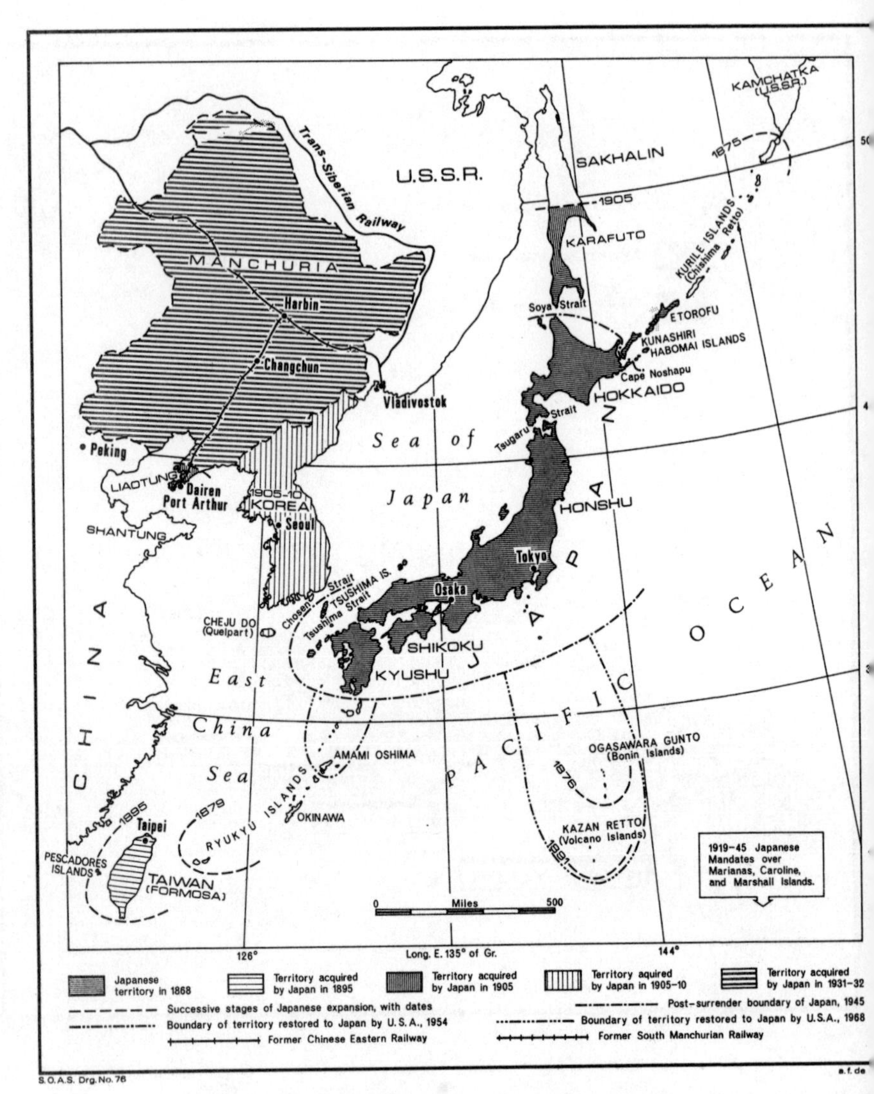

The maritime fringe of East Asia 1868-1968

8. THE BRITAIN OF THE EAST?

Nature did not tailor the resource pattern of Japan to a scale befitting a great nation.

Glenn T. Trewartha

Whether such lyrical propensities as those displayed by Captain Suzuki were as typical of Imperial Japanese Army officers as they were untypical of their British counterparts I do not know, though I suspect that some of the more inspired phrases had been culled from travel brochures intended to appeal to American tourists. Nevertheless the sentiments expressed were remarkably tolerant for so late a period in the war when, as a result of long sustained and extremely intensive Allied bombing and devastating submarine warfare, conditions in Japan were becoming extremely grim. Certainly, however, Captain Suzuki was right in assuming that, in order to appreciate what an unfamiliar country and its people are like, one should begin by seeking to understand something of the geography which sets the stage for the human drama.

At the outset, therefore, it is necessary to place Japan in its true geographical perspective as a very small country by comparison with its great neighbour China, which in area is some twenty-five times—and in population roughly ten times—as large as Japan. In short, China completely overshadows all the other states of eastern Asia put together, and moreover has a historical tradition reaching back over forty centuries, or roughly three-and-a-half times as long as that of Japan, which in comparison appears little more than a parvenu.

In such a context it is easy to understand why the Chinese have come to regard their country as the centre-piece of the Asian-Pacific world or, to use their own more poetic phrase, 'the single sun in the sky', surrounded by a series of satellite luminaries, such as Korea and Mongolia to the north, Sinkiang and Tibet to the west, Burma, Siam, the Indochinese lands and Malaya to the south, and Japan—all on its own save for the minute Ryukyu islands—to the east.

At first sight the four main islands of Japan, namely Honshu, much the largest and most important, in the middle; together with Shikoku and Kyushu—the two smallest—in the south-west; and Hokkaido in the far north, seem to present an obvious parallel with the British isles, in that both these island kingdoms lie off the opposite extremities of the vast Eurasian landmass stretching from Brittany to the Bering Straits.

Nevertheless there is a profound difference between the twenty-two miles of the Straits of Dover and the hundred-and-twenty miles of the Straits of Korea. And, particularly in the early days of dependence on small sailing craft, the effect of this difference was intensified by the usually much greater roughness of Korean waters.

Undoubtedly the high degree of isolation imposed upon Japan throughout most of its history by some five hundred miles of often tempestuous sea between itself and the China coast, and the four thousand miles of the remote, bleak, and ironically miscalled Pacific to the east, has conduced to pronounced cultural introversion and an associated lack of confidence *vis à vis* peoples from other less secluded lands. Nevertheless geographical isolation is only one of several inhibiting factors which have persistently plagued Japan. For, besides the problems posed by so pullulating a population in so small a national territory, which moreover is acutely deficient in most of the more important natural resources, the Japanese cannot escape the fact that at least three-quarters of their predominantly mountainous country is too steep for normal methods of cultivation or for use as sites for domestic, commercial or industrial buildings and installations.

Moreover, although so far as temperature is concerned, the Japanese climate is generally well suited for intensive cultivation—providing the local terrain is not too steep—most parts of the country are subject to heavy and often torrential rain during the summer monsoon, and more especially so in the extreme conditions of individual typhoons. Thus, given the steepness of the almost ubiquitous mountains, such intensive rainfall often causes catastrophic erosion and landslides, as well as disastrous flooding of the coastal lowlands at their feet.

Inevitably the effects of such catastrophes are apt to be seriously aggravated by the ever increasing concentration of human settlement within these already acutely congested patches of flat low-lying land. And, as if all this were not enough, Japan is exceptionally prone to the ravages of earthquakes, and to the devastating tidal waves (*tsunami*) to which they give rise. Understandably, therefore, this combination of an exceptionally small percentage of good agricultural land and an extreme paucity of mineral wealth, together with an almost unique proneness to natural hazards, goes far to explain why, at least until very recently, Japan has been an intrinsically poor country.

On the other hand, however, the natural beauty of Japan, and especially of Seto Naikai (the Inland Sea) with its infinite variety within a very small compass, is breath-taking, and there is a kind of natural logic in the way that the whole vista of southern Japan culminates in Mount Fuji, which accordingly has come to symbolize all that is most majestic and sublime within the country as a whole. In such circumstances it is not surprising that the Japanese people have developed an intense artistic awareness which seems to be a purely spontaneous response to the natural beauty surrounding them. And this is not only a matter of landscape in the wider sense, but also of vegetation—notably the majestic pines and cryptomerias (Japanese cedars), the graceful and ubiquitous bamboos, the flowering shrubs, and the various tufted grasses which have a loveliness that is all their own.

Moreover the Japanese take an intense delight in beautiful—but not necessarily precious—stones, which they arrange to exquisite effect, both in their minute gardens and even inside their houses. Probably more than any other advanced peoples in the modern world, the Japanese have retained an intimate sense of affinity with nature, which is closely linked with the strong animist tradition embodied in Shinto, the ancestral system of primitive beliefs, myths and legends which antedates—but, at least until recently, has not been extinguished by—the Buddhist and Confucian concepts subsequently introduced from China.

This deep-rooted sense of harmony with nature is revealed in all kinds of ways, particularly in the skill and care with which buildings are blended into the natural landscape in a way that enhances even the beauty of nature itself. Traditional houses and Buddhist temples are built almost exclusively of wood—which is often left entirely unpainted but lovingly preserved and polished, though the larger Shinto shrines and *torii*—large ornamental gates—are usually painted a rich red.

Significantly the typical roofs of Japanese houses—heavily tiled and steeply pitched, with wide gutters on both sides—are really diminutive models of the mountain-backed Japanese islands themselves, the steep slopes facilitating the rapid run-off of heavy rains so as not to flood or otherwise damage the underlying structure. But at the same time the Japanese roofs are gently curved, and the curve is identical with that of the branches of the pines which, above all other trees, the Japanese most admire.

Yet, by contrast, there has been almost equally widespread agreement among foreigners that the Japanese people are not particularly prepossessing, and in fact many Japanese have themselves been even more outspoken on this subject. Thus, for example, Komakichi Nohara, in *The True Face of Japan* clearly implies that Japanese women are not beautiful, and that such attractiveness as many of them undeniably do manage to convey is achieved by skilful grooming, and tasteful dressing in exquisitely patterned silks, supplemented by elaborate coiffures and other accessories. Or, as one of my old teachers sardonically put it, 'a kimono can cover a multitude of sins', a phrase which may also be extended to apply to the apparently monumental dishonesty, and hypocrisy evident, for example, in the statement (see p. 74) from the *Nippon Times* of 30 March, 1943, about Japanese 'humanism' towards prisoners of war. However, this element of hypocrisy, or at least evasiveness—as it seems to the outsider—may well be a by-product both of the deep-seated Japanese sense of inferiority and of the extreme formalization of behaviour which developed during the Tokugawa Seclusion, when the whole social structure tended to be frozen into immobility.

Likewise the Japanese art of making the most of what little one possesses, and invariably trying to put on the best face possible, extends into many other aspects of life—from ordinary social relations to international diplomacy—and while it often works well enough, disastrous results may follow if the 'face' in question unexpectedly comes unstuck. Undoubtedly, the intensity of the concentration of population within narrowly restricted areas has been one of the most significant factors in moulding Japanese culture. To live tolerably in such conditions calls for a high standard of social discipline, and in the event this has clearly been forthcoming, even though both individuals and groups—and on rare occasions the entire nation itself—may react explosively against the prolonged continuance of such constraints.

Similarly, in all kinds of lesser ways, such as the cultivation of dwarf trees and the highly skilled art of *ikebana* (flower arrangement) shortage of space has clearly influenced culture and behaviour. Thus the traditional house type is an almost perfect example of the economic use of space, and indeed the only room in which the Japanese tend to spread themselves is the bathroom, which I suspect is basically a model of an irrigated ricefield, the only real difference being that the bath water is—by Western standards—uncomfortably hot. The normal practice is to fill the bath—usually a tall rectangular wooden box—to the brim and then climb in, thereby displacing a substantial volume of water on to the tiled floor, which is slightly concave and so allows the surplus water eventually to drain away through a pipe from the lowest point in the centre of the room. The same basic principle could be seen in operation, at least until recently, over vast flights of terraced ricefields in the Shinano valley, where the water successively irrigated —by flooding over into them—the whole series of fields from top to bottom.

Perhaps most important of all, however, has been the way in which the geographical limitation of space has given a unique degree of intimacy to Japanese culture. This is seen to perfection in the exquisitely beautiful and mostly well sheltered Inland Sea which, with its innumerable islands functioning as stepping stones to link this entire maritime basin together, has provided an ideal nursery for Japanese seamanship.

Nevertheless, it was essentially as a result of cultural contact with China, via the Korean bridgehead, that the Japanese first began to develop a civilization of their own which, though recognizably an offshoot of the Chinese, subsequently achieved maturity and indeed brilliance in its own right. In the event, Kyushu in the far south-west was the main avenue of entry for incoming peoples and cultures, and also served as the original core area within which the Japanese developed as a distinctive people. Between the third and the first century B.C. the Chinese-derived Yayoi bronze and iron culture entered Japan, also via Korea and Kyushu, and it was by these means that irrigated rice cultivation was first introduced into the country.

Moreover the fusion of the Yayoi peoples with the earlier neolithic Jomon hunters and fishers led to the emergence of the Yamato peoples who, between the fifth and seventh centuries A.D., produced within the Nara basin, near the eastern end of Seto Naikai, the first recognizably Japanese civilization, which was characterized by the use of the Chinese ideographic script and the practice of Buddhism and Confucianism, superimposed upon a strongly developed foundation of animist beliefs expressed in traditional Shinto—'the way of the gods'.

After an attempt had been made during the seventh and eighth centuries to remodel Japan on the pattern of China, by introducing the centralized administrative system of T'ang China and building at Nara a new capital designed as a replica of Ch'ang-an, the Japanese during the Hei-an period (794–1185) once again developed a more distinctively Japanese civilization, this time centred on Kyoto. But the problem of maintaining unity in so mountainous and fragmented a land, while simultaneously struggling to drive back the more primitive Ainu peoples of the interior and north, helped to bring about the development of a new political pattern more akin to that of medieval

European feudalism, in which powerful regional *daimyo* (barons) were supported by their own *samurai* (military retainers).

Thereafter, while the imperial capital remained at Kyoto, one of the daimyo families, the Minamoto, which was based much further to the east in the Kanto plain, seized power in 1192 and its leader, Minamoto Yoritomo, became the effective ruler of the country under the title of Shogun (barbarian-subduing generalissimo). Recognizing that Kanto was not only the largest plain in Japan but also formed the strategic hinge which linked the southern and northern halves of the country together, he established his military headquarters at Kamakura near the southern edge of the Kanto plain.

However, under the Ashikaga Shogunate, from 1339 to 1573, there was an almost complete breakdown of law and order, and in the fifteenth and sixteenth centuries this found a new form of expression in piratical raids along the China coast. Meanwhile the waters between China and Japan for the first time came to be frequented by European mariners, as the Portuguese explored northwards from Malacca after 1511, to be followed in the 1570s by the Spaniards, likewise advancing northwards from Manila in the Philippines. Moreover, during the next half-century Portuguese and Spanish missionaries together made some hundreds of thousands of converts to Catholicism, mostly in Kyushu.

Inevitably, however, such developments on so great a scale were bound in the end to produce a reaction, which in turn served to aggravate the existing internal chaos. From this Japan was eventually freed by the initiative of the daimyo Oda Nobunaga, who made full use of the new smooth-bore muskets which Portuguese traders had introduced into central Japan, where they soon began to be manufactured in much larger numbers by local Japanese gunsmiths. Thus in a succession of local battles Nobunaga, with the support of two very able and loyal henchmen, Toyotomi Hideyoshi and Tokugawa Ieyasu, succeeded in establishing effective control over the previously warring feudal elements in the strategically critical area of central Japan.

In some respects Hideyoshi—notwithstanding his dwarfish stature and allegedly simian physiognomy—seems to have been the most effective of the three, thanks above all to his exceptional talents as a military strategist, and it was largely due to him that by 1590 the greater part of Japan had been pacified. However in 1592 Hideyoshi made a gross miscalculation in planning both to invade China, via Korea, as a first step towards the conquest of the whole East Asian mainland, and to make a parallel thrust southwards by sea via Taiwan and the Philippines into South-east Asia.

Viewed retrospectively this extraordinarily grandiose venture, which in fact failed ignominiously[1], smacked of megalomania, in a manner, moreover, which curiously foreshadowed the equally disastrous strategy of the Japanese military and naval leaders during the Second World War. However, it is possible that an alternative—or supplementary—motive was a desire on Hideyoshi's part to resolve the rivalries among his followers in Japan by diverting their energies overseas. In any case, however, Hideyoshi's escapades proved to be essentially irrelevant to Japan's more immediate concern over the growing volume of Western maritime activity in the surrounding seas.

In 1603 a new Shogun, Tokugawa Ieyasu, chose Edo, the ancestor of the modern Tokyo, as his headquarters, and during the two centuries which followed, successive emperors, shorn of all effective power, were compelled to reside in virtually complete seclusion in Kyoto. During this period a solution was found, at least for a time, to the problem of maintaining internal peace and unity. Fundamentally this was a geographical problem resulting from the attenuated, fragmented, and extremely mountainous nature of the country over which the Japanese people had been slowly spreading out from the south-west towards the north-east since proto-historic times, though they were still very unevenly distributed, being for the most part concentrated in scattered patches of lowland south of the 37th parallel.

The Tokugawa solution to the problem of national unity was in effect to revive the old Japanese tradition of emulating China, in particular by re-emphasizing the Confucian concept of the rigid hierarchical ordering of society, and by reintroducing a centralized administrative system, completely by-passing the imperial court which was left to stagnate in Kyoto. From its new base in Edo, the Tokugawa *Bakufu* (military headquarters) established a system of rigid control over the daimyo, and through them over their retinue of samurai and indirectly also over the peasantry, whose labours supported the whole of this feudally-based economy and society.

The method of control adopted centred in the practice of compelling all daimyo to reside in Edo for part of each alternate year, and to leave their wives and other dependants there while they themselves were in their fiefs. To make this possible the rudimentary road system of Japan was greatly improved, to include two major trunk roads, namely the Tokaido, following the southern coastal zone from south-western Honshu, with feeder roads from the islands of Kyushu and Shikoku,

[1] The king of Korea had warned Hideyoshi that his proposed invasion of China had no more chance of succeeding than would a bee trying to sting a tortoise through its shell.

to Edo, and the Nakasendo, which also extended from the south-west to Edo, but followed an inland route, via Kiso Fukushima, mostly through ruggedly mountainous country. In addition a centralized form of police control was established over movement along the main roads and also over the lives of the people within the areas which these roads served.

However, although by these various means designed to hold the entire country in a kind of geopolitical straitjacket, Japan achieved a prolonged and much needed era of internal peace and stability, this in turn created new problems. Over a period of many centuries the Japanese had shown remarkable skill in adapting Chinese methods of rice cultivation to the very different geographical character of their own islands, but no amount of skill could wholly compensate for the extreme scarcity of land suitable for such cultivation. Meanwhile population had built up to the astonishingly high figure of some eighteen million by the late sixteenth century, probably the highest density in the world at that time.

Against this background it is not surprising that during the fifteenth and sixteenth centuries individual Japanese, particularly from the coastal regions and islands of Seto Naikai, should have begun to look overseas for wider opportunities, whether by maritime trading or by the acquisition of new but hitherto relatively sparsely populated territories. Thus began the first sporadic and small-scale attempts by Japanese pioneers to establish themselves in the *Nanyo* (South Seas) a process which initially took the form of buccaneering and piratical raids. Later, these gave place to more peaceful trading activities, and so led to the establishment of small nuclei of Japanese settlers in various parts of maritime South-east Asia. Indeed, it has been estimated that in the seventeenth century there were some 15,000 Japanese living in the Philippines and eight hundred in Siam, as well as smaller numbers in Annam and Cambodia, and in 1623, in the so-called 'Massacre of Amboyna' (known to the Dutch as 'the Ambon Incident') the victims included nine Japanese.

However, well before that time, other Western sea powers had begun to explore the seaways of south-eastern and eastern Asia. In the decades after 1511 the Portuguese from Malacca took the lead, and the first recorded Europeans to reach Japan were two Portuguese whose ship had been blown off course in 1542/3, to be followed by the Spanish Jesuit missionary, Francis Xavier, who arrived in Kyushu in 1549.

While both the Portuguese and the Spanish missionaries—mostly Jesuits—made many converts in Japan and at first were well received by the Tokugawa authorities, the latter eventually concluded that the Christian faith could not be reconciled with Japan's accepted religious beliefs. Moreover the behaviour of many of the Spaniards—who wielded much more power than the Portuguese—began to cause growing alarm in Japan over the possibility that the Spanish authorities in Manila, who had already tried unsuccessfully to take over Taiwan in 1593, might now attempt to extend their rule northwards into Japan itself. Thus, partly out of fear of such foreign conquest, and partly from a sense of internal insecurity and instability, the Tokugawa Bakufu made the drastic decision to promulgate a series of edicts aimed at effectively sealing off Japan from direct contact with the outside world. In particular, therefore, it was decreed in 1637 that any Japanese attempting to leave the country would be executed, and the same fate would await any other Japanese who sought re-entry to Japan after having left it without being detected.

Throughout the entire period of the Tokugawa Seclusion, the only foreigners to have any direct dealings with Japan were small numbers of Dutch and Chinese traders operating from the minute island of Deshima near Nagasaki in the far south-west. Apart from this minuscule flow of trade, and a trickle of new ideas from western Europe via the Dutch in Deshima, Japan was for most practical purposes completely isolated from the outside world for over two hundred years.

Whether this extraordinary decision should be seen as an early symptom of the inferiority complex from which the Japanese as a nation have often appeared to suffer, perhaps ironically as a consequence of their age-old geographical isolation from other peoples, it is impossible to say. But certainly there can be no denying that such a policy represented the very reverse of what was needed to solve the economic and demographic problems from which Japan was already beginning to suffer, and inevitably these now became even more intractable.

Admittedly, as a result of the introduction, via the Spanish link with the Philippines, of maize, sweet potatoes, peanuts, and other unfamiliar Latin American food crops, and also of the reclamation of extensive coastal areas and the terracing of upland slopes, the population-carrying capacity of Japan was raised still further to some 23 million in 1650, and approximately 30 million by the 1720s. This, however, appears to have been virtually the tolerable limit under a pre-scientific agricultural system, and thereafter, primarily through widespread recourse to abortion and infanticide—together known as *mabiki* which literally meant thinning out a row of rice plants—the population was held at that level, with certain fluctuations reflecting intermittent epidemics and local famines, during the remainder of the Tokugawa period. In these circumstances of acute demographic congestion, the rigid Confucian ordering of society took on a new meaning, and the highest social virtue came to be that of recognizing—and keeping to—one's proper place within the tightly organized social structure which Frank Gibney, in *Five Gentlemen of Japan*, has aptly called 'the web society'.

Nevertheless, new forces were already working in the cities to bring about fundamental changes in the existing social order, based as it was on territorial control of the means of agricultural production. Indeed, as far back as the fourteenth century the growth of Japanese overseas trade had prepared the way for a change-over from rice to money as the medium of exchange in the Kansai towns of Osaka, Kyoto and Kobe, and during the Tokugawa period, despite the near cessation of external trade, this tendency increased. Meanwhile, with the daimyo and the samurai compelled to spend long periods at great expense in Edo, far removed from their territorial sources of income, the practice grew among both these classes of disposing of their rice revenues for cash to traders and brokers in Osaka, which was geographically well placed to become the central rice market of the country.

Thus the practice of biennially concentrating a rurally based aristocracy in Edo, the administrative capital, which also came to contain a large population of artisans, servants, and entertainers, enabled Osaka—nearer the geographical focus of the traditional agricultural economy—to become the economic capital of Japan. Already, well before the nineteenth century, a high proportion of daimyo and samurai were deeply indebted to the new commercial community of Osaka, which had emerged as the second largest city, and the principal supplier of foodstuffs and other bulky produce—by sea—to Edo, whose population at times exceeded a million, thus making it the largest city of the pre-nineteenth century world.

By the early nineteenth century, therefore, Japan was becoming increasingly restive within the Tokugawa straitjacket. In the overcrowded countryside the peasantry—from whom had to be squeezed the surplus foodstuffs and other essentials for the largely unproductive population of Edo and other towns—was suffering increasing hardships. Thus the early nineteenth century saw severe famines and rural revolts. Meanwhile, within the towns, as economic power was slipping away from the traditional aristocracy to the *nouveau riche* commercial element, the Tokugawa obsession with Confucian propriety was leading to a new questioning of the right of the Bakufu to usurp the imperial authority. In short, behind the façade of apparent stability and unity during the mid-nineteenth century, Japan was already changing, and indeed ripe for still greater changes, when the West, itself in process of being transformed by its own Industrial Revolution, attempted once again to force an entry into eastern Asia.

*

Throughout all this time the large northern island of Hokkaido—traditionally known as Yezo, a name which meant 'savages' and implicitly referred to the indigenous Ainu—had remained essentially an area apart from the rest of Japan. Since the climate of Hokkaido was almost as cold and bleak as that of Newfoundland, it was understandable that the Japanese, whose whole history, traditions and life-style originated in the sub-tropical south, should feel little liking for so apparently inhospitable an island. Moreover, since it was assumed first that rice cultivation would be impossible in such a climate, and secondly that people who did not eat rice were *ipso facto* barbarians—as the Ainu were automatically considered to be—it was not surprising that there were barely a few thousand Japanese living in Hokkaido at the beginning of the nineteenth century, and even as late as 1869 its total population, nearly all of whom were Ainu, was under 60,000. Indeed, had it not been for the fact that Russian seafarers had begun exploring southwards from Kamchatka, via the Kurile islands, and also along the coast of Siberia and Saghalien in the seventeenth century, Yezo might have remained unoccupied for even longer. But the appearance of the Russians alarmed the Japanese, and this situation was aggravated by further and more effective prying and probing during the eighteenth century. So in 1798 the Shogunate sent a commission of enquiry to Yezo, and followed this up with plans to populate the island with Japanese settlers, some 60,000 of whom were believed to have arrived there—mainly from the nearby areas of northern Honshu—between 1800 and 1821.

Following the Opium War in China (1839–42) the Russians became alarmed at the growing naval presence of the British, Americans and French in these offshore waters of north-eastern Asia, which they feared might undermine their own position in that area. It was for this reason that a Russian naval squadron, under Admiral Putyatin, was in 1852 sent to the Orient and arrived at Nagasaki in August 1853, some six weeks after Commodore Perry's American squadron had reached Uraga near the entrance to Edo Bay.

Thereafter, as the Western maritime powers embroiled themselves more and more in this remote corner of the world, Japanese fears over the insecurity of Yezo increased. Not the least frustrating of the problems which this almost empty island presented was the extremely high incidence of fog, whose sudden descent might provide almost impenetrable cover under which intruding forces could surreptitiously establish themselves ashore. But a more specific problem was posed when the Commander of the Shogunal navy, Admiral Enomoto, who sought to continue resistance against the Meiji Restoration, fled to Hakodate in December 1868. Although Enomoto was captured in the following spring, he was pardoned and allowed to enter the imperial service.

Clearly, however, considerations of national security now called for much more effective control of this strategically placed but inadequately administered island, and accordingly in 1869 the new Meiji government established the *Kaitakushi* (Colonial Office) to organize the development of Yezo, which was thereupon renamed Hokkaido (Northern Sea Circuit) and definitively incorporated within the Japanese administrative system.

9. FROM DAI NIPPON TO GREATER EAST ASIA—AND DEFEAT

Wider still and wider, shall thy bounds be set;
God who made thee mighty, make thee mightier yet.

A. C. Benson, *Land of Hope and Glory*

The Words of Confucius and Mencius have lost their strength.
Scientific learning from the West has yet to reach us. It is
as though the sun has set and the moon has not yet risen.

A scholar of Meiji times (quoted by Shigeru
Yoshida, *Japan's Decisive Century: 1867–1967*)

The period of a decade and a half between the arrival of Commodore Perry's American naval squadron in Edo Bay and the establishment in 1868 of the new Meiji government, with its headquarters at Tokyo, witnessed the most momentous and rapid change in the whole of Japanese history. For the potential ability of Perry's 'black ships'—steam-powered naval vessels—to force an end to the two and a quarter centuries of almost total isolation from the rest of the world faced the Japanese nation with an unprecedented challenge. Either it must attempt to defy the United States—and by implication also the other Western naval powers—and continue to live in the Middle Ages, or else it must come to terms with the fact that, in having completely side-stepped the Industrial Revolution, it had been left far behind Europe and North America technologically, economically and strategically.

The choice was by no means an easy one to make. Japan was not alone in having its blinkered traditionalists, and indeed in China, its hitherto much respected neighbour, similar ideological backwoodsmen had torn up the first railway to be built in their country, in the firm belief that the locomotive was an invention of the devil, if not indeed the devil in person. (Britain also had similar reactionaries who thought almost identically about Stephenson's 'Rocket', especially after it inconsiderately ran over and killed the ex-President of the Board of Trade, William Huskisson, at the opening of the Liverpool and Manchester Railway in 1830.) Nevertheless, Japan's need for drastic change was more urgent than China's, if only because of its greater population pressure which was no longer being effectively contained by *mabiki*.

In these circumstances, therefore, some of the more perceptive young samurai realized that the opening of Japan to the outside world, far from being an unmitigated calamity, in fact offered the only real solution to Japan's most pressing problem.

According to any normal standards Japan was grossly overcrowded, and meanwhile virtually all the great powers were steadily extending their trading relationships overseas, as Japan itself had begun to do well before the Tokugawa seclusionist policy had been introduced in 1637. Indeed, effective seclusion had originated even earlier, in 1628, after which the only traders allowed in at all were a few Chinese and Dutch, who were confined to the minute island of Deshima, adjacent to the port of Nagasaki in the far south-west.

By a remarkably favourable turn of events the Japanese, during the 1850s and 60s, were given adequate time in which to take stock of the highly critical situation which now confronted them. For initially Western pressure had been directed not against Japan itself, but—by the British—against China, with its vastly greater potential market on which the new Lancashire cotton industry was now casting envious eyes. So Japan, which was near enough to observe what was happening to its great neighbour, but far enough removed to avoid direct involvement, was in effect provided with an invaluable object lesson directly relevant to the formulation of its own new policy.

What in fact had happened was that the Chinese, pre-eminently a land-minded people who had never seriously considered the possibility of invasion from the sea, had been completely nonplussed by the naval power which the British deployed in the Opium War of 1839–42 and in the resultant débâcle their entire imperial structure had begun to disintegrate. Japan, by contrast, a small insular country, had for centuries been aware of its own vulnerability to stronger external sea-powers—which of course was one of the reasons why it had sought for so long to seal itself off from them—though it now realized that steam-powered navies presented a far greater potential threat than the archaic wind-propelled men-of-war.

However, since such marginal naval pressure as Japan had begun to experience from the United States in 1853 soon abated with the outbreak of the Civil War of 1861–5, the Japanese had a further breathing space wherein to adjust to the immense changes which the leadership now recognized must be made.

Meanwhile, although the Japanese continued to regard China with the traditional respect to which it had long been accustomed, this had begun to wane following the débâcle of the Opium War. In such circumstances, therefore, the contemptuous condescension which the Chinese still displayed towards the Japanese as 'the island monkey peoples' or 'the black dwarfs of the eastern seas' was bitterly and understandably resented. Yet in reality this supposed blackness was only a somewhat darker shade of yellow resulting from the suntan acquired in sub-tropical southern Japan, and similarly the Japanese were 'dwarfs' only in so far as many of them were stunted and bandy-legged as a result of malnutrition. However others have claimed that this trait resulted from the Japanese habit of squatting on their heels, though the American anthropologist, Ruth Benedict, has attributed it to the extremely tightly bound, heavy cloth diapers which Japanese babies have traditionally been made to wear during the first few months of their lives.

Whatever the precise cause—or causes—of this deformation, there can be no denying that many Japanese have been acutely embarrassed by their small stature and the related ugliness of their gait, which all too often has provoked undisguised mirth on the part of taller and straighter-legged peoples. And this in turn has certainly exacerbated the deep-rooted inferiority complex which has bedevilled the Japanese throughout almost the whole of their subsequent history. Yet so intensely engrained was this feeling of inferiority—which persisted in spite of the traditional Shinto belief in the divine origin of the Japanese nation—that when China itself had manifestly demonstrated its own unsuitability as a model, the Japanese instinctively sought an alternative in the West, instead of trying to devise a new one appropriately adapted to Japanese conditions.

Nevertheless it is absurd to criticize the Japanese of the 1860s for being 'mere copyists'. Having by-passed two-and-a-quarter centuries—and these the most revolutionary in the whole history of technology—they were understandably obsessed with the need to make up for lost time, and the quickest way to catch up was not by retreating into prehistory and re-inventing the wheel, but by mastering for themselves the intricacies of the latest relevant inventions of the West. So an infatuation with modernity became—and has ever since remained—a prevailing characteristic of the Japanese ethos. In a world whose technology was advancing exponentially, Japan has persistently sought at all costs to get to the front of the queue with the minimum possible delay, and was already styling itself 'the country of the twenty-first century' before it had reached the end of the first two-thirds of the twentieth.

In seeking a new model the Meiji reformers had three main concerns.

First, and transcending everything else, the survival of the nation's territorial integrity against all possible external threats to its security must be ensured, and to this end it was necessary to modernize both the army and the navy with all possible speed. But secondly, and almost equally important, was the related need to preserve internal social cohesion and stability through what was manifestly going to be a period of unprecedented change, occasioned by the opening of this hitherto hermetically sealed country to a tidal wave of totally unfamiliar ideas emanating from the opposite side of the world.

The magnitude of the psychological readjustment which Japan would have to make was acutely and sympathetically perceived by Dr Erwin Baelz, who on 25 October 1876 wrote in his diary:

> . . . less than ten years ago the Japanese were living under conditions like those of our chivalric age and the feudal system of the Middle Ages . . . but . . . betwixt night and morning, one might almost say, and with one great leap, Japan is trying to traverse the stages of five centuries of European development, and to assimilate in the twinkling of an eye all the latest achievements of western civilization.

Inevitably such a 'giant's leap' was fraught with danger, though in the event the transformation was made without disaster. But it certainly had its comic side, as Baelz himself described in his account of New Year's Day 1877, when innumerable Japanese, many of them mere ten-year-old boys, turned out in top hats, white gloves, and excruciatingly ill-fitting frock-coats. Nevertheless the high—or perhaps I should say the low—spot was reached when, according to Honor Tracy's delightfully hilarious *Kakemono*, members of the Diet first attired themselves in European clothing, though with their trousers worn back to front! However, such gaffes as these were soon forgotten, as the new generation of Japanese applied themselves with intense energy to the daunting task of completely remodelling their ancient homeland.

With remarkable wisdom the new Japanese leadership realized that the key to the preservation of internal stability lay in harnessing the intensely powerful forces of patriotism to the pressures of strategic, social and economic necessity. Since the new strategic focus of Japan was the Kanto plain, within which was situated Edo, by far the largest city in the country, Commodore Perry's American naval squadron had already seized the opportunity to show the flag in Edo Bay. Yet while this selfsame area had for centuries been controlled by the Tokugawa

Bakufu, the Emperor still languished in seclusion within the ancient capital in Kyoto.

By an astonishingly perceptive decision the monarchy was restored to its proper place and status by bringing the Emperor out of his enforced isolation in the distant Kinki lowlands, and establishing him at the supreme geographical focus of the country, in a new Imperial Palace at Edo, now renamed Tokyo, or 'eastern capital'. Thus, most appropriately, Tokyo turned its back on China and the rest of the Asian mainland, and instead looked out on to the Pacific, which the Americans were already beginning to call 'the Ocean of the Future'.

Yet although the psychological consequences of this relocation were truly revolutionary, there had been no political revolution. Continuity and stability had been preserved by *restoring* the young and very astute Emperor, who thus—in assuming the reign name of Meiji—inaugurated the era of modernization under the Meiji restoration of 1868. From the outset, the new Emperor set an entirely new style, as was evident in the famous words of his Charter Oath: 'Knowledge shall be sought all over the world and thus shall be strengthened the foundations of the imperial polity.'

Finally the third of the new Japan's most pressing concerns was the modernization of its economy by the setting up of Western-style manufacturing industries and the creation of a modern transport system with both rail and steamship services. And significantly, in view of the recent rise of Osaka to pre-eminence as the commercial focus of the country, where the traditional rice revenues were replaced by modern currency, the first of Japan's modern factories was the new mint at Osaka.

Inevitably the achievement of so comprehensive a programme as this, within the space of a few decades, called for the acquisition of modern expertise of many kinds, a process which in the event was achieved by simultaneously hiring appropriately skilled experts from overseas, and by sending talented young Japanese—especially well educated samurai whose historic role as feudal retainers had meanwhile become redundant—to undertake professional and/or technical training in the West. In thus seeking knowledge 'all over the world', in accordance with the Emperor's Charter Oath, the Japanese displayed an innate shrewdness in not relying excessively on any one single source, and in effect they countered the characteristic imperialist ploy of 'divide and rule' by a more subtle one perhaps best described as 'select and survive'.

In a feudally minded country which had been so long sealed off from the sea it was only to be expected that the military should take precedence over the naval forces. But now that the most obvious threats seemed likely to come from overseas, it was all the more necessary to modernize and strengthen the navy, and from the late 1860s the growing rivalry between these two forces became a crucial feature of Japanese political life.

While the obvious source of advice on the expansion and modernization of the Japanese navy was the United Kingdom, the samurai leadership, with its engrained military traditions, put greater store on the improvement of the army. And since in 1868 the French military tradition still retained the prestige it had acquired under Napoleon I, the Japanese unhesitatingly chose French experts to train their new army. However, with the unexpected defeat of the French in the Franco-Prussian War of 1870–71, the Japanese hard-headedly replaced their French instructors by Prussians. This decision was amusingly reflected in an immediate change of style in the uniforms of the Imperial Japanese Army, with the result that in photographs taken in 1870 members of the Japanese army all looked like pocket Pétains, while those photographed a year or two later had clearly undergone a remarkable transmogrification into diminutive Kaiser Bills.

Nevertheless the largest number of foreign experts employed by the Japanese were engineers and technicians of all kinds, and since the United Kingdom was then the unchallenged pacemaker in these fields, it is not surprising that out of the total of 214 foreign experts of all kinds employed by the Japanese government in 1872, 119 were British, followed by fifty French, sixteen Americans, nine Chinese, eight Germans—mostly medical men—two Dutch, and one each from several other, lesser countries.

Given such a preponderance of Britons among the expatriate community in early Meiji Japan, together with the fact that the United Kingdom was firmly established as the metropolitan state of the richest and most powerful empire in the world, it is understandable that in his book, *Problems of the Far East*, published in 1894, G. N. (later Lord) Curzon should have commented thus:

> Placed at a maritime coign of vantage upon the flank of Asia, precisely analogous to that occupied by Great Britain on the flank of Europe, exercising a powerful influence over the adjoining continent, but not necessarily involved in its responsibilities, she sets before herself the supreme ambition of becoming, on a smaller scale, the Britain of the Far East.

Moreover, in *Dai Nippon* in 1904, another British observer, Henry Dyer, stated:

> When I arrived in Japan (in 1873) the highest ambition of all the officials with whom I came in contact, and also my own students, was that their country might become the Britain of the East, and they not infrequently got laughed at by foreigners for what was considered their conceit. During the thirty years that have elapsed since that time they have kept their ideal steadily in view, and few will deny that they have gone a long way towards its realization.

Nevertheless, at least until shortly before the United Kingdom agreed to a revision of its unequal treaty with Japan in 1894, the official British view was that Japan was a rather ridiculous country, trying to do too much too quickly.

Yet in that same year Japan invaded Korea—then under Chinese suzerainty—and in 1895 China, having been roundly defeated, had to accept the Treaty of Shimonoseki, whereby it was required to cede both Formosa (Taiwan) and the Liaotung Peninsula—the key to Manchuria—in addition to paying a large indemnity and granting commercial and other privileges to Japan.

It was at this juncture that, in accordance with the prevailing armigerous imagery of the day, the so-called 'continental bloc'—France, Germany and Russia—affected to see in Liaotung 'a pistol aimed at the heart of China', and accordingly despatched a note to Tokyo stating that they 'would give a new proof of their sincere friendship for the Government of H.M. the Emperor of Japan, by advising him to renounce the definite possession of Liaotung'. By any standards this astonishing *dêmarche* must rank as one of the most insolent pieces of diplomatic hypocrisy ever recorded. Clearly, with friends such as these Japan had scant need of enemies, though the Russians nevertheless rubbed salt into the wound by acquiring for themselves a twenty-five-year lease over the tip of the Liaotung Peninsula in 1898.

Yet while the Sino-Japanese War was still in progress another Englishman, Henry Norman, had made a far more perceptive analysis of Japanese ambitions than Curzon's bland statement that Japan aspired to become, '*on a smaller scale*, the Britain of the East' (my italics). Specifically, after forecasting the Shimonoseki peace terms with a close approximation to accuracy, Henry Norman in his book, *The Peoples and Politics of the Far East* (1895), stated bluntly that these terms would not satisfy the Japanese. What Japan wanted could be 'summed up in four words: "Asia for the Asiatics" '; and, he added, 'In other words I am able to say from positive knowledge that the Government of Japan has conceived a parallel to the Monroe Doctrine for the Far East, with herself as its centre.'

Meanwhile, out of the indemnity obtained from China for the privilege of having been defeated by Japan, the latter in 1901 set about building the largest steelworks in Asia, at Yawata in Kyushu, the jumping-off ground for a future invasion of the continental mainland via Korea. Likewise in 1901 the so-called *Kokoryukai*, or 'Black Dragon Society' (the term 'Black Dragon' was a symbolical Japanese name for the Amur River), was founded with the aim of extending Japanese power on the mainland in order to hold back Russia to the Amur River frontier. Clearly Japan was now a power to be reckoned with, and in 1902 it became the partner of hitherto splendidly isolationist Britain in the Anglo-Japanese Alliance.

Some two years later the Japanese, defying accepted international practice, by employing the tactics of the undeclared war—later to become known as the blitzkrieg—were victorious in the Russo-Japanese War, a primary purpose of which was to soften up Manchuria and still further to isolate Korea, which Japan proceeded to annex in 1910. Manifestly, in the sardonic words of my former and greatly revered teacher, the late W. S. Thatcher, M.C., 'The Japs *must* be civilized. They know how to fight.'

Nevertheless the irony in this comment was double edged, and the Japanese had skilfully and cynically played the West back at its own game. For it was the West which had taught them that, even if they had, with consummate speed and tenacity, mastered the West's achievement in the mechanized mass production of slaughter, they were still not accepted as the white man's social equals. But, no less significantly, throughout the whole of Asia, 'little' Japan's defeat of the Russian colossus was hailed as proof that the days of white supremacy were numbered. Japan was acclaimed as the new champion of the East against the West, and one Burmese newspaper suggested that Japan might shortly formulate a 'Monroe Doctrine for the Far East' (cited by Lothrop Stoddard in *The Rising Tide of Color*). Meanwhile Kaiser Wilhelm II, who boasted of the deadly prowess of his own 'Huns', did not hesitate to refer to the Japanese and Chinese as the 'Yellow Peril'. But what of the White Peril which had already ranged over a much wider area of the globe?

In a world dominated by the white man, who was not notably outstanding for his modesty, particularly when a long way from home, it was scarcely surprising that the Japanese, who had long been exposed to Chinese racial prejudice, now found themselves to be the butt of Western denigration. For the Westerners, who in the middle and later nineteenth century had produced the spectacular advances of the scientific and industrial revolutions, were only too ready to read into the Darwinian biological doctrine of the survival of the fittest a self-gratifying belief in the intrinsic intellectual and moral superiority of the white man over all other members of the human species.

Moreover, within the specifically Meiji context, the very fact that the Japanese were having to rely on white tutelage served only to intensify their age-old feelings of inferiority. Unfortunately and unforgivably, fuel was added to the fires of resentment by the—at best inconsiderate and at worst deliberately cruel—manner in which not a few of the well-paid Western experts ridiculed almost any unfamiliar, and therefore presumably comic, aspect of Japanese behaviour. Worse still, in these circumstances it was probably inevitable that the traditional—and still surviving—practice of *mabiki* should be singled out for particularly scathing criticism: obviously people who openly practised abortion—not to mention infanticide—were barbarians, while those others who relied instead on charms, or the naming of a second or third child by such names as 'Stop' or 'Be the last', were merely regarded as superstitious fools.

Thus, notwithstanding the extremely impressive beginnings which the Japanese had made in the modernization of their country, particularly since 1868, they had not succeeded in overcoming their sense of racial inferiority, now strongly reinforced by supposedly scientific social Darwinism. Probably the most remarkable manifestation of this attitude was expressed in a book by Yoshio Takahashi, published in 1883 and entitled *Nihonjinshu Kairyoron*—'The Improvement of the Japanese Race', which included the following statement:

> Having accepted the hypothesis that the physical and mental constitution of our Japanese is inferior to that of European peoples, it follows that in the event we persist on an inferior level there is a danger that we may soil the historical record of our blameless Empire . . . The only solution is to improve our racial quality by means of inter-marriage (with the Caucasian race) . . . When we marry European women there is an additional benefit in the custom of following a meat diet.

So seriously was this argument taken, at the highest level, that the Prime Minister, the great Hirobumi Ito, arranged for the English sociologist Herbert Spencer to be consulted on the advisability of adopting such a course. Perhaps it is not surprising that the guru of Gower Street advised against positive thinking on so uncertain a matter.

However, since the modernization of the Japanese economy was beginning to make possible the support of a substantially larger population, *mabiki* was itself encouraged to die a natural death, a development which was particularly welcome to the armed forces who were anxious that Japan should not lack the military man-power it wanted for further imperial expansion. Thus in 1907 a certain Mr Tokugoro Nakabashi, arguing that the requisite for a world power was a great population, went on to state that while thirty to fifty million were enough to maintain great power status in the nineteenth century, eighty to a hundred million would be needed by the end of the twentieth. This advice was taken to heart, and with characteristic thoroughness the loyal Japanese put their patriotic duty first and duly delivered the goods, bringing the total population of Japan up to well over one hundred million, thirty-two years ahead of schedule, and most appropriately so in 1968, the centenary year of the Meiji Restoration. Truly the Japanese are a remarkable people: as one American researcher (John Gunther, author of *Inside Asia*) was told when he asked how the ordinary Japanese preferred to spend their spare time, 'I should advise you to consult our vital statistics.'

Little men often tend to talk—and to act—big, so perhaps it was not accidental that the little Japanese should have called their own relatively small country Dai Nippon (Great Japan) or that it was they who invented the super-tanker, the most monstrous yet of all the man-made dinosaurs. But even more dangerously, the Japanese craving for bigness, and for the power that is assumed to go with it, found its most obvious expression in imperialistic expansion, a tendency which was further stimulated by the post-Tokugawa Seclusionist psychology of the young man in a hurry.

Thus, shortly after the outbreak of the First World War, while the Western powers were fully occupied on the European fronts, and Japanese manufacturers and traders were busily capturing the markets which their hard-pressed British ally could no longer effectively supply, the Japanese expansionists seized the opportunity in 1915 to press upon the clay-footed colossus of China the famous, or rather infamous, Twenty-one Demands, which turned that country into a *de facto* Japanese satellite, and so marked the first major step towards the 'Greater East Asia Co-prosperity Sphere'.

Already, less than a quarter of a century after its newly modernized armed forces had proved their prowess against China in 1894–5, Japan's prestige had risen from a level described in the early 1890s by the then British Ambassador to Japan, Sir Harry Parkes, as 'a potential Latin American Republic', to that of one of the world's major powers. Even so, however, the Japanese people were still not accepted as being on the same footing as Westerners, and although at the Versailles Peace Conference in 1918 the Japanese delegation had appealed for racial equality, the proposal was not carried. Thus while no other country in the entire world suffered such acute population pressure as did Japan, nearly all the most obvious outlets for aspiring Japanese seeking better opportunities overseas were rigidly restricted, and all kinds of linguistic legerdemain were employed to cover up the obvious racial prejudice of the white powers, which everyone knew was the fundamental reason for restricting, or in some cases completely excluding, Japanese and other Asian immigration into Australia, Canada, Hawaii and the continental United States.

Admittedly, in November 1907, the 'Gentleman's Agreement' had been reached between the United States and Japan, whereby Japan agreed to refuse passports to what were then called coolies, desirous of emigrating to the United States. For, despite its high-sounding title, the Gentleman's Agreement rested on the implicit assumption that white gentlemen were superior to yellow gentlemen. And unfortunately this situation was greatly exacerbated by extremely short-sighted behaviour on the part of the United States Senate in 1924.

On 1 September 1923 Japan suffered one of the most devastating earthquakes ever recorded, and as a result over 150,000 people, mostly in Tokyo and Yokohama, lost their lives. Both at the national and the individual level, the United States excelled itself in the scale of its generosity to help the surviving victims, and this in turn generated a veritable tidal wave of Japanese gratitude. Yet at this of all times, when—amid the ruin and chaos occasioned by the earthquake—American-Japanese relations were at their warmest, the Senate suddenly sprang a surprise by passing a new immigration law which, in the words of Inazo Nitobe, *Japan—Some Phases of her Problems and Development*, 'was aimed, though not explicitly, at the discriminating exclusion of Japanese immigrants'.

Although no less a person than Charles E. Hughes, then Secretary of State, said that the new law would inevitably be regarded by the Japanese as 'a legislative enactment fixing a stigma upon them', the Act was placed on the Statute Book of the United States. To quote further from Mr Nitobe, one of the closest Japanese friends the Americans and British have ever had:

> The repercussion of this legislative act on Japan was profound. She felt as though her best friend had, of a sudden and without provocation, slapped her on the cheek. She questioned the sanity of American legislators. At heart, however silent, she does not now and never will accede to this law . . . whatever may be the 'legal' rights of a country as regards its own enactments. Each year that passes without amendment or abrogation only strengthens and sharpens our sense of injury, which is destined to show itself, in one form or another, in personal and public intercourse. All talk of peace and goodwill is vain, so long as one nation sows in the heart of another the seeds of suspicion and resentment.

Mr Nitobe did not exaggerate. Some twenty years later, in the very different circumstances of a Japanese prisoner of war camp on the Thailand-Burma Railway, a senior Japanese officer, Colonel Nagatomo, in the course of addressing a motley collection of bedraggled Allied soldiers, of whom I was one, made the following comment:

> The Great Asiatic War has broken out due to the rising of the East Asiatic nations whose hearts were burnt with the desire to live and preserve their nations on account of the intrusion of the British and Americans for past many years.
>
> There is therefore no other reason for Japan to drive out the Anti-Axis powers of the arrogant and insolent British and Americans from East Asia in co-operation with our neighbours of China and the East Asiatic nations and to establish the Greater East Asia Co-prosperity Sphere for the benefit of all human beings and to establish ever-lasting peace in the world.
>
> During the past few centuries Nippon has made extreme endeavour and has made sacrifices to become the leader of the East Asiatic nations who were mercilessly and pitifully treated by the outside forces of the Americans and British, and Nippon without disgracing anybody has been doing her best up to now for fostering Nippon's real power.

Clearly, even at this late date, neither the Anglo-Americans nor the Japanese had yet learned to see, let alone to solve, the crucial problem so acutely expressed in 1943 by Pearl S. Buck in *What America means to me*: 'The main barrier between East and West today is that the white man is not willing to give up his superiority and the colored man is no longer willing to endure his inferiority.'

Nevertheless Colonel Nagatomo's claim that what he called the 'Great East Asiatic War' was fought by Japan 'in co-operation with our neighbours in China' cannot be accepted at its face value. For, in fact, by far the greatest victim of the Japanese attempt to establish the Greater East Asia Co-prosperity Sphere was China itself, which, having first been undermined by Japan's Twenty-one Demands in 1915, was deprived of its three Manchurian provinces by the Japanese invasion of 1931—which area, under the new name of Manchukuo, became a Japanese puppet. Then, following a further invasion in 1937, the Japanese proceeded to extend this process to the remainder of China proper, which thus became another Japanese puppet regime, under the nominal rule of the Chinese opportunist Wang Ching-wei. (The co-operation with China mentioned by Colonel Nagatomo, thus being no more than co-operation with Japan's puppet regimes.) In short, the sequence of events from the First Sino-Japanese War of 1894–5 to the Second Sino-Japanese War, beginning in 1937, fulfilled almost to the letter the forecast made by Henry Norman in 1895.

Nevertheless, although by the end of the 1930s Japan had established its hegemony over the whole of East Asia, it had no intention of stopping there. Indeed, in 1936 the American Ambassador to Japan, Mr Joseph C. Grew, recorded the remark of a 'highly placed Japanese' during the Washington Conference of 1921–2: 'There is absolute unanimity in Japan on the proposition that we must expand.' The only questions which remained were the timing of such expansion and whether it should begin by a deeper military penetration, via Korea, into Manchuria and beyond that into Inner Asia, or by a new naval thrust southwards against the colonial territories of the Western powers in South-east Asia.

More specifically, on 5 October 1940, the Japanese Foreign Minister, Mr Yosuke Matsuoka, outlined his view on the establishment of a new order in East Asia. Under this, 'Japan would establish the relationship of common existence and mutual prosperity with the peoples of each and every land in Greater East Asia, including enterprises, trade, and emigration in and to every land in Greater East Asia and thereby be enabled to solve its population problem.'

In all of this Japan was obviously copying Western imperialism, both in its objectives and its self-justifying propaganda, though with the distinctive Japanese characteristic of the young man—or the diplomatically immature power—in a hurry to make up for lost time. Moreover, by the 1930s the tempo was clearly accelerating. Between the first Sino-Japanese War of 1894–5 and the Russo-Japanese War of

1904–5 the interval amounted to ten years, whereas between the invasion of Manchuria in 1931 and its extension into the rest of China in 1937 was a mere six years, after which the acceleration reached its catastrophic climax only four years later with the simultaneous and totally undeclared attacks on Pearl Harbor, Hong Kong and Singapore in December 1941.

By this stage the Japanese, intoxicated by their series of increasingly euphoric victories, all too easily achieved against militarily far weaker powers, had cast caution to the winds and were fast losing touch with reality. Thus, in taking on the two greatest naval powers in the world, they had deprived themselves of any possibility of retaining their hold over the Nanyo (South Seas) territories which they had coveted for so long, only to hold them for less than three years. For, owing to what the Japanese Prime Minister, Mr Shigeru Yoshida, with typical kimono-mindedness, subsequently called 'the great miscalculation', it had become clear before the middle of 1944 that Japan's appallingly heavy losses of both naval and merchant shipping (by mid-1945 about nine-tenths of both fleets had been lost) had deprived it of the means to control the vital sea routes without which the Greater East Asia Co-prosperity Sphere could no longer be held together.

Nevertheless Japanese morale—or, as many Westerners regarded it, fanaticism—was such that, inspired by their *kamikaze*[1] pilots who committed suicide by crashing their bomb-laden planes on to their targets, ordinary citizens in Japan were preparing to fight the expected Allied invaders with bamboo spears. It was widely believed, too, that should the Allies succeed in landing the Japanese would fight to the last man or, if prevented from so doing, would commit ritual suicide, either individually or *en masse*. (Westerners commonly refer to ritual suicide by the colloquial name *hara kiri*, though the Japanese prefer the formal usage, *seppuko*.)

By any rational assessment, Japan in the early summer of 1945 was virtually at the end of its tether. Already on 7 May, Germany—its only significant surviving ally—had surrendered unconditionally, a development which made possible the Soviet Union's undertaking to its Western Allies to attack Japan within three months. Meanwhile the British took the offensive against the Japanese forces in Burma, and American Superfortresses, operating from strategic islands in the

[1] *Kamikaze*—'the Divine Wind' was the name given by the Japanese to a severe typhoon which in 1281 suddenly destroyed the Mongol fleet, thus preventing the Mongol warriors from invading Japan. During the Second World War the Japanese suicide pilots appropriated the name.

western Pacific, steadily stepped up their conventional and incendiary bombing of Japanese cities, as a prelude to the Allied demand, expressed in the Potsdam Declaration (convened on 26 July after the Allied defeat of Germany had ended the war in Europe in order to co-ordinate policies and devise a post-war settlement) for Japan's unconditional surrender. With the exception of Kyoto and Nara, which for cultural and historical reasons were spared, all the major Japanese cities experienced severe devastation.

However, the Japanese, continuing blindly to believe in their own invincibility, made tortuous behind-the-scenes attempts to end the war by trying to persuade the Soviet Union to act as a mediator. Inevitably, in view of the Russians' prior commitment to their Western Allies, and of their deep-rooted resentment over the defeat they had sustained at Japanese hands in 1905, this suggestion was bluntly rejected. Instead the U.S.S.R. declared that, as from 9 August, it would consider itself at war against Japanese aggression, thus helping to shorten the war, reduce casualties and restore peace.

Throughout the late spring and the summer of 1945 the life of the ordinary people of Japan must have been one of almost intolerable strain, severely aggravated by hunger, poverty and accumulating tiredness verging on total exhaustion. Nevertheless, for the senior scientists and other top decision-makers—who already knew that work on the atomic bomb was proceeding fast, though its success had yet to be demonstrated—the tension must have been even greater. Moreover, the situation was further complicated by the suddenness with which the two great leaders of the West, President Roosevelt and Prime Minister Churchill, were respectively replaced—as a result of the death of the former in April, and of the political defeat of the latter in July—by Harry S. Truman and Clement R. Attlee, both of whom were almost unknown outside their own countries.

By the evening of 16 July, the day on which the Potsdam Conference was due to begin, Truman had received news of the successful detonation of the first atomic bomb in the wastes of New Mexico, and Stalin declared that the Red Army would be willing to attack Japan in early August. Meanwhile Truman had been informed that the first bomb to be used in action would be ready between 4 and 10 August. In the event it was dropped on Hiroshima in the early morning of 6 August, by which time the Soviet Union had well over a million troops in position confronting much smaller forces on the opposite side of the frontier in the Japanese puppet state of Manchukuo.

Thus, in view of the demoralizing inferiority of the Japanese military situation, highlighted as it was by the unprecedented destructive potential demonstrated by the two atomic bombs, the second of which had been dropped on Nagasaki on 10 August, the Japanese were now left with no feasible option but to accept Allied demand for unconditional surrender which they had rejected for so long. And, indeed, it may well be doubted whether they would have done so even then but for the unexpected courage and unsuspected perceptiveness of the Emperor, notwithstanding his uniquely isolated life and exceptionally exalted position. For it was he who, following the dropping of the second bomb on 10 August, took the momentous decision to call upon the senior members of his armed forces and the Cabinet—several of whom by this time had broken down and were sobbing uncontrollably—to 'bear the unbearable': a phrase which had been used by his illustrious grandfather, the first Emperor Meiji, when the Triple Intervention of Russia, Germany and France had deprived Japan of the hard-won Liaotung Peninsula in 1895.

No doubt Professor Margaret Gowing, in her 1977 J. D. Bernal Lecture, 'Science and Politics', was fully justified in saying that there had been 'much discussion and heart searching' about whether to use these bombs, and that, since 'there was evidence that Japan was blind to defeat whatever the logic of her position', the decision was made mainly to prevent the appalling slaughter which it seemed almost certain would otherwise ensue. Perhaps, also, it was significant that, while Western experts were prepared to forecast the probable number of Allied deaths by 'conventional' means at between one and a half and two million, no comparable forecasts seem to have been published of the corresponding slaughter to be expected from the dropping of the two nuclear bombs. In fact, however, while the populations of Hiroshima and Nagasaki at that time were approximately 400,000 and 250,000 respectively, the deaths caused by these two bombs were 'at least 200,000' in Hiroshima and 74,000 in Nagasaki—approximately 50 per cent and 30 per cent respectively of the total population of these two cities. (These estimates were made by local experts in each city; they are cited by John Toland in *The Rising Sun*.)

Clearly, however, in calling these two monstrosities not bombs but 'devices', the West has not been slow in learning to practise the art of 'kimono-minded' hypocrisy. Yet, for my part, and I write as one of the one-million-plus Allied service men whose survival has been widely attributed to this revolutionary resort to nuclear warfare, I cannot but agree with the judgement expressed in 1948 by Major General J. C. E. Fuller in *The Second World War*:

> Though to save life is laudable, it in no way justifies the employment of means which run counter to every precept of humanity and the customs of war. . . . If the saving of lives were the true pretext, then, instead of reverting to a type of war which would have disgraced Tamerlane, all President Truman and Mr. Churchill need have done was to remove the obstacle of unconditional surrender, when the war could have been brought to an immediate end.

Moreover, we need to remind ourselves that it was not Japan but Germany, the most sinister—as well as the most affluent and most technologically advanced—of the three Rome-Berlin-Tokyo Axis powers, which precipitated the Second World War. But of course the Nazis were white men and, as all red-blooded right-thinking white men know, to use white men as guinea pigs would obviously be to sink to the level of Tamerlane and his Mongol hordes, whose skin colour was the same as that of the Japanese.

No less surprising than the extent and the manner of Japan's defeat were the rapidity and co-operativeness with which the Japanese people thereafter accepted the Allied Occupation under General Douglas MacArthur, an arrangement which lasted until the end of April 1952. Here again the Emperor displayed unforeseen qualities of leadership in his readiness to divest himself of his supposed divinity and to accept his much diminished role as 'the symbol of the State'. This decision greatly facilitated the nation's return to stability, notwithstanding the terrible loss of more than two million Japanese lives, a quarter of a million square miles of territory—representing nearly half the pre-war empire —together with some two million dwellings and innumerable other industrial and commercial buildings and installations of all kinds.

Yet, despite these severe blows—as well as much initial scepticism concerning the suitability of an elderly American general to inculcate democracy into what had hitherto been the most inward-looking and traditionally minded of all surviving Oriental despotisms—the experiment proved remarkably successful. Here, unquestionably, the strength and resilience of the Japanese family system, based as it is on the Confucian virtues of filial piety, discipline and hard work, proved to be of decisive importance in maintaining the continuity of established values which, in combination with unusual adaptability to both social and technological innovations, provided the foundations upon which this remarkably resilient nation has begun to rise above the material chaos and the shattered dreams of the Japanese Götterdämmerung.

10. TOKYO RESURGENT, 1961

Nor shall this peace sleep with her; but as when
The bird of wonder dies, the maiden phoenix,
Her ashes new create another heir
As great in admiration as herself.
Shakespeare, *Henry VIII*, V, iv

From the outset of this, my first visit to Japan, the emphasis was on the two inter-related themes of rebuilding and modernity, both represented in the new Japan Air Lines symbol—the phoenix rising from the ashes—of the plane which was to take me, by one of the early polar flights, from London to Tokyo via Paris, Copenhagen and Anchorage in Alaska.

Since my only previous flight had been in an R.A.F. Dakota belonging to a squadron engaged in ferrying ex-prisoners of war out from Bangkok to Rangoon after the Japanese had capitulated, the flight to Tokyo promised to be an exhilarating experience. And, indeed, in anticipation of this prospect, I spent several hours map reading and making related calculations before I succeeded in proving to my own satisfaction that, given reasonably good visibility, it should be possible to see Mount McKinley, the highest peak in North America, from Anchorage airport.

Unfortunately, however, our take-off from Heathrow was delayed for several hours by an electrical fault, and this trouble repeated itself at Copenhagen. Besides being somewhat disconcerting when one is about to fly more than ten thousand miles over totally uninhabited polar wastes, the combined effect of these delays was that a twenty-two-hour journey which should have been wholly in daylight in fact took place almost entirely in the dark, though we did experience a brief semi-twilight for about half an hour somewhere near the North Pole, before reverting to total darkness. This caused much mystification—bordering indeed on consternation—to the hitherto silent Italian gentleman sitting next to me.

In the process of trying to divert him with a little light-hearted conversation, I discovered that he had been invited to Japan on account of his having won the 'Golden Scissors' prize, of which I had never previously heard. Doubtless because of my own addiction to scissors and paste, I asked him if he was a journalist; clearly, to judge from his reactions, this was a monumental gaffe. For in fact the award was for his exceptional skill as 'Tailor of the Year', and this was why he was now on his way to Tokyo to make a suit for the Emperor of Japan. Mustering all my self control, I suppressed my facetious desire to ask if this was because the Emperor hadn't got any clothes, but fortunately the arrival of an exceptionally sumptuous meal—at the somewhat unorthodox time, according to my watch, of 4.30 a.m.—speedily reduced us both to a satiated silence which slowly lapsed into total somnolence. However, a few hours later, we were wakened in preparation for our stop at Anchorage, which enabled us to stretch our legs and reorganize our stomachs. So far as I could make out through the darkness the entire surroundings were heavily snowbound, though the log-cabin-style airport was overpoweringly hot, and I was a trifle disconcerted to observe two very tough-looking Arctic frontiersmen, each with revolvers on both hips, and distinctly heard one say to the other: 'Say, why don't we go get a glass of milk?' Clearly, like the old grey mare, the frontier wasn't what it used to be.

As I was flying first class, at a level of luxury I had never previously experienced, the total impact of the journey was entirely consistent with the new image which Japan was beginning to create for itself as 'The country of the twenty-first century'. Nor was this image significantly tarnished by the accumulated delays we had suffered, resulting in our arrival at Tokyo well past midnight, though I confess that, at this late hour, I was beginning to feel a little apprehensive as I recalled Erwin Baelz's account of his first arrival in Japan—by sea at Yokohama—in 1886. For on that occasion there was no one who spoke any English, no interpreter, let alone the Japanese Government official he had been told would meet him—a newly appointed Professor of Medicine—and indeed he had to wait several hours on deck before a small and primitive local boat eventually appeared and a ship's officer arranged for it to take him and his baggage ashore, where he eventually arrived soaked to the skin.

In the sharpest imaginable contrast to this, what I experienced seventy-five years later was a model of courtesy and extreme efficiency. As our aircraft came slowly to a halt on the arc-lit tarmac, a red carpet was instantly laid down for a V.I.P., who proved to be the new Swiss Ambassador, and was obviously considered to be someone of exceptional significance. For at this time there were many Swiss hoteliers acting as advisers to new Japanese-owned Western-style hotels, which were springing up like a multitude of mushrooms to cater mainly for

American visitors suffering from post-Occupation nostalgia, and longing to be back in 'Lotus Land' complete with the 'Tea-house of the August Moon'.

The Ambassador having duly been whisked away at once, the rest of us received almost equally efficient treatment. I was met by a Mr Tsutsumi (whose name, most appropriately, was pronounced 'it suits me'), an official from Gaimusho, who got me through the passport, health and immigration procedures in a couple of minutes, while my baggage suddenly materialized swiftly, silently and in perfect order, from the other side of the airport. Whereupon Mr Tsutsumi hustled me into a taxi and we sped off down the main highway to my hotel, where, after forty-eight hours' non-stop travel, from Sheffield to Tokyo with barely three hours' sleep overall, I was only too glad to get to bed.

Next morning, the English-language *Japan Times* slid silently under my bedroom door a split second before my morning tea put in an equally welcome appearance at a somewhat more exalted altitude and, thus refreshed, I decided to take a stroll before breakfast. Since I had seen virtually nothing since I left London, it was a fascinating experience merely to walk out of the hotel, in blazing September sunshine, and to find myself in the very heart of Tokyo, within a couple of minutes' walk of the Ginza, the local counterpart to Oxford Street, which was already crowded with shoppers and traffic.

My first—and lastingly dominant—impression of Tokyo was one of intense energy and vitality. Half the buildings were either new structures under construction, or else old and usually damaged ones now being knocked down to clear the way for bigger and more modern blocks of offices, flats and shops. Likewise at least half of the streets seemed to be undergoing some major modification to make them more suitable for modern motor traffic, now rapidly increasing in volume, and by far the commonest of all street signs was a black pickaxe rampant, on a yellow ground, accompanied by the arresting words (in English and Japanese) UNDER CONSTRUCTION.

In fact this was Tokyo's second major reconstruction within the memory of the majority of its citizens, the first having followed the great earthquake of 1923 when some attempt was made to decentralize the old urban pattern so as to help prevent excessive concentration of destruction in the centre of the city in the event of another earthquake of similar magnitude.

Certainly no other city in the world has ever sustained a comparable succession of two such monumental disasters as had Tokyo in the early decades of its development as a modern city. While only rough estimates are available of the casualties involved, it is clear that war-time bombing reduced the population of Tokyo from nearly six million in 1935 to some two million immediately after the war, though the greater part of this decline was due not to direct casualties but to large-scale movements of people out of Tokyo into less dangerous areas at varying distances from the capital itself.

Although the centres of almost every significant Japanese city consisted almost entirely of small antiquated wooden houses, packed together cheek by jowl, the intensity of the overcrowding in central Tokyo was in a class of its own. Thus it was that, following some nine months of predominantly high-explosive bombing, which had begun with a devastating Superfortress raid on the great Yawata steelworks at Kita-Kyushu in the far south-west, the single, sudden and wholly unexpected mass incendiary bombardment of Tokyo on 9–10 March 1945 caused an even heavier loss of life than the appalling 1923 earthquake, for which the death toll was approximately 80,000, as against the two hundred thousand or so victims of the first atomic bomb, which was dropped on Hiroshima on 6 August 1945.

Ironically, it seemed, humanity was hellbent on displaying its superior capacity for slaughter over the worst that nature, unaided by the most that modern technology had yet achieved. Meanwhile, by comparison with these apocalyptic human casualty statistics, the United States Air Force, in its massive raid of August 9–10 lost only four per cent of the aircraft—and presumably also a similarly low proportion of the aircrews—involved.

The most vivid account I ever heard of the extent of the devastation in Tokyo immediately after the end of the war was given to me by one of the senior Foreign Ministry men whom I met in 1961. He was about my own age and, again like me, he had spent the war years in the army overseas, though naturally on the opposite side. Eventually, after it was all over, he, along with thousands of others, defeated, dejected and disillusioned, was squeezed aboard a troopship and, after seemingly endless days of hunger, seasickness and innumerable other kinds of discomfort, was finally decanted on to what appeared to be a completely featureless waste of rubble which a few years earlier had been one of the greatest complexes of docks and warehouses in the world.

Since he did not know who—if any—of his relatives were still alive in Tokyo—nor was there any quick means of finding out—he began simply and instinctively to walk in the general direction of where the old city centre had been. At first all around him seemed dead; but as he got nearer to the centre he saw occasional flickers of light in the gaps beneath his feet, where groups of people were living a kind of troglodyte existence in cellars, dugouts and even open holes. But not until he had trudged several miles was he able to identify a single recognizable landmark in this—once the greatest city in the world—which he had known since his boyhood.

The only thing more remarkable than his story was the complete absence of bitterness with which he told it to me. But several subsequent experiences have taught me that this was not exceptional. Former serving men, even if they had been fighting on opposite sides, seem far less hostile to one another than former civilian enemies, whose experience tends to be distorted by its very vicariousness. By contrast, the great majority of those who have been caught up in such a 'mortal storm' know only too well that the holocaust was not of their choosing, nor had they the power, once entangled, to do anything which could possibly have stopped it. Over and over again in Japan—and for that matter, in Germany too—I have found an almost instant and intuitive *camaraderie* among soldiers from opposite camps, and some of my own deepest and most abiding friendships have developed from such beginnings.

One of the most memorable examples of this tendency concerned a delightfully friendly and humorous man, Professor Futagami, who had spent the war years in the Japanese air force as a rear gunner and had in consequence sustained a severe wound in his foot, though this did not prevent him from being remarkably agile and a splendid host. Immediately after our first meeting he invited me to his home to spend the evening with his family. After meeting his charming wife, who had prepared a lavish meal, I was greeted by their three young children, each of whom had been taught a little speech of welcome in English.

So, after scarcely a moment's hesitation, the youngest—a little girl about six years old—stepped forward, bowed demurely, and said impeccably and without hesitation: 'Good evening, Meesta Feesha—my name is Mami. How do you do?' This was followed in ascending age and descending pitch by the two boys, whose names I have forgotten; and after one of the most enjoyable and relaxed evenings I have ever spent, all three children insisted on running and waving to me as they tried to keep up with the car which was taking me to the station. Some ten years later, on learning that Profesor Futagami was planning to visit London, I wrote at once to make sure that he called on me, and I asked him to remember me to his wife and Mami. From his reply it was clear that he was amazed that I had remembered his daughter's name, and then he added: 'Mami is now at high school. She is what we call a *moga*, which means *modan garu* (modern girl). As I know you also have a daughter you will understand why my head's hairs are now turning grey.' I did.

*

A few years previously, owing to still vivid memories of the Tokyo earthquake of 1923, as well as of other more recent ones in various parts of the country, an upper limit of thirty metres (a little under a hundred feet) had been set on new buildings, and in fact the great majority of these were much longer than they were tall. This applied also to the old Imperial Hotel, specially designed by the great American architect, Frank Lloyd Wright, in order to withstand earthquake shocks, which it did successfully in 1923, and in so doing prepared the way for a new and exciting era in Japanese architecture under the inspiration of Kenzo Tange. Meanwhile, however, owing to rocketing land values in central Tokyo, the original Imperial Hotel has been dismantled and re-erected somewhere in rural Japan as a museum piece; a new and very trendy Imperial Hotel has been built on an equally central—but much smaller—site, and is some thirty to forty storeys high. In the hotel's brochure, so I was informed, visitors are told not to be worried in the event of an earthquake, when the building 'will sway gently like a willow in a breeze'. Some willow—or perhaps a will o' the wisp?

Crammed into the interstices between new blocks of offices and shops of the 1961 city centre was a chaotic assemblage of assorted wooden buildings, mostly unpainted and many of them distinctly dilapidated. Although it was late September when I first visited the area, and there had been plenty of rain, everywhere in Tokyo seemed to be covered in dust and the whole city looked as though it needed a good hoovering. Basically this was caused by the fact that most of the roads, other than the main thoroughfares, were unsurfaced and the heavy volume of both vehicular and pedestrian traffic inevitably churned up enormous quantities of dust.

In fact the existing roads, like the buildings, presented an extremely sharp contrast between old and new, and in turning out of a well-surfaced road as broad as Regent Street, into one of the many lesser streets at right angles to it, a car might suddenly drop six inches or more, giving a disconcerting jolt to its back axle, and scraping its nether regions excruciatingly on the unsurfaced road-bed. Deep ruts and sudden breaks in the surface made driving a constant hazard, and since most of the population had until recently been unfamiliar with cars, the standard of driving was positively nightmarish. Cars cut in from left or right, and back again, at hair-raising speed, and an ordinary taxi ride was periodically punctuated with sudden squealings of brakes—your own, or somebody else's, or more probably both—and it was most unusual not to collect at least two or three visible bumps and dents in a mile's drive through central Tokyo.

Nevertheless, whenever a collision occurred, causing any significant damage to either or both vehicles, it was customary for both drivers to get out and bow politely to one another, as a kind of cooling-off process, before attempting to sort out the responsibility of each party. So far as I could make out, the only difference in reaction to a red light and a green light was that, while going flat out in both cases, the driver sometimes sounded his horn at the red! It was difficult to avoid the impression that every vehicle was driven by a teenager, and though that was certainly not true, I suspect that the average length of experience of Tokyo drivers at that time was little more than a year, if that long. Apparently the number of motor vehicles had trebled in two or three years, to reach some 650,000 in 1961.

As in Western countries all drivers of motorized vehicles were required to take tests before obtaining a licence, though to judge from the standards of driving in 1961 the tests must have been pretty perfunctory. Much of the greater part of the 650,000 motor vehicles in Tokyo were trucks, taxis and buses, and only a minute proportion of Tokyo's population could in those days afford—or were brave enough —to run a car of their own.

Thus almost everybody relied either on American-style street cars or the various electric railways, predominantly elevated rather than underground, which together served virtually the whole of greater Tokyo. Alike in street cars, buses and the electric railways the degree of overcrowding was appalling, and one Tokyo Municipality official told me that all services were operating at over 200 per cent capacity. Probably the most overcrowded of all were the Tokyo railways, and at peak hours virtually the entire platform area was packed solid with row upon row of people waiting for the trains, which in turn were so crowded that scores of passengers were pressed tight against the windows and the doors, so that their noses and lips were positively flattened and did not resume their normal shape until several minutes after their respective owners had managed to struggle out of the trains.

My culminating experience of Tokyo's overcrowding came one day when I arrived rather earlier than usual at Tokyo Central Station and so got caught in—or rather was swept involuntarily into—the vortex of the early morning rush hour. The experience provided a fascinating demonstration of what I believe is nowadays called social physics.

Tokyo Central Station is an impressive edifice, dating from the Anglophile days of the turn of the century, and accordingly built in red brick, which the older generation of Japanese still for some obscure reason regard as exceptionally handsome. So much so, in fact, that when a few years ago a colleague of mine, who was suddenly called upon to show three Japanese lady professors of needlework round London, after beginning with the Albert Hall and then moving on via the Royal College of Music to the Royal School of Mines, found the ladies gazing enraptured at this last somewhat stereotyped edifice and simultaneously exclaiming: 'How very beautiful—just like Tokyo Central Station.'

But, to return to social physics, I should explain that, although the platforms are all more or less at street level, passenger access to the trains is via a very broad underground passage, extending beneath the entire width of this exceptionally large station. At each end there are wide flights of steps leading down to the main underground passage-way, and at intervals of about ten to fifteen yards somewhat narrower stairways, at right angles to the main passage, leading upwards to the platforms.

On the morning of my first visit to the station thousands of commuters were streaming into and out of it, and almost equally large numbers of other passengers were arriving to catch the morning long-distance expresses to the various major cities elsewhere in Japan. Already some twenty or thirty yards from the top of the steps I felt myself—along with hundreds of others—being sucked into the surging stream of humanity, which rapidly gathered momentum before plunging over the top step in its descent to the nether regions. I suppose it was rather like going over Niagara Falls without a barrel. Having survived the descent, I was immediately sucked into the main transverse current, and, being some inches taller than the great majority of the Japanese, I was able to observe, with a somewhat precarious detachment, the fascinating and indeed rather soothing wave-like motion produced by the rhythmical bobbing up and down of hundreds of sleek black heads somewhere between five and five and a half feet above the floor level of the passage-way.

However, the corresponding motion on the surface of the streams of people descending the staircase was considerably more agitated—like that of a mountain stream cascading down ultimately to join the broader and much more majestic current of the arterial river flowing confidently through the main passage-way. But the really interesting places to observe were the confluences where these several tributary streams flowed into the main river, for here the scene was one of extreme turbulence as some people were lifted off their feet, while others stumbled and sank, apparently without trace, below the surface level.

Indeed, so exciting was the spectacle that I forced my way, against the current, up one of the stairways from where I could get an all-embracing vista of this fascinating study of human hydrology. For several minutes I gazed in spellbound admiration at the Japanese capacity for self-preservation; but clearly I was not one of the fittest for survival and, predictably, I missed my train as a result.

Inside the trains it was likewise an enormous advantage to be a Westerner and therefore on average several inches taller than most Japanese, for one could at least breathe a little more freely—though it helped to breathe out while one's neighbour breathed in—and it was also possible to see enough through the window to read the name of the station at which one was hoping ultimately to struggle out. So efficient, though, were the guards at keeping the traffic moving that the less nimble often got carried several stations past their intended destination. However, it is only fair to add that, while this intense overcrowding on public transport was basically a reflection of the exceptionally high density of population in Japan, conditions in 1961 were still far from normal owing to severe wartime damage both to the vehicles and the roads and railways on which they ran.

At the time of my visit in 1961 the population of Tokyo had just climbed back from its wartime low of two million to a little over eight million. This figure refers to Tokyo Municipality, which is commonly known as the 'ward area', that is the area which is subdivided administratively into wards. However, since the drift of people into Tokyo, so far from abating was now accelerating, it was clear that special measures would be needed if the total population of the Tokyo ward area was to be prevented from exceeding the supposed optimal figure of nine and a half million. Presumably this figure was optimal in the sense that twelve is the optimal number of sardines in a tin, and on this basis the obvious solution was to obtain more tins, or in other words to build a series of satellite towns. Already in 1961 thirteen such towns were being built in the environs of the Tokyo ward area, though I was told that the total number would rise to about fifty in the course of the next twenty-five years or so.

While in 1961 there were still many yawning gaps in the built-up area of the central business district, these were no longer devoted to growing pumpkins and similar produce, but were undergoing a process of frenzied preparation as sites for scores of new office blocks, hotels and similar buildings, together with new expressways, flyovers and the like, in anticipation of the forthcoming Olympic Games in 1964.

Indeed 1961 probably saw the reconstruction of Tokyo at its most confused, with old and new juxtaposed in roughly equal proportions wherever one looked. The main downtown shopping thoroughfares were spacious, with broad sidewalks, and the roadways were well surfaced. But very few of these had any recognized names, and although one of the biggest—roughly comparable to the Strand in importance—had recently been designated Z Street, the side streets were a complete jumble of anonymous criss-crossed alleys, rather than streets in the Western sense of that term.

In the absence of properly named streets, let alone serially numbered houses or apartments, which seemed to be distributed wholly at random, like confetti at a wedding party, finding one's way to someone's private address called for far more than even a professional geographer's sense of place and skill in map reading, and belonged more appropriately to the realm of what the late Professor Eva Taylor called 'the haven-finding art'. Certainly in the Tokyo of 1961 few if any of its 15,000 taxis were likely to be of much help, for although they were normally quite roadworthy, their drivers were mostly newcomers from the countryside, who were often almost completely ignorant of the whereabouts of anything in Tokyo other than the Imperial Palace, Tokyo Central Station, and the Dai Ichi Life Insurance Company Building, which had been General MacArthur's headquarters during the Occupation. Moreover, even if the taxi driver had some inkling of where a particular address was to be found, the way thither was apt to be barred by the narrowness of vital alleys, major road repairs, or new highway construction which, in preparation for the Olympics, took precedence over everything else.

So, if the weather was reasonably fine it was often wisest simply to walk, providing that, before setting out, one studied the street map meticulously, if possible with the collaboration of a life-long Tokyoite. In fact, if one was not pressed for time, such explorations could be thoroughly enjoyable. The ordinary Japanese man in the street, even if he had only half a dozen words of English, was always only too willing to help a Westerner to find the place he was looking for, by the simple device of steering first in the general direction of where the ward in question was thought to be, and stopping from time to time to ask complete strangers the way. Such tactics quickly produced a positive surfeit of conflicting—if not always very relevant—information, and the relative merits of widely differing appraisals were carefully considered in an essentially constructive and—doubtless thanks to General MacArthur—democratic spirit, enlivened by much hilarity and ultimately culminating in mutual congratulations all round when the place in question was finally tracked down—often only a few hundred yards from where the original expedition had been launched.

Although this method, which was basically akin to that of a paper chase or a run with the local hounds, was apt to be rather time-consuming, everyone thoroughly enjoyed it, and in time I came to believe that I knew my way around Tokyo almost as well as I knew London. There, however, I had over-reached myself, as I soon discovered one very sunny morning, when, to my surprise, I had been invited to lunch at the British Embassy. As there were still two full hours before the appointment at one o'clock, I decided to stroll past the Palace moat and take a few photographs. As I always tend to do, I found more and more pictures to take, before I suddenly noticed that it was already half past twelve, and I was still a couple of miles from the Embassy. Being a brisk walker I felt sure I could safely manage this in the time available, but as I had my best dark suit on, and the temperature began to soar into the eighties, I decided to take a taxi.

As luck would have it, one materialized there and then; I hailed the driver and said, very slowly, 'Can you take me to the British Embassy?'

'Hai.' (Yes) he replied, 'Shimbashi'.

'No,' I said, '*not* Shimbashi,' (the Tokyo counterpart to Piccadilly Circus underground station). 'I want Bri-tish *Em-bass-y*.'

'Hai,' he answered, and off we went. After a mere thirty yards or so he took a right turn, though I knew it should have been left. So I repeated, 'British Embassy'; and he cheerfully repeated, 'Hai'. A moment later, before I could stop him, he took another right turn, accelerated to make up for lost time, and off we went, flat out in the opposite direction from the Embassy. After a few minutes of verbal ping-pong between Briti-shembassy and Shimbashi, I suddenly caught an unexpectedly welcome glimpse of my hotel on a distant horizon, and firmly ordered the driver to take me 'speedo' to Okura Hotel. Fortunately, and notwithstanding his surprise, he did so, and even more fortunately the porter there understood English; so at 1.20 the taxi started back on the road to the Embassy, where I arrived a little after 1.30. To my horror I found that it was a large luncheon party, with various V.I.P. guests, some of whom I recognized from their photographs in the Tokyo newspapers. All of them had been waiting, though luckily well fortified by the Embassy staff, over half an hour for my arrival.

Covered with embarrassment, I went straight to the Ambassador—whom I'd never met before—introduced myself, and apologized profusely, giving him a brief résumé of what had happened. 'My dear chap,' he said, 'there's nothing whatever to apologize for. It often happens to me. We've had just the right time for our drinks, and there's still some left for you. As a matter of fact our car took me to Shimbashi instead of bringing me home only the day before yesterday. Come and have lunch.'

Whatever one may think of the state of Britain, one has to hand it to the Diplomatic Service.

Amid the hectic reconstruction and modernization of their country it was understandable that many Japanese in 1961 still tended to be embarrassingly apologetic about Japan's supposed backwardness. But my own reaction, based on what I could see for myself of the prodigious effort that the nation had already put into its rebuilding, while continuing to carry on 'business as usual', was one of unstinted admiration.

Moreover whatever may have been the situation up to the 1930s, it seemed clear by the early 1960s that modern Westernized Japan had already come of age. Most Japanese no longer seemed ill at ease in Western clothing, or in the environment of Western-style hotels, even though they retained Japanese habits of behaviour among themselves. Whenever groups of them met, for example in the hotel where I was staying, there was much, and prolonged, bowing from the waist to an almost horizontal position. But the same people would instantly turn to greet a Western visitor in a perfectly Western manner without any gaucheness or apparent selfconsciousness. From what I could gather, all this was very different from what it had been a mere twenty or thirty years previously, and while the change arose in part from a further generation of exposure to Western culture, it was in the main a result of the American Occupation.

Nevertheless, while the Westernized Japanese, whom one met in the hotels, on the airlines or in the universities, now seemed quite at home in both worlds, and one felt that a successful synthesis was being achieved culturally in many fields, the contrast between generations, between young and old, and between traditional and Western, was still the most striking and ubiquitous feature of life in the Japan of 1961. Perhaps nowhere else in the world was there at that time such an international atmosphere as in Tokyo. For the Japanese had largely

Westernized themselves—instead of having had it done for them like the Indian upper class, who sent their children to English boarding schools—and in the end this process of self-education tended to be much more durable. Certainly it was difficult to doubt that Japan was already by far the most Westernized state in Asia, in the sense that a much higher proportion of Japanese had assimilated a great deal more of the Western outlook than was the case in India or colonial South-east Asia.

Probably the most striking aspects of this were the extremely widespread appreciation of Western music, and the remarkably high quality of performances of chamber music and perhaps even more so of major symphonic works by orchestras of eighty to a hundred or more players, virtually all of whom were Japanese. Moreover, although in the early 1960s conductors and leading soloists in concerto performances were mostly Westerners, that phase did not last long, and it is now commonplace for Japanese conductors and leading soloists to give first-class performances with some of the most distinguished orchestras in Europe and North America.

While undoubtedly many thousands of Japanese now possess a deep and appreciative love of what was once European but is now universal music, the Japanese in the 1960s still showed a tendency to affect Western styles in many other respects, apparently purely for modernity's sake. Thus in the early post-Occupation period the thoroughly practical habit among Japanese city workers of eating a sandwich lunch led to bread's replacing rice as a middle-class status symbol among the younger set, and some ten years later European-style wine, mostly produced locally in Japan, began to be regarded as more modern and trendy than the traditional *sake,* beloved of the older generation.

In order to promote this somewhat expensive new fashion, the hotel in which I was staying began to place a bottle of wine on each table in the main dining room, together with a little note about the pleasures of winemanship. The label on a bottle of red wine on my table read as follows:

CHATEAU LION
Vin rouge de premier qualité.
Mise en bouteilles dans mes cuves.
Suntory Ltd., Osaka and Tokyo.

It seemed only fair to give it a trial, so I did, and rather to my surprise it proved to be remarkably palatable.

In short, it was no longer true (if indeed it ever had been) to say, as Bertrand Russell rather cruelly did, that 'the Japanese have adopted our faults and kept their own'. On the contrary they were no longer comic caricatures of Europeans, but an increasingly self-confident and extremely impressive people, even if some superficial aspects of their behaviour did seem a little odd to Westerners. No doubt much of their new confidence had come—and deservedly so—from their 'economic miracle' of post-war recovery, which, like Germany's, had benefited greatly from the forced destruction of antiquated equipment and its replacement—largely with American aid—with brand-new machinery. But there had also been a magnificent and sustained effort, based on sturdy national discipline—likewise uncannily reminiscent of post-Nazi Germany—in facing and overcoming the consequences of military defeat.

Nevertheless Japan always has its surprises, and a couple of days before I was due to go on a tour of southern Japan, I received a phone call at my hotel saying that I was invited to be the guest of honour at a special dinner that very evening (indeed in less than an hour's time) at which all the leading Tokyo geographers would be present. My informant told me that it was to be at a place apparently called the Shirrutoppu Hoteru, which continued to fox me even after the name had been repeated several times. Fortunately the sudden arrival of Mr Tsutsumi saved the situation, as he explained diplomatically that the name of the place was in fact the Hilltop Hotel, and even more important, he proposed to take me there forthwith.

It was a most amicable occasion. We had an excellent dinner and the assembled geographers proved to be congenial company, though—like most academics, regardless of nationality—we spent most of the time talking shop. However, after these proceedings had been going on for some time, one of the more senior members made a little speech to the effect that Japanese, whose black hair rarely turns grey except in extreme old age, were usually thought by Westerners to be much younger than in fact they were. Whereupon I was asked to guess the age of each of the venerable professors in turn. Without exception I undershot the runway by between ten and twenty years in every case, provoking much laughter and wagging of heads, before finally I did what I assumed was expected of me, and asked if they would like to guess my age.

This suggestion was received in a constructive and co-operative spirit, with extended discussions and consultations—of course in Japanese—among those present, before a consensus emerged and was finally and very diffidently put to me. They had weighed the matter up very carefully and concluded that I must be a little under fifty, and after further deliberation they finally settled for forty-eight. This was absolutely correct (the occasion being, of course, a longer time ago than I now care to remember) but I congratulated them all warmly on their skill in so effectively penetrating the secrets of an inscrutable Occidental like myself. We departed in high spirits and low taxis, but it wasn't until next morning that I discovered that everyone at the dinner had received a detailed copy of my *curriculum vitae* (age, of course, included) from Gaimusho.

The next day, when I was to be the guest of the Asano Boys' High School, served only to increase my mystification. Asano, I learned, was a Japanese pioneer of land reclamation who, in the nineteenth century, had begun to realize that in so rugged and overcrowded a country as Japan, with scarcely any spare land left, a major expansion of heavy industry could not take place unless new land could be reclaimed from the sea for that express purpose. So Asano travelled to the Netherlands to learn how this could be done, and was later instrumental in organizing extensive reclamation of the foreshore south of Yokohama and thus providing the basis on which the great Kawasaki steel plant was subsequently erected.

Having visited the steelworks and also the statue of Mr Asano, looking threateningly at the sea like a Japanese Canute, we went on to the Boys' High School named after him. We were graciously received by the diminutive and rather obsequious headmaster, who, after saying what a great honour it was for the School to have a visit from me, proffered us some green tea. Like virtually all other pedagogues, the headmaster automatically assumed that we wanted to see the School's library, and added that he very much hoped I would be willing to autograph one of its books. Having agreed, I was told 'Unfortunately we do not have your book so please autograph a book by Professor Dudley Stamp.' When I asked whether he wanted me to sign L. Dudley Stamp or Charles A. Fisher he seemed at as big a loss as I was to know what was expected of me, but eventually he decided that I should sign my own name.

Perhaps in order to change the subject, and/or to make up for any snub I might think I had received (though I didn't) he said: 'Tomorrow every boy in this School will write an essay entitled "The Visit of Professor Fisher to the Asano Boys' High School".' This reminded me of what had been puzzling me during the previous two hours, namely the uncanny silence, so unusual in a boys' school. So I asked, 'When am I going to meet the boys?' only to be told 'Very sorry, no boys here today; today is public holiday.'

For some obscure reason this conversation reminded me of what someone had told me years before, namely that among the Zen sect of Buddhists one of the great philosophical problems is phrased as follows:

> We know the sound made by two hands clapping.
> But what is the sound made by one hand clapping?

Perhaps if I had signed Dudley Stamp's name as well as my own it might have helped to solve this profound philosophical problem.

From an empty boys' school I was taken next day to what seemed to be an exceptionally crowded Womens' University, at Ochanamizu, where I met two male faculty members—Professor Akira Watanabe and Dr Yasuo Masai—who have remained among my closest friends ever since. Much to my delight Masai took me to see his parents' apartment in a new block, several miles from the city centre. This block was part of a new housing estate, designed—like a hundred or more similar new estates—each to accommodate some ten thousand people. The buildings were modern-style reinforced concrete—some two storeys and others four storeys high, though each individual apartment was on a single floor. Masai's own apartment was on the ground floor and I instantly committed the inexcusable, if totally unfamiliar, sin of entering without first removing my shoes. However, all was forgiven and I was taken outside to see the small garden, in which they grew flowers and hung out the washing for all the occupants, who included his parents as well as his brother and sister-in-law.

The whole apartment was about eight feet high, and the total floor space about fifteen by twenty-five. Apart from the modern kitchen and the new 'flush toilet' there were no doors, though partitions separated the rest of the space into three rooms, and the monthly rental was about fifteen U.S. dollars (at that time around £4). Heating—by either electric fire or gas stove—was usually necessary for four months from December to March, but its cost was not very great. Already by 1961 many industrial workers, even in slum areas, had television aerials on long bamboo poles, and Tokyo took great pride in the fact that its Television Tower was taller than the Eiffel Tower in Paris and hence—needless to say, though everyone did—the tallest building in the world.

Even more interesting than Masai's flat was his father, a remarkably alert man of seventy or thereabouts with thick black hair and not a trace of grey, who was an English teacher at a High School. Although Masai, who had spent some years in the United States, said his father read English but did not speak it, on the contrary Mr Masai senior spoke it extremely well—a little slowly but completely correctly, clearly and idiomatically, and far better than many British language teachers speak French or German.

Like so many of his generation who remembered the Anglo-Japanese Alliance, the older Mr Masai was full of admiration for things British, and told me how much he wished he had been able to visit England once in his life. When he heard that I came from Sheffield he immediately enquired how far Sheffield was from Stratford-upon-Avon, and also from the Lake District. After extemporizing an answer to both questions, I said to him, 'I suppose that your favourite English authors are Shakespeare and Wordsworth?' His face lit up instantly as he asked, 'How did you know?' Then, after a brief silence, he said there was something else he wished to ask me: was the water of the Thames in London really as clear as a mountain stream? I hated to disabuse him so late in life and only assuaged my conscience by saying that, although this was no longer so, the Thames was a good deal clearer than the Sumida River in Tokyo. But that wasn't saying much.

*

On returning from Ochanamizu University to my hotel I remembered having noticed amid Professor Watanabe's extensive collection of books on geography and geology an exceptionally large and solitary tome dealing with racial problems and the colour question, and I wondered what lay behind his interest in this particular field, so apparently remote from his own. Yet in fact the question virtually answered itself. As victims of Western racial prejudice themselves, the Japanese in general—and their politicians and academics in particular—were inevitably deeply concerned about such matters, especially in view of the seriousness with which they had been taken by their great Prime Minister, Hirobumi Ito, as long ago as the 1880s.

To what extent General MacArthur's post-war Occupation forces, which included a proportion of black American G.I.s, had refocused attention on this sensitive subject it was difficult to say, though my impression was that there was remarkably little obvious friction on this or any related score. Indeed, having at first regarded the General's policies with some scepticism I ended by being very impressed with nearly all of them, except for some minor misgivings relating to educational matters. Certainly, however, the Occupation introduced several important and overdue changes, particularly in the universities, the numbers of which increased rapidly as a result of up-grading numerous less advanced centres to full university status, though even so the demand for such higher education far exceeded the supply.

Clearly this in turn called for a rapid multiplication of supporting services, as was most appropriately illustrated for me when one unusually garrulous professor took me to the room where the correspondingly multiplied secretarial staff were now ensconced. With a magnificent sweep of his arm in the direction of four dainty pairs of girls' slippers neatly parked outside the office door, he exclaimed with a resounding chuckle, 'Obsarve: Perkinson's Raw.'

I had the impression that he too had an eye for the perks.

11. SOUTH AND NORTH—THE DISSIMILAR HALVES OF JAPAN

Paradoxically, Tokyo, like many other capital cities, is at once the focus, and in many respects represents also the quintessence, of the nation it symbolizes. Yet by the very fact of its being by far the greatest city in Japan—and indeed the largest in the world—it cannot but be untypical of the rest of Japan. Certainly no one who concentrates his attention predominantly on Tokyo will ever really understand Japan, for it is only by visiting and savouring for oneself the extraordinary diversity of its landscapes and its associated traditions that the foreigner can begin to perceive the true richness of Japan's cultural tapestry.

Tokyo, originally Edo, grew up on—and subsequently sprawled over—the flat and rather dreary Kanto plain, the largest of Japan's relatively few and far from expansive stretches of lowland. Besides Kanto there are two other lowlands lying to the south-west: the Nobi and Kinki plains, respectively the sites of Nagoya and Osaka; and to the north the somewhat smaller Sendai plain of north-eastern Honshu and the Ishikari plain in western Hokkaido.

While in latitude the Kanto plain is virtually central within Honshu, climatically it belongs unmistakably with the warmer southern half of Japan. Having originated in the south-western extremity of the country, Japanese civilization slowly expanded eastwards and northwards, subsequently penetrating to the northern limits of Honshu by the end of the eighteenth century and finally extending into Hokkaido in the nineteenth. Nevertheless the agriculturally more productive and climatically much pleasanter south has from the outset remained much the more densely populated, and today at least three-quarters of the total Japanese population, and seven of its eight cities with a million or more inhabitants—namely Tokyo, Osaka, Yokohama, Nagoya, Kyoto, Kobe and Kita-Kyushu—are within the southern half, leaving only Sapporo, in Hokkaido, in the northern half.

The city of Shizuoka now extends over nearly the whole of the Oi plain, formerly covered by ricefields.

A corner of Kumamoto Castle showing the highly skilled craftsmanship of the dry stone walls.

The *torii* (ornamental gateway) at Miyajima. Note how the curve of the *torii* roof resembles the curve of pine branches.

洋服
ファルコン印
赤ちゃん用品
子供服
エプロン
株式会社 黒松
タオル

The deer park at Nara.

Dobuike is the main clothing centre in Osaka, the second largest city in Japan.

The great Buddha at Kamakura.

The Ginza, main shopping street of Tokyo.

Rush hour in Tokyo: queuing for buses and overhead railway.

The port city of Kobe provides a striking example of the problems caused by building on excessively steep slopes. In recent years many buildings have been completely swept away by landslides.

Typhoon damage at Nara Park. Many of the trees are over five hundred years old.

The Nakasendo highway near Kiso Fukushima.

Crater of Mount Aso, Kyushu, the largest active volcano in Japan.

In order to prevent landslides on steep slopes many hillsides are revetted with concrete blocks.

Hiroshima provides an appalling example of the desecration of scenery by the reclamation of vast rectangular slabs of foreshore for industrial use.

The southern shore of Dokai Bay in Kyushu viewed from Hobashira-yama, some 1,900 feet above sea level.

Lumber camp in the depths of the Hokkaido forest.

Rice cultivation on the Ishikari Plain, Hokkaido. The fields here are much larger than those of central and southern Japan.

Ainu man and woman against a background of totem poles adorned with bears' skulls.

Spring returns to Hiroshima. The burnt-out building in the background is the old city hall of Hiroshima.

In these circumstances it is understandable that the maps of Japan produced during the Tokugawa period greatly exaggerated the scale of the southern half of the country, and indeed this area is shown on one such map as comprising some ninety per cent of the country! Moreover, this cartographic distortion was carried to even greater extremes in a Dutch map published by Johannes Vrient in 1596, which shows virtually nothing but the southern half of the country. In effect, these old maps of Japan were remarkable precursors of the 'mental maps' produced by some modern geographers; and since the Dutch, the only Westerners who were permitted to trade with Japan during the Tokugawa Seclusion, were confined to the minuscule artificial island of Deshima, off Nagasaki, it is not surprising that their maps presented what may be called a 'Nagasaki- (or Deshima-) eye view' of Japan.

*

My first visit to southern Japan took place in the autumn of 1961, and although I travelled alone I was met at each major stop by local geographers who showed me round their home areas. Fortunately, since my knowledge of Japanese was both fragmentary and rusty, I was seen into the train by Mr Tsutsumi and so learned the basic Japanese routine relating to tickets and other formalities. However, my first impression on boarding the train, and claiming my very comfortable first-class reserved seat by the window, was one of unusual informality. Admittedly, it was already remarkably warm for early morning, but even so I was astonished to see a well-dressed Japanese gentleman on the other side of the central aisle calmly take off and hang up first his jacket and then his trousers, after which he sat in his vest and long white underpants for the entire journey. Despite the typically English addiction to following established precedent, I did not do so on this occasion, if only because I was not wearing long white underpants myself.

The journey began along the Tokaido line, which should not be confused with the New Tokaido Line, nowadays better known by its Japanese name *Shinkansen*. This extremely impressive new railway, now world famous for its 'bullet' express trains, was just beginning to be built in 1961, more or less alongside the original Tokaido railway, though with more gentle curves, and on the standard gauge adopted by nearly all European and North American railways, in contrast to the narrower gauge of the original Tokaido line and also of most other Japanese railways.

Although in more recent times I have greatly enjoyed travelling, often at well over 100 miles per hour, on the *Shinkansen*, I am glad that my first journey to the south was on the original Tokaido railway, itself named after the still older southern highway by which, in feudal times, the daimyo and their retinue of samurai and others made their biennial journey to Edo. For since the old Tokaido line wound its way around the sinuosities of the southern coast of Honshu, usually from well above sea-level, its trains moved at a relatively leisurely pace, so that one could savour to the full this entrancingly beautiful area, which was uncannily reminiscent of the French Côte d'Azur. Never, I am sure, could there have been a more beautiful day than this one, on which for the first time I made the acquaintance of these gleaming cliffs, looking out over a cobalt-blue sea beneath a totally cloudless mid-blue sky. Except for the widespread and extraordinarily graceful bamboos, virtually all the main forms of vegetation—acacia, cactus, and a wide variety of aromatic bushes—seemed almost identical with those of the southern Alpes Maritimes. And it was a sheer delight to observe how each new bend in the line brought into view yet another diminutive cove, with its shining white sand accompanied by a pale green fringe of offshore seaweed, and its cluster of fishermen's dwellings, packed tightly together so as to leave as much as possible of the minute extent of cultivable land for productive use.

Throughout almost the whole of the way to Shizuoka, our first stop, I sat with my face glued to the window, like a schoolboy on his first train journey. So much so, in fact, that it was only when an unusually sharp bend presented a sudden view inland of a gigantic volcanic cone that it occurred to me that this might be Mount Fuji, which had captivated my imagination in early childhood. But scarcely had I had time to recognize this than the train plunged into a tunnel, and shortly afterwards we were slowing down for our arrival at Shizuoka.

Here, I had been told, I should be met by the tallest geographer in Japan—'almost as high as Mount Fuji'—but, perhaps because of the strain of maintaining such an exalted posture, the great man did not appear, though two other geographers—one of medium height and the other minute—did their limited best to fill the gap. But much the most interesting member of the group who met me was a very distinguished economist who had spent a long time in the United Kingdom and spoke excellent English. His high international reputation was such that he could almost certainly have obtained a key post in one of the leading Tokyo universities, for he was already the author of an award-winning classic in his field; but as both he and his wife preferred to live in more attractive surroundings, where they could enjoy both the coastal scenery and a spectacular view of Mount Fuji, he chose to work at a less prestigious university nearby. Had I been in his position, I should like to think that I would have acted as wisely as he did.

Shizuoka, then with about a quarter of a million people, was a typical middle-rank Japanese city, which had grown up on a small delta and by 1961 had spread itself over the greater part of its available rice land. Although it was not a place of any great importance, either economically or strategically, it had not escaped Allied bombing. Indeed the city centre had been almost totally destroyed, though it was now in process of being replaced by a new central business district, with modern blocks of offices, shops and flats, whose spick and span appearance contrasted sharply with the drabness of the tightly packed one-storey wooden dwellings in which the majority of its population lived. In addition it had a small tea factory, producing both black and green tea; a large cannery, concentrating increasingly on oranges (satsumas) which were now tending to displace tea from the hillsides as they were distinctly more profitable. Strawberries also were beginning to be cultivated commercially here with encouraging success, and in addition there was a busy fishing industry, particularly concerned with tuna and bonito which were also processed at the cannery, though presumably not in the same containers as the oranges. The fishing boats, including some large ocean-going vessels, used the harbour at nearby Shimizu, an expanding coastal town already within sight of merging with Shizuoka and so producing another major city.

As I have implied, Shizuoka was famous as a centre from which to see Mount Fuji, the preferred viewpoint being a ridge of hills to the south, on which tea and oranges were grown. We drove up to the top of the ridge and from there had an excellent view over the city and the nearby orange groves, strawberry beds, and tea gardens, but Fuji was completely covered in cloud. After I had waited with my camera at the ready for over an hour, a minute speck of the top of the cone emerged; I snapped it but it was gone in an instant. Since then I have often shown this photograph to illustrate what Professor Frederic Starr considered to be the essence of the Japanese concept of scenic beauty (quoted by Inazo Nitobe, *Japan*):

> Fuji bare and naked in a blaze of sunshine is beautiful;
> Fuji with its summit wrapped in cloud and mist is more beautiful;
> Fuji blotted out by fogs until but a hint line is left is most beautiful.

On this basis my own photograph, of which the 'hint line' occupied much less than one per cent, would seem to represent the fulfilment of the Japanese concept of scenic perfection. Alternatively, in the words on the back of a Japanese picture postcard: 'Mt. Fuji is a valuable classic property, which Japan is proud of, and matches well to Tomei highway.' *Chacun à son goût.*

After leaving Shizuoka in the early evening my journey continued in the dark to Nagoya, then Japan's third largest city (recently displaced to fourth by Yokohama). Before the First World War its population had passed one million, and by 1961 it was over 1.6 million. This growth was the more remarkable because in the intervening period Nagoya had sustained greater setbacks in proportion to its size than any other Japanese city with the possible exception of Hiroshima. Thus in 1942/3 Nagoya—already the primary centre of the Japanese aircraft industry, suffered a severe earthquake which knocked out the most important aircraft factory. In so far as aircraft production had begun to be resumed, it was again set back by massive American air raids in 1945, and, as if by an afterthought fourteen years later, Nagoya—and in particular its harbour—caught the full blast of the Ise typhoon, one of the worst ever recorded.

Yet by 1961 Nagoya was in many respects the most impressively rebuilt of all the great cities of Japan. For it was the only one which, instead of rebuilding on the old congested street plan, like London after the great fire of 1666, had had the vision to replan from scratch, and had been realigned along a spectacular new highway a hundred metres wide, comprising a vast dual carriageway with a wide green strip between the two roads. Admittedly, many of the earlier blocks of offices, apartments and other kinds of accommodation, which had been put up with great rapidity, were hideously ugly, but among the more recent ones—particularly those flanking the 'hundred metre highway'—were many very handsome modern buildings. Thus, even though I arrived, as a complete stranger, late at night, I quickly sensed something of the intense dynamism and vitality of the city, in which reconstruction work was continuing far into the night while, down below, the new and very impressive underground shopping centre was nearing completion and work was already in progress on Nagoya's new underground railway.

By way of contrast to all this modernity, it was also at Nagoya that I had my first experience of staying alone at a Japanese-style hotel or *ryokan*, though I was briefly introduced to its mysteries by my host, Professor Matsuda, who met me at the station and looked after me during my stay in the city.

Putting first things first, and following instinctively the dictates of my professional discipline, I naturally began by exploring the local geography in search of what, in my earlier days as a prisoner of war, I had learned to call the *benjo* (literally 'the convenient place') though I soon discovered that in the more polite circles in which I now moved it was known as the *gofujo* ('the great unmentionable place'). Despite its duality of names, it was neither convenient nor great, being tucked away in the remotest possible corner, and so diminutive that I invariably banged both elbows and nearly removed my scalp every time I went in or out of the door. By comparison with these sufferings, which arose from my being substantially larger than most Japanese for whom the facilities had of course been designed, sleeping on the floor—or rather failing to do so with the doubtful assistance of a wooden pillow—was a mere bagatelle.

However, such trivialities were more than offset by the excellence of both the service and the food, which at Matsuda's invitation I now proceeded to sample, beginning with a steak which he strongly recommended. To my surprise he did not eat anything at all, but sat in complete silence opposite me (both of us cross-legged on the floor) until I had finished my meal.

Then came what he clearly regarded as the high spot of the evening: we should go and drink beer. He hailed a taxi and we dashed across the city at a hair-raising speed to what from the outside appeared to be a deserted office block. But Matsuda clearly knew his way around, and we took the lift up to the penultimate floor which opened onto a wide but dimly lit saloon in which were arranged a series of semi-private tables. At almost every one of these was an elderly, and apparently well-heeled Japanese businessman in process of being plied with beer by a bargirl, who invariably topped up the glass after each gulp or even sip, with the insidiously dangerous result that the drinker quickly lost count of how much was being stowed away between decks.

At an early stage the girl serving me spilt a few drops of beer on the sleeve of my jacket, and was overcome with acute embarrassment; so I made soothing noises and took another sip to reassure her. A long conversation followed, in Japanese, between the girl and Matsuda, who then translated slowly for my benefit. 'She says English Professor very kind man. I spill beer, but he not angry. Very kind man. *Very* kind man.' By this time, as things seemed to be warming up in one way and possibly another, I removed my slightly beer-stained jacket, revealing the not very disconcerting fact that I was wearing a short-sleeved sports shirt. Whereupon the girl began stroking my arms, and talking to Matsuda who translated once again. 'She says English Professor has very beautiful *white* arms'; to which the only reply I could think of on the spur of the moment was 'thank you very much!' There followed more beer, more Japanese, more stroking, and finally, in English via Matsuda, the blockbuster. 'She says, please change your beautiful white skin for my ugly yellow skin.' It seemed to me that at this point it was time for me to take a stand—until I suddenly began to have vague misgivings regarding my capacity to do so. Nevertheless, broad-minded and tolerant though I endeavour to be, I felt that there were limits to what I was prepared to do in a bar, even in Japan, and even with the lights dimmed.

Fortunately Matsuda, doubtless on the basis of much past experience here, realized that it was time for him to intervene. Suddenly he rose to his feet and, by way of a little diversion, delivered a succinct but slightly unorthodox lecture on the geomorphology of Nagoya, beginning with the words: 'This building is situated on a diluvial terrace . . .'; after which—being understandably in need of further sustenance—he announced, 'Now we go to another bar,' which we did.

There, at this second hostelry, which was already well populated with both men and women comprising a single and highly informal community, the main activity seemed to be singing, either individually or collectively, as the spirit moved, which it seemed to be doing with considerable fluidity. I have a hazy recollection of having given a profound rendering of 'Old Man River', which seemed to go down well (indeed all the way to a bottom B flat) followed by the Japanese Navy March, to which I had written some facetious Japanglo words several years previously in Chungkai camp. Officially the march had been banned under the Occupation, and certainly my words ought to have been banned, Occupation or not, but since nobody appeared to understand them no harm was done and, on the contrary, I became the hero of the evening.

This performance was followed by what seemed to be a very melancholy solo by one of the ladies present, and I was duly told that it was the song of a man pining for his wife who was looking after aged relatives in a distant village. Then suddenly the singer turned to me and asked if I had a wife, and if so didn't I feel sad because she wasn't with me in Nagoya? I answered both questions in the affirmative, and proudly produced a photograph of my wife in support of my assertions. The photo was passed round and everyone—both men and women—expressed their approval: 'Ah—bery beautiful, *bery* beautiful wifu. You bery happy man when you with beautiful wifu.' I expressed general agreement with these sentiments, and was just beginning to sit back and bask in the reflected glory of my wife's photograph, when one of the women suddenly exclaimed, 'Prease kiss photo of your wifu.' When I demurred I was immediately assured by a growing chorus, which soon included everyone present, that 'In Japan man always kiss photo of his wifu. *You* prease kiss photo of *your* wifu.'

Being of a somewhat philosophical turn of mind I decided that perhaps it would be ungracious of me not to follow the old rule, 'when in Nagoya do as the Nagoyans do'. So, feeling more than a little ridiculous, I did what was required of me. Whereupon the whole company burst into torrents of uncontrollable laughter. 'Bery punny; *bery* punny; in Japan we do *not* kiss photo of wifu. You bery punny man.' Quite obviously I was, and so I joined in the 'pun', even though it did seem to confirm General MacArthur's waspish quip that the Japanese were a nation of twelve-year-olds. But at least it's more enjoyable, and certainly far more fun, to laugh—especially at oneself—than to sting other people. So to celebrate this general bonhomie the entire company decided to sing 'Goddu Savu Queenu' in my honour, and then we all linked arms and sang another vaguely familiar song, apparently called 'Orrud akwaint', which further research revealed to be 'Auld lang syne'.

Certainly Matsuda was a marvellous host, and next day he had arranged for the Nagoya civic authorities to entertain us both to lunch in the City Hall. While we were enjoying this civic repast Matsuda—like most Japanese a compulsive photographer—solemnly and silently took out his camera and photographed me on the opposite side of the table. Not to be outdone, I reciprocated with my newly acquired Japanese camera, and was very pleased later to discover that the photograph had come out remarkably well, notwithstanding the absence of any artificial lighting in the room. After my return home I wrote to thank Matsuda for all his hospitality and added that 'under separate cover I am sending a copy of the photo I took of you at the City Hall'. By return of post I received a delightful letter which had obviously been written with the aid of a Japanese-English phrase book. It began: 'Dear Professor Fisher, It does my heart good to have my portrait under cover.' My heart got quite a kick out of it too!

Unlike the Nobi plain which is dominated by the single great city of Nagoya, Kinki, the third major plain in southern Japan, contains a veritable cluster of cities which together present a bewildering diversity of urban functions, styles and traditions. Nevertheless, both in size and wealth, Osaka is clearly much more than the *primus inter pares* of Kinki, and its population, now of some three and a half million, is greater than that of all the other Kinki cities put together.

In modern Japan's salad days, when the 'Britain of the East' cult was much in vogue, Osaka, as the great commercial metropolis, quickly succeeded in establishing its reputation as the 'Manchester of Japan'. During this transitional phase the already recognized differences of emphasis between Tokyo—combining the roles of the nation's capital, the Imperial Residence, and the primary cultural and educational centre—and Osaka—as the leading provincial city, concentrating mainly on industry, commerce and banking—came to present a striking parallel to that between London and Manchester. As a Lancastrian—if not exactly a Mancunian—I had a strong impression that the self-confident, no-nonsense citizens of Osaka were totally assured in their belief that what Osaka thought today, Tokyo would not get around to thinking at least until the day after tomorrow.

Moreover this self-assurance, which was obviously characteristic of the Osakans, seemed also to be shared to the full by their opposite numbers in the great port of Kobe, which stretches in a narrow ribbon between the steep mountain ridge behind, and the shore of Osaka Bay looking out to the Pacific. One day when I was being shown round Kobe harbour—including the vast Mitsubishi ship-building yards—I asked the deputy harbourmaster if Kobe was still regarded as the ocean port of Osaka, now that air travel was tending to supersede ocean-liner traffic. With a satisfied smile he replied: 'No. Kobe has never been the port of Osaka. Osaka is the port of Kobe!' However, whether I was in Kobe—whose 'baby beef', nurtured at least partly on beer, is a great delicacy, or in Osaka—whose most beautiful cherry blossoms grow in the congested and unprepossessing precincts of the mint—I felt thoroughly at home in what I have ever since thought of as 'the Lancashire of Japan'.

However, during the critical post-1945 reconstruction period, Osaka—while remaining indisputably the second largest city in Japan—tended to lose out relatively, though certainly not absolutely, to Tokyo. For it was in the capital that General MacArthur had his headquarters, in the monumentally squat and poker-faced Dai Ichi Life Insurance Building, condescendingly looking out on to the Imperial Palace. Accordingly many of the vital decisions affecting Japan's commercial, industrial and economic future, which in more normal times would probably have been taken in Osaka, came increasingly to be handled in Tokyo.

Thus, during the Occupation years, Japan slowly at first, but later with gathering momentum, underwent a significant geographical reorientation. From the early days of the twentieth century when, following the first Sino-Japanese War, the great Yawata steelworks were built and Korea was transformed into the bridgehead for the invasion of the continental mainland of Asia, the new demilitarized Japan began to turn its face towards the Pacific—'the ocean of the future'—and to its new-found American mentor on the road back to recovery and rehabilitation, both physical and psychological.

Nevertheless Osaka had no intention of adopting what the Japanese call 'a low posture' during the post-war refashioning of Japan. So, while Tokyo was reshaping itself from a chaotic and overgrown latter-day Edo into an impressively modern city in preparation for the 1964 Olympic Games, Osaka assiduously, and ultimately successfully, negotiated for the role of host city for the next International Exposition —or Expo '70 as it came to be called. And just as the 1964 Olympics had provided the psychological and economic stimulus for the impressive new architecture of Kenzo Tange, a host of new luxury hotels, and the magnificent new expressways soaring above the existing street pattern of downtown Tokyo in broad sweeping curves, so Osaka began to follow suit in order to cater for the greatly increased flow of traffic and tourists which Expo '70 was bound to generate.

Unfortunately, however, the terrain of Osaka—prevailingly flat and very congested—offered less scope for aesthetically pleasing urban renewal. In particular, the core of the city was aligned along both sides of the Yodo river, where several historic and attractive rice-merchants' warehouses still survived, overlooked by the very imposing English-style redbrick City Hall and Law Courts. But if these landmarks of Osaka were to be preserved, the only way of building the most vital section of the new expressway was to erect it on a series of massive concrete stilts over the Yodo river.

In purely practical terms this has obviously been very successful, but visually, as I discovered on a more recent visit, the result is deplorable. For, in contrast to those in Tokyo, the overhead highways in central Osaka twist themselves tortuously in and out of the remaining gaps between the main surviving buildings, completely destroying the once attractive urban skyline which I remembered nostalgically from 1961. Indeed the whole contemporary impression reminded me vividly of the great ruins of Angkor in Cambodia (Kampuchea) which, during the centuries after its downfall in the fifteenth century, has been overgrown with dense tropical rain forest, whose massive roots and branches have wrapped themselves around many of these once magnificent buildings which have been undermined or virtually strangled in the process. While, needless to say, none of the handsome new hotels, office blocks and other buildings of present-day Osaka are threatened by any such destruction, it nevertheless seemed to me that aesthetically the city centre had come unpleasantly close to strangulation.

Simultaneously with the refashioning of Osaka in the late 1960s the continuing drift of population to the cities has led to the building of more and more dormitory suburbs, or sleep towns as my Japanese friends called them. While some of those I visited in 1961 were attractively laid out, with well planned blocks of apartments, each having its own kitchen and bathroom, and with very colourful and pleasantly landscaped shopping centres, I am bound to say that the huge and controversial new town at Senri, adjacent to the site of Expo '70, looked more like a barracks or a prison—indeed quite remarkably similar to the one at Princetown on Dartmoor—than it resembled any town I would care to live in.

At the time when I visited Senri New town in 1967 it contained 50,000 people, accommodated in 15,000 'dwelling units', but it was already scheduled to expand in order to house 150,000 people in the course of the next few years. The town was subdivided into 'neighbourhoods', each of 2,500 dwellings, accommodating a total of about 10,000 people. Each such neighbourhood had one primary school and two neighbourhood centres, and in addition there were to be three high schools and three large car parks.

But the most remarkable thing about Senri was that none of its individual 'dwelling units' had its own bathroom, and instead everyone had to go to the public bath-house at the neighbourhood centre. For many people this might entail half an hour's walk which during the winter months might well be bitterly cold, wet, and on occasion made distinctly hazardous by deep snowdrifts. Obviously the practice of concentrating on a few central bath-houses, and thus eliminating one room from each dwelling unit, represented a significant saving in scarce and expensive space, but—in accordance with the Japanese habit of drawing a veil over what one does not wish to reveal—the policy was dressed up as a modernized version of the traditional Japanese custom of communal bathing.

In commenting on the Kinki plain I have hitherto concentrated on its two great modern cities, Osaka and Kobe, but there are also several lesser industrial towns, notably Sakai, Fusei, and Amagasaki. In the most literal sense, however, it is arguable that Kobe, Amagasaki, and Sakai do not belong within Kinki, whose name means 'Neighbourhood of the Imperial Palace' and refers to the vicinity of the old palace at Kyoto. With some one and a half million people, Kyoto is slightly larger than Kobe, and as such ranks as the second city in Kinki.

Far more important than its size, however, is the immense historic and aesthetic significance of Kyoto, which is much the most attractive of all the so-called 'million cities' of Japan. By contrast with the intense bustle symptomatic of modern Japan's obsessive desire to become the first country of the twenty-first century, Kyoto treasures and delights in the peaceful seclusion of a tradition which goes back over a thousand years. For amid the quiet serenity enshrined within its beautifully chiselled stone walls, one can still sense something of the grace and elegance of its ancient but exquisitely preserved temples and shrines. And in so doing one can also experience a sense both of gratitude for the past and hope for the future when one recalls that Kyoto—the cultural treasure-house of Japan—was deliberately spared the kind of unforgivable devastation which tore the heart out of every other great Japanese city.

Yet to my view Kinki has one even more delectable city than Kyoto, and that is the still older—and now much smaller—capital city of Nara, which dates from the eighth century. Thus while Kyoto includes also a considerable and typically modern industrial sector, Nara remains essentially a historic—yet living—monument. For it is here that the Japanese genius for blending and harmonizing the man-made beauty of temples and shrines with the exquisite natural scenery of the Nara Basin and the adjacent coast of Seto Naikai achieves its most perfect expression. And it is in the nearby village of Ikaruga that the early-seventh-century Horyuji Temple, the oldest and surely the most beautiful Buddhist temple in Japan, is to be found, though in terms of tourist appeal the greatest interest seems to centre in the eighth-century Todaji Temple, with its enormous bronze Buddha, over fifty-three feet high and said to weigh over four hundred tons.

Nevertheless, neither this nor most of the other temples in Nara compare in delight with the bucolic charm of the deer park, extending over much of the large area which, well over a thousand years ago, comprised the original city of Nara. For here one can wander at will along innumerable quiet paths, flanked by hundreds of beautifully carved stone lanterns, beneath the shade of the great cryptomerias, many of which must be almost as old as Nara itself. And, in strolling thus, one is rarely alone, for in this haven of peace and harmony with nature the incredibly graceful 'bambi' deer seem to be wholly unafraid of humans, and so provide amiable and elegant companionship on what must surely be the archetypal 'Walk to the Paradise Garden'.

*

Although southern Japan does not end at Kobe, or even at Okayama, about a hundred miles farther to the south-west, the areas beyond that point contain no lowlands remotely comparable in scale even to Nobi and Kinki, let alone Kanto. Indeed, in this remote south-western corner of Honshu, together with the adjacent islands of Shikoku and Kyushu which complete the perimeter of Seto Naikai, the proportion of flat land falls to its lowest level, amounting barely to five per cent of this entire area. Significantly the only two lowlands of any importance in this south-western extremity are completely occupied by Hiroshima and Nagasaki respectively, though there is also a series of industrial towns strung out along the shores of the Shimonoseki Strait and Dokai Bay. This group of towns, which is centred on the great steel complex of Yawata, has recently become recognized as the conurbation of Kita-Kyushu (Northern Kyushu) which with 1,050,000 inhabitants now ranks as Japan's newest 'million city'. Although Yawata had already suffered intense bombing by conventional means before the atomic bomb was ready for use, its great steel complex has since been rebuilt and considerably extended.

Owing both to its remoteness and extreme ruggedness, this south-western corner of Japan is severely isolated—except by air and, for bulk transport, by sea—from the rest of the country, and most obviously so from Tokyo. Whether Hiroshima and Nagasaki were selected for atomic bombing in the hope that their remoteness might in some degree reduce the amount of justifiably hostile publicity which these outrages would inevitably provoke, I do not know. But if the bombs were dropped in order to terrify the whole Japanese nation into instant capitulation, it would seem that that objective might have been much more effectively—and infinitely less outrageously—achieved by dropping them offshore, with due warning, within visible but not destructive range of Tokyo.

To turn now from the southern to the northern half of Japan, it is necessary first to retrace our steps to Kinki, from which I made the first of my two visits to northern Japan in October 1961. To begin with, my journey to the north involved going by train from Osaka through the mountains, along a route close to that of the Nakasendo as far as Kiso Fukushima, historically a major post station on that road, and in more recent times an important centre of the lumber industry. Perched on the side of a narrow valley, Kiso itself provides the most striking example I have ever seen of a town managing to exist virtually without any flat land at all: it merely clings to a narrow artificial ledge along the bank of the Kiso river which, at least when I saw it after heavy rain, seemed more like a torrent than a river. Behind the houses poised on the edge of the torrent, two or three parallel rows of others rose on narrow man-made terraces at successively higher levels, but above these the steep mountainside was covered with magnificent and obviously carefully tended trees.

It was at Kiso, after having spent the night in company with a Japanese friend, in a rather spartan *ryokan*, that I experienced the well-meaning but somewhat disconcerting considerateness of Japanese hoteliers. For, realizing that I was an Englishman, and therefore presumably addicted to a cooked breakfast, usually referred to as 'hammu eggu', the lady in charge gave me a special dish consisting exclusively of the two most softly fried eggs I have ever been introduced to. Unfortunately the only weapons I possessed in this strange encounter were a pair of chopsticks. Being ravenously hungry, I found these impedimenta particularly frustrating, but in the end I picked up the bowl containing my breakfast *à l'Anglais*, put it to the side of my mouth, tipped it up, and steered the honourable eggs into the abyss with my chopsticks. Whereupon I was immediately congratulated by my companion, who had watched the performance with intense fascination, and was most impressed that, as he put it, I ate 'just like a Japanese peasant'.

From the rather wild and windswept Kiso valley we continued northwards by rail through the heart of the Japanese Alps to Nagano, near the lower end of the beautiful and very fertile Shinano valley, which was particularly renowned for its huge and luscious apples, known as 'twenty-first centuries'—presumably because they were bigger and better than any of their predecessors. In the early 1960s the Shinano valley was still one of the main rice bowls of Japan, and at the time of my visit in 1961 the rice in the fields had fully ripened into a rich golden colour before being suddenly flattened by a violent typhoon. To my inexpert eye it appeared that the whole harvest was ruined. And indeed, if the farmers there had gone over to the new mechanized methods of reaping that were just coming into fashion in Japan, most of the crop would probably have been wasted; but in fact, as I learned a week later, it was nearly all successfully harvested by hand. In such a congested farming area, with holdings so small that an individual family could effectively provide all the labour that it needed, the case for mechanization did not entirely convince me, and in so far as it was practised I suspected that the motive was at least partly a matter of status—based on modernity—as of economics, though I was not able to check this.

Even more interesting, and extremely spectacular, were the vast flights of terraced ricefields, extending upwards for some two thousand feet along the western, and not very steep, side of the valley for several miles, though the slopes on the opposite side were mostly too steep for terracing. In fact these terraces dated from the Tokugawa period, when population pressure was becoming acute, and the local peasants accordingly turned to intensive dry cultivation of upland maize, sweet potatoes, tomatoes and peanuts, all of which had been introduced into Japan from Latin America via the Philippines. However, long before the time I visited this area, rising standards of living had led to the gradual replacement of dry cultivation by wet rice farming on these terraces, which were irrigated simply but effectively by intermittently deflecting small hillside streams to bring water to the fields. More recently, however, I have been told that with still higher standards of living 'it no longer pays' to cultivate in this way, though I remain unconvinced that it was wise to abandon such magnificently cultivated hillside fields which seemed to be yielding heavily.

The second stage of my travels in northern Japan involved my returning direct by train to Tokyo in order to catch the late afternoon flight from Haneda airport to Sapporo, the chief city and administrative centre of Hokkaido. Although I was the only Westerner on the plane, all announcements were repeated in excellent English for my sole benefit, which besides striking me as being exceptionally courteous also allayed any alarm I might otherwise have felt when take-off was considerably delayed to the accompaniment of ominous sounds of tinkering with one of the two engines.

Immediately after take-off we climbed very steeply and then banked suddenly at an angle of nearly ninety degrees, from which, if we felt so inclined, we could look down vertically—and vertiginously—over the centre of Tokyo. This somewhat curious manoeuvre, which rather disturbed some of the passengers, seemed to suggest a hurried attempt to avoid a collision in the exceptionally congested air space over Tokyo, and a few minutes later, after we had flattened out again, the flight became very bumpy and the aircraft seemed to be vibrating rather alarmingly, which was not surprising as there was a typhoon in the vicinity. However, a quarter of an hour later we began descending smoothly and steadily towards the lights of Sapporo, where we arrived a little behind schedule but otherwise in good order.

On awakening next morning in brilliantly crisp autumnal weather, I felt as if I had arrived in another continent, wholly remote from the still hot and humid south of Japan in which I had spent most of the preceding month. And this impression was quickly intensified when, immediately after breakfast, I went out for an exploratory walk around Sapporo, a city of some half a million people, with massive civic and commercial buildings, laid out on a rectangular street plan, strikingly reminiscent of such mid-Western centres as Minneapolis and Winnipeg. But what above all made Hokkaido seem so totally unlike the over-crowded cities and congested countryside of southern Japan was the feeling it conveyed of spaciousness and abundant elbow room, together with extensive agricultural and forest potential, as well as other natural resources which as yet remained largely untapped.

At the time of my visit in 1961 Hokkaido had a population density of some 170 to the square mile, or about a quarter that of Japan as a whole. Yet in 1869, less than a century previously, the total population of Hokkaido was a mere 58,000, nearly all of them Ainu, with a density of less than one-sixtieth that of 1961.

It was, of course, no accident that this spectacularly rapid advance in Hokkaido had occurred during the century immediately following the Meiji Restoration. For, with the collapse of the last lingering resistance of the Shogunal forces under Admiral Enomoto in Hakodate, the way was open for a new forward policy in Hokkaido under the administration of the newly founded Kaitakushi, the Colonial Office. This new policy aimed at the planned colonization of the island, primarily by Japanese soldier settlers, drawn at least partly from the samurai class, to form a militia able to defend Hokkaido against any further threat of Russian invasion.

Since even the supposedly tough samurai hated the Hokkaido climate and began to drift back to Honshu, it was fortunate that the task of colonization had been entrusted to an outstandingly able man, Kuroda Kiyotaka, who had the good sense to seek advice from American agricultural experts, particularly New Englanders and Middle Westerners, whose home areas were broadly similar climatically to those of southern and central Hokkaido. Thus in 1871 Kuroda persuaded the United States Federal Commissioner of Agriculture, General Horace Capron, to serve as adviser in Hokkaido from 1871 to 1875, and shortly before his return home Capron succeeded in getting the government to set up an agricultural college at Sapporo, under the direction of Dr W. S. Clark, in 1876–7.

Notwithstanding a significant difference of outlook between Capron—who was convinced that permanent Japanese settlement in Hokkaido could only be achieved by developing effective means of rice cultivation there—and Kaitakushi—whose overriding concern was military and political rather than economic—this unprecedented period of Japanese-

American co-operation in colonization and land settlement laid the foundation for what has since become a vigorous, flourishing and essentially modern Japanese community and economy in a uniquely attractive area of Japan which a century earlier was almost virgin territory thinly occupied by a handful of Ainu tribespeople.

Yet while it was Kuroda and Capron who laid the material foundations of the new Hokkaido, perhaps the most revolutionary innovation of all was the motto with which Dr Clark inspired his students: 'Boys, Be Ambitious'. For here was the genuine spirit of the frontier pioneer and go-getter, an ethos which was poles asunder from the Confucian-based tradition of knowing and keeping to one's proper and pre-ordained station in an ancient and overcrowded land.

On my first full day in Sapporo I had an appointment at 9.30 a.m. to meet the Governor of Hokkaido, Mr Kingo Machimura, a former Member of the Diet who had also served for a time as Governor of another prefecture. He proved to be a most likeable individual—unusually well-built for a Japanese, and very much a man of the world, though he spoke to me entirely in Japanese which an interpreter translated very fluently. In the course of conversation it emerged that the Governor had been told by Gaimusho that I had been invited to visit Japan because English and other Western textbooks of geography dealing with Japan contained many errors, and Gaimusho was anxious that reliable and accurate information about their country should be disseminated in foreign textbooks.

The conversation then turned to politics, and the Governor went on to say that the boundary question with the U.S.S.R. was 'a big headache' The Russians adopted the twelve-mile limit at sea; but some of the nearby Kurile islands, which had been taken over by the Soviet Union after the war, reached to within three miles of the coast of Hokkaido and many Japanese fishermen were captured while fishing in what they thought to be perfectly safe areas, where in fact they had fished for most of their lives. Since there seemed to be no prospect of these islands reverting to Japan in any foreseeable future, a considerable migration eventually had to be organized, in harsh, rough and bitter weather, to enable these unfortunate Japanese islanders to re-establish themselves in Hokkaido.

Fundamentally this Russo-Japanese dispute is both a matter of strategy—which goes back well into Tsarist times—and of economics, for these offshore northern waters, remarkably like those off Newfoundland, are exceptionally rich fishing grounds. At the time of writing, this dispute remains unresolved, and so far as I know the only good thing to emerge from it has been the production of the finest film I have ever seen. Its title—a translation from the Japanese—was, I think, *The Angry Sea*, and it presented a truly epic account of the maritime exodus, in the towering sub-Arctic wintry seas, of the Japanese Kurile islanders —from babes in arms to aged and infirm men and women—to Hokkaido, where those who survived the terrible journey landed at Abashiri. And here they started, with equal courage and determination to that which I had seen among the people of Tokyo after the war, to rebuild their severely disrupted lives.

Shortly after my return to England late in 1961, the Japanese Embassy showed this film to an invited audience, and Ambassador and Madame Ohno invited me accompany them. After having seen several rather tawdry—and often virtually incomprehensible—Japanese films in prisoner of war camps, I was absolutely astounded by the quality of this one, which convinced me that the Japanese are unequalled in the art—in the fullest sense of that word—of cinematography. Immediately the film was over I expressed my enthusiastic congratulations to my hosts, and added, 'I was in Abashiri last week.' Completely flabbergasted, Madame Ohno said, 'You—an Englishman—are the first person I've ever met who has been to Abashiri!' But, after all, as I pointed out to her, I am a geographer.

*

In many ways this visit to Hokkaido was the high spot of my entire trip to Japan. To begin with, the tinglingly crisp New England-style 'fall' weather was intensely stimulating and invigorating after the heat and humidity of the south. But by far the most attractive feature was the superb autumn colouring, with the flaming scarlets and the almost unbelievable ochres of the maples standing out all the more vividly against the deep rich greens of the ubiquitous pines and the brilliant azure of a totally cloudless sky.

After spending a day or two looking round Sapporo, I was driven north through the main farming area of the Ishikari plain, and—as indeed throughout most of my time in Hokkaido—I felt I was back in North America. By contrast with the minute farm holdings of southern Japan, here in Hokkaido were spacious farmsteads, with fine well-built timber and brick houses, often accompanied by Dutch- and Danish-style farm buildings, and when at dusk we stopped to collect some information brochures at Asahigawa City Hall, the intensity of the central heating nearly took my breath away.

This was an area wholly unlike the rest of Japan, a frontier region of great potentiality, peopled with dynamic, forward-looking and well-educated individuals who, on much larger holdings than those in the south, had risen, through their own determination to master this unfamiliar environment, to a level of living well above the typical peasant standard of central and southern Japan. Moreover, all this potential—in timber, water-power, coal and fish, as well as such temperate agricultural produce as sugar beet, potatoes and salad crops—conveniently filled much of the gap in the Japanese economy caused by the loss of Japan's formerly dependent territories in Korea and Manchuria as a result of the war.

Shortly before leaving Sapporo I had received an unexpected invitation to visit its university—which had grown out of the Agricultural College and was now under the direction of one of Japan's leading chemists, Dr Suginome who, besides being Rector of the University was Chairman of the Hokkaido Planning Board—all of whose members had been assembled especially to brief me on their astonishingly enterprising plans for the future. Above all, Dr Suginome emphasized, Hokkaido must be more effectively linked, via northern Honshu, with Tokyo. The obvious way was by tunnel, which would need to be half as long again as the proposed English Channel Tunnel, partly because it needed to go so much deeper under the Tsugaru Strait, and clearly the tunnel must be wide enough to take the two tracks of the proposed northern extension of the *Shinkansen* railway into Hokkaido.

As I listened with a mixture of admiration and astonishment verging on disbelief, I wondered where on earth, in a formerly impoverished country, still only beginning to recover from a catastrophic military defeat, the money could be found for even a fraction of what was proposed in the new Hokkaido Plan. And in fact progress to date has been much less than Dr Suginome had hoped, though the record of achievement is nevertheless an impressive one.

Before I said goodbye, Dr Suginome asked me to sign his visitor's book, and I must admit that I felt I had moved up several notches in the pecking order when I found myself signing my name only a few lines below the great Dr Arnold Toynbee, who himself—perhaps also stimulated by the invigorating Hokkaido atmosphere—had forecast a similarly exhilarating future for this still only marginally developed but promising island.

Just as I was about to leave Sapporo, a present arrived for me from the Governor, consisting of a bottle of Hokkaido's finest whisky, which I managed to take home with me where I knew it would be of even greater interest to my father-in-law, who regarded himself as a connoisseur in such matters. After some initial deprecatory comments he condescended to sample it, and eventually ended a process of slow escalation by pronouncing it 'not at all bad', though I doubt whether he would have been equally approving of another Hokkaido brand, which advertised itself for the international market as 'Finest quality whisky made from genuine imported Scottish grapes'.

*

For the rest, my Hokkaido trip was spent mainly in travelling through the mountainous interior, which I found strikingly reminiscent of the Canadian Rockies, with its numerous snow-capped summits, interspersed with still and silent ice-blue lakes, all the way to Nemuro in the far north-east, where big yellow caterpillar tractors were clearing the forest for cultivation, near a promontory from which one could look out across the cold grey seas to the southernmost Kurile islands of Etorufu and Kunashiri which had recently passed under Soviet control.

This almost empty area—in which a rather pathetic remnant of indigenous Ainu lived like North American Indians in reservations where they scraped a little extra pocket money by carving trinkets for—and allowing themselves to be photographed by—tourists, nearly all of whom came from other parts of Japan. Except for the industrialized south, where the principal coalmines were located, Hokkaido was genuine frontier country, and at least as much so economically as politically. Nevertheless, and most uncharacteristically, the frontier appeared to be far more prosperous than its hinterland in Honshu. Its mainly wooden and brick dwellings were massively built, well heated, insulated and double-glazed, and the great stone and concrete civic buildings in Sapporo were even more imposing. Yet of all the things which most impressed me there, perhaps the most unexpected was the sophistication and modernity of outlook of so many of the people I met, and I suspect that these were really enterprising types who had had the courage to brave the harsh northern climate, which most southern Japanese detest, in order to able to farm on relatively large holdings in a progressive and comparatively affluent North American style.

What brought this home to me was the behaviour of the people when we stopped first at a coffee bar one day and then at a small roadside restaurant for a snack on the day following. In both cases, the first involving a group of teenagers and the second a number of ordinary workmen, everyone present was sitting in silence watching and listening to television. But it wasn't pop music or Westerns; the first time it was a televised performance of Brahms's austere Fourth Symphony, and the second was a cello recital. Both were obviously appreciated—and this on the edge of the primeval forests of sub-arctic north-eastern Asia.

Certainly it was here in Hokkaido that I first sensed the immense latent potential within the Japanese people to go far beyond what they had yet accomplished, and at the time it seemed to me that this ruggedly beautiful island, with its relatively sparse but intensely vigorous population, might one day provide a new and even more constructive leadership for Japan as a whole. But, at least as yet, this has not happened, and indeed Hokkaido is better known now as a vast tourist region, partly for skiers, skaters and other winter sports enthusiasts, and even more so for large groups of honeymoon couples who, whether simply in accordance with Japanese communal traditions or in order to gain a little moral support from others similarly placed, prefer to honeymoon on package tours rather than *à deux*.

As it happened, the train which took me to Asahigawa (after which everyone transferred to taxis or buses which completed the journey to a hot-spring hotel at Sounkyo in the mountains) was full of such couples and, shortly after we arrived there, so did the complete package of forty shy young couples. My companion thereupon told me that if I wanted to bathe in the indoor hot spring, I should have to do so, like everyone else, Japanese-style, in the communal bath, which did not deter me unduly. 'Everyone else' of course consisted almost entirely of the honeymoon couples, as well as my companion, who promised to collect me at the appropriate time and show me where to go. At the appointed hour there was a loud knock on my door, and there he was, with nothing on at all except his heavy-framed spectacles, which he kept on throughout the entire performance. Some people are never satisfied.

However, it was at Abashiri, even farther north, that I encountered for the first time the supreme mystery of the Japanese art of bathing. Whether this remarkable discovery occurred purely by chance, or whether my hosts had excelled themselves in honouring a foreign visitor, I never found out, but they had certainly booked me in to a palatial *ryokan* during what, though it was only early October, was already bitterly cold weather. As I had been travelling almost continuously for a day and a half, I was greatly relieved to find that the *ryokan* was well heated, and even in my bedroom there was a large charcoal brazier. Thanks to the foresight of the Japanese colleague who had made the arrangements for me, a gargantuan meal was already laid out on a table in my bedroom, comprising a vast steak of grilled salmon, and, side by side with the hollowed-out shell of an even larger crab, was a spectacular cone of crab-meat, arranged like a perfect replica of Mount Fuji. It was at this juncture that the hotelier himself appeared, in order to show me the acknowledged *pièce de résistance* of the *ryokan*, namely what he called 'our husbandu and wifu bath'.

Certainly the bath was of palatial proportions, big enough indeed to have accommodated an entire family, though obviously that would have been a wholly self-defeating act of supererogation. Unfortunately, however, I was travelling alone so, notwithstanding my aesthetic appreciation of languishing in such unaccustomed luxury in so magnificent a receptacle, my satisfaction alas was only vicarious.

However, I found some partial compensation in the prodigious evening meal, which had been prepared specially on my behalf according to the recommendation of the Hokkaido Tourist Office, and beyond any doubt it was the most monumental repast I had ever consumed. Inevitably, before very long the combination of traveller's tiredness, an overheated room, and a surfeit of succulent seafood reduced me, via stupor, to complete somnolence, even though my bed consisted of a narrow wooden platform, only a few inches above floor level, and my pillow—doubtless for aesthetically harmonious reasons—was made of the same unyielding material.

I slept remarkably soundly until some time around three a.m., when I awoke, rather befuddled, to see in the dim light of a solitary flickering candle a daintily kimonoed figure tiptoeing slowly, with intermittent stops and glances in my direction, past my bed. Was this, I began to wonder, what the Japanese refer to as a 'second wifu'? Perhaps—though it seemed rather odd—the Japanese preferred to take their bath in the middle of the night? As I pondered drowsily over these new mysteries of Japanese etiquette, repletion slowly but inexorably overcame receptivity, and I relapsed once more into slumber.

Vaguely, as I dozed off, I recalled two curiously successive sentences in my English-Japanese phrasebook, under the enticing sub-heading 'In Cupid-Land':

> You are the most beautiful girl in the world.
> Please may I have a glass of water?

But by then I had forgotten the Japanese translation; so I had to forgo my glass of water.

Following a week spent in enjoying the delights of a perfect autumn in Hokkaido, I knew that anything else was bound to be somewhat deflating, and so it proved to be. For the heavy industrial area centred on Tomakomai in southern Hokkaido—through which I now had to travel *en route* to Hakodate, the large port near the southern tip of Hokkaido—had an atmosphere of early Industrial Revolution squalor only equalled in my experience by that of the English Black Country between Birmingham and Wolverhampton.

By the time we reached Hakodate, where I was to take the night ferry to Aomori in northern Honshu, my rather morose companion—who seemed not to have recovered from having had to leave Manchuria when it ceased to be a Japanese satellite after the war—was obviously relieved that his task as my guide was now coming to an end. So, after he had shown me where to buy my ticket, we exchanged goodbyes and he departed, while I sat and waited for the ferry. Although I had been told that my first-class ticket was for a private room, it was in fact merely for an upper berth in a large room containing eight pairs of upper and lower units, and anything less private would be difficult to imagine. Everyone—men, women and children, including numerous babies—seemed to be mucking in together and, to judge from what I could see through the curtains of my exalted upper berth, a good time was being had by all. Heaven alone knows what fun it must have been travelling second class!

The crossing to Aomori was smooth and I had ample time in which to catch the train to Akita where, after following the other alighting passengers, I suddenly discovered that I had not reached the station exit as I assumed, but was on the second floor—'Ladies Clothing Department'—of a large department store, from which I was eventually rescued by my old friend 'Emperor' Isida, who was carrying a white paper flag bearing my name in both English and Japanese.

The purpose of our stop at Akita, I now discovered, was to show me round a huge new land-reclamation scheme, the largest in Japan, at Hachiro Gata (Hachiro Lagoon). This was a national project modelled on Dutch practice in turning extensive areas of the Zuyder Zee into polders, and at that time, then still in its early stages, the intention was to devote the newly reclaimed land almost wholly to wet rice cultivation, in order to reduce Japan's heavy dependence on imported rice. Meanwhile the authorities were planning to experiment with different intensities and styles of cultivation in adjacent blocks of reclaimed land, in order to find out which combination was most suited for local conditions. At the time of my visit the planners were talking of five hectares of land for the average farm, though in view of the extreme shortage of flat land in most other parts of Japan this seemed an unduly optimistic figure.

Beyond any doubt, however, this was a most ambitious project. The original water surface of the lagoon covered some fifty thousand acres, and an even larger area drained into it. Clearly its construction must have entailed a very heavy expenditure. Yet long before the reclamation work was completed, the experts had concluded that large-scale wet rice cultivation of this kind would never pay its way in this part of Japan, mainly because of the huge surplus of rice which had already accumulated in Japan as a result of government subsidization and the introduction of more intensive methods of cultivation in other parts of the country. Eventually, therefore, a substantial part of this newly reclaimed land was made available instead for the construction of a new airport to serve the nearby and relatively small Akita City, then with a population of less than 125,000.

On our way to visit Hachiro Gata we had travelled in a large, sleek and very comfortable car, which greatly impressed me, until the driver took a sharp bend too quickly, and the car skidded right off the road into an irrigation ditch where it landed up on its side, and I only just managed to lift my suitcase—containing all my clothes, notes and photographs—above my head before the water, pouring in through the broken window, had reached my knees.

As I continued my journey by train, after mopping up and drying myself out, I began to wonder whether perhaps there was something in common—and even symbolical—about these two incidents. In short, were they not both, in their very different ways, typical expressions of the disconcerting restlessness of the Japanese, expressed in the urge always to move too quickly, without stopping to consider the cost, and to rush forward into the twenty-first century before the twentieth had run its course? And was not this tendency itself a belated legacy of the hasty and ill-considered decision which in 1637 initiated the Tokugawa Seclusion, whose most serious consequence had been to leave Japan more than two hundred years behind in the development of its technology and its knowledge of the outside world?

During my brief farewell stops, first at Osaka and then at Tokyo, I was astonished at the enormous number of parting gifts which were showered upon me from my new-found friends in these two great cities, and indeed I was so weighed down with this addition to my original (maximum permissible) baggage load that I felt sure I should never be allowed to take it all on board the aircraft. However, since the giving of presents is the most ubiquitous—as well as one of the most charming—of Japanese customs, the ground staff at Haneda airport never even mentioned the matter, so that eventually, a few days later, I arrived home in England bowed down and bedecked with an immense assortment of packages, for all the world like a walking Christmas tree.

*

After the exhilarating experience of visiting Japan for the first time, and getting to know its people—no longer as enemies and captors in a land which was as unfamiliar to them as it was to me, but as friendly, warm-hearted folk in their own country which they loved with such intensity—my long flight home by the southern route, with a brief stop-over in Hong Kong, provided at least a breathing space in which to try to sort out some of the innumerable new impressions and ideas which I had acquired during my stay. In fact, however, there was little sorting to be done since one thing stood out to such an extent as to overshadow everything else. For in the course of little more than a month my attitude towards the Japanese had undergone a complete *volte face*: so much so, indeed, that on my return home some of my former prisoner of war acquaintances seemed to regard me as at best a hypocrite, if not indeed something akin to a traitor. Yet, so far from being put off by their attitude, I was now resolved to do all I could—by writing, teaching and public speaking—to try to persuade my fellow-countrymen to discard their outdated and all too often distorted views about Japan and its people. In this connection, therefore, it was one of the happiest achievements of my life to have been able, some two years later, to assist in the process of creating in the University of Sheffield the first British Centre of Japanese Studies.

Nevertheless, South-east Asia remained my primary area of professional concern, so that when in 1964 I accepted an invitation to build up an entirely new Department of Geography at the School of Oriental and African Studies, with exceptional opportunities for field work in my chosen area, I thought it most unlikely that I should revisit Japan in the foreseeable future. In fact, however, it was precisely because of my work in South-east Asia—including the organization, under the auspices of the United Nations E.C.A.F.E.[1] Mekong Committee, of an extended survey of agricultural innovation and changing land-utilization in north-east Thailand—that I was invited a mere five years later to go once again to Japan, which by then was vigorously reactivating its interests in that part of Asia.

So in 1969 I agreed to become, for a third time, a guest of the Japanese, this time under the auspices of Mombusho—the Ministry of Education—in collaboration with the Japan Society for the Promotion

[1] E.C.A.F.E.—Economic Commission for Asia and the Far East—founded in 1947, was one of the four regional Commissions of the United Nations Economic and Social Council. In 1974 E.C.A.F.E. was replaced by E.S.C.A.P., the Economic and Social Council for Asia and the Pacific.

of Science, with the primary task of delivering a course of thirty lectures on South-east Asia at the University of Hiroshima, to an audience with interests in South-east Asia which I was told to expect would number some three hundred people, drawn from all over southern Japan.

PART THREE

A GUEST OF MOMBUSHO AND THE JAPAN SOCIETY FOR THE PROMOTION OF SCIENCE—1969

The moral is that little Boys
Should not be given dangerous Toys.

Hilaire Belloc, *George*

12. HECTICALLY IN HIROSHIMA AND TORTUOUSLY THROUGH TOKYO

So far as I was concerned, the proposed timing of my visit to the University of Hiroshima, in the early spring of 1969, was wholly fortuitous, but once again it chanced to coincide with a major turning point in the post-war history of Japan. For, sandwiched between 1968—the centenary of the Meiji Restoration—and the year of the great Osaka Expo '70, the year 1969 aptly exemplified the new era of unprecedented affluence which another eight years of intense and sustained effort by the Japanese people had now produced.

Yet while much of what I saw during this visit—including some outstandingly fine modern architecture and the superb new 'bullet express' trains of the New Tokaido Line (*Shinkansen*) between Tokyo and Osaka—greatly impressed me, I was also deeply disturbed by the extent to which the surpassingly beautiful scenery bordering Seto Naikai had been ravaged in the process, and at least equally alarmed by the widespread evidence of mounting political instability and extremism. These last phenomena were particularly evident in the universities, many of which were virtually paralysed for a year or more at a stretch. Thus, whereas my first period as a guest, albeit a reluctant one, had certainly been both gruelling and harrowing—though I probably learned more from it than during all the rest of my life hitherto—my second experience of Japanese hospitality was, by contrast, intensely stimulating and wholly delightful. But the third period in 1969 defies any such categorization, and in retrospect I can only say that I felt all the time as though I was watching a kind of surrealist parody of Gilbert and Sullivan's *Mikado* and George Orwell's *1984* rolled into one.

From the outset I sensed that there was something odd about this particular visit. To begin with, the invitation came right out of the blue, by direct telephone call from Hiroshima to my home near London, whence it was re-routed to me at the School of Geography at Oxford, just as I was about to deliver an invited lecture on 'The New Japan'. Moreover, Professor Yamaguchi, who had telephoned me from Hiroshima, wanted me to go almost immediately—within a week if possible—and stay for at least a month. Although such frantic haste seemed unnecessary, and was certainly inconvenient, I finally succumbed to his reiterated and plaintive pleading: 'What is the matter? *Please* come to Japan.' So I went.

After an enjoyable trans-polar flight which, in marked contrast to my previous one, was in daylight nearly all the way, with a superb azure sky over the polar regions, I arrived at Haneda airport, Tokyo, where, in the middle of a milling mass of travellers, I was both surprised and relieved to see Professor Yamaguchi, who had come all the way from Hiroshima to meet me, and had also arranged for me to spend a few days with him in Tokyo before we took the train down to Hiroshima. Yet while this little interlude had obviously provided ample time for conversation, it was not until we had arrived at Hiroshima, and taken a taxi to the University, whose entrance was blocked by a towering pile of desks and other educational paraphernalia, and adorned with innumberable protesting posters, that the awful truth came out at last: 'Very sorry, University on strike. After next week probably open again. So next week please take a holiday and visit other places.'

As it happened, my colleague, John Sargent, one of the best English speakers of Japanese I have ever met, had meanwhile arrived in Japan on study leave, though I didn't know precisely where he was based. However, with the help of various Hiroshima staff members, who quickly put through a complicated series of calls to several parts of the country, we finally tracked him down in Shikoku on the opposite side of Seto Naikai, barely an hour's journey by hydrofoil from Hiroshima.

So, to fill in time until the strike was over, the two of us made an extensive tour of this south-western corner of Japan, in what proved to be quite abnormal weather. The usually tranquil Seto Naikai was so rough that we were nearly seasick by the time we reached Beppu—a place which provides the unusual combination of a major naval port with a hot spring resort—and the 'skyline' bus trip over the central mountains of Kyushu had to be abandoned because of exceptionally heavy snow. Worst of all, however, what should have been the culminating event in our programme—a visit to the spectacular coastline of western Kyushu—was completely ruined by an almost impenetrable haze which was incomprehensibly accompanied by near-gale-force winds, though above it all we could intermittently see the sun shining brightly in a clear blue sky.

On returning to our hotel we learned from the television weather report that this astonishingly dense and persistent haze had been produced by a freak anti-cyclone over north-western China which had generated winds powerful enough to blow enormous quantities of fine loess dust over a thousand miles from the deep interior of China to south-western Japan, where it had instantly been called the 'Motsotu dust' in honour of Chairman Mao Tse-tung.

Since, much to our relief, the weather next day seemed to have regained its composure, we did likewise, and were able to travel by bus to a point from which we could climb, literally to the crater's edge, Mount Aso, the largest and most violent volcano in Japan. There for a time we enjoyed the entertaining company of a really delightful group of Japanese students who, to judge from their demeanour, were not on strike but merely, like ourselves, taking a short holiday.

It was on that occasion that I first became aware of the curious way in which the Japanese, when printing in English or any other Western language, are apt to break up words at any point in order to fit them into the space available. What drew my attention to this was a new advertising gimmick whereby the larger shops in Kumamoto (and doubtless elsewhere) attempted to publicize the modernity and cosmopolitanism of their goods by presenting customers with large white carrier bags, adorned with supposedly English slogans.

One such bag, belonging to the pretty little conductress of our bus, read as follows:

> Your charm and da-
> ndyism is began wit-
> feet. All time, all
> seasons MAEHARAS sho-
> es moody up your dre-
> am ware.

It would be difficult to put it more romantically.

After this agreeable and relaxing interlude I returned by train to Hiroshima on the Sunday evening before I was due to give the first of my lectures on the following morning, and was met at the station by virtually the entire staff of the Geography Department, headed by Professor Yamaguchi in person. With what proved to be excessive optimism, I had assumed that this mass welcome implied that the strike had now blown itself out, and indeed I was reassured in this belief by Professor Yamaguchi's remark that he and his colleagues would call at my room in the University Guest House, where I was now staying, at eight o'clock next morning, to take me to the lecture room.

Since this was to be my first public appearance in Hiroshima, I got up particularly early and, having checked that my notes and slides were in good order, I waited until well past nine, before two of the staff made a belated and effusively apologetic entrance, after which everyone relapsed into silence. Meanwhile, like Brer Rabbit, I lay low, and eventually Professor Yamaguchi decided that it was time to make a move, and led the way from the Guest House across the campus square, to a large block of buildings on the opposite side, in one of which was the lecture hall that I was to speak in.

As we entered the building it appeared at first sight to be totally deserted, and the sound of our footsteps on the bare stairs echoed and re-echoed along the empty corridors as we climbed to the upper floor where we were ushered into Professor Yamaguchi's vast room, whose expansive rows of book shelves were completely devoid of books. Indeed the only sign of human habitation, apart from the Professor himself, was a teapot and a large collection of teacups. Professor Yamaguchi briefly explained that, because of possible trouble from the students, he had taken all his books home, and meanwhile he busied himself by making tea, though thus far there were only three of us present.

However, at this juncture a pleasant-looking young man entered the room, bowed deeply to me, and said, 'I am Mr Takahashi; I am very pleased to meet you; how do you do?' After proffering me a cup of green tea and drinking one himself, he bowed again and disappeared. In the course of the next half-hour about a dozen other young men, of similar age and appearance, made their entrances and their exits, though whether they liked it or not, all played identically similar parts, except for the last one, who varied the procedure by asking me if I had any slides to illustrate my lecture, which it was now time to begin. I replied in the affirmative, handed over my slide box, and he departed with them to the lecture room. But as I was just getting up to go there he returned to say, 'Very sorry; students have removed projector. So please lecture without slides.'

Feeling rather like one of the children of Israel called upon to make bricks without straw, I prepared myself for the ordeal of facing my class of three hundred Japanese, all of them reputedly interested in Southeast Asia, only to discover that my audience consisted of a solitary front row comprising the dozen or so young men I had recently met, together with Professors Yamaguchi and Wada. Beyond that front row lay an empty waste land which stretched all the way to the back of the room.

However, as the loyal fourteen looked up at me, each with a beaming smile of welcome, it seemed clear that face had been saved on both sides, and the lecture could now really begin, after an introductory welcome to me from Professor Yamaguchi. Presumably the other 286 prospective members of the audience had concluded—and rightly so—that the strike was still on, and that it would therefore be better from every point of view for all of them to absent themselves.

Eventually, having been formally introduced, I began my lecture some three hours late, and after about ten minutes I felt that I had established a satisfactory rapport with my small but obviously select audience, and that all would now be plain sailing. But suddenly, only a few minutes later, all hell seemed to break loose. A huge loudspeaker, fixed to the outside wall of the room inside which I was lecturing, began blaring out at full volume a Bach organ fugue, while several thousands of students, packed into the main square of the campus, were all yelling their heads off. Although I continued speaking I couldn't hear a word of what I was saying, while the outer wall of the room was vibrating so violently that I wondered whether an earthquake had hit Hiroshima.

However, the upheaval proved to be essentially vocal and political rather than seismic, though little, if at all, less dangerous on that account. In the middle of the turmoil a furtive note was passed to me by Yamaguchi which read: 'Please try to go immediately to back door of building. We will try to get you out safely. Important Faculty meeting called for this afternoon. We will come to your room in Guest House tomorrow morning, as usual, to take you to your lecture.'

By now, however, the situation was almost completely out of control. While I was trying to find my way to the back door Yamaguchi suddenly caught up with me and asked if I would be willing to store the departmental typewriter, for safety, in my room at the Guest House, as students probably would not go there. At least in the short run he was quite right, but only because they were already snake dancing (this appeared to be a kind of warming-up process before going berserk) around the Guest House where I was soon marooned in almost solitary confinement, apparently cut off from contact with the rest of the University, let alone the great world outside. But before he could get anywhere near the Guest House, Yamaguchi, complete with typewriter, and accompanied by other staff members, was driven back into the building where I had recently tried to lecture, and from whose roof the Red Flag was flying high.

Late that night somebody came to tell me that the faculty members had just been released from their room by the students, and that thereafter the University would be closed, though for how long nobody seemed to know. In the meantime Yamaguchi, drawing no doubt on his wartime experience as one of General Yamashita's Staff Officers, executed a skilful strategic withdrawal to his own house, which thenceforward became, in effect, the strategic headquarters of the Department of Geography. Whether the honourable typewriter ever found its way thither I do not recall. However, it soon transpired that this ingenious tactical diversion had made it possible for me to lecture in Yamaguchi's house-cum-headquarters to an even more select but still smaller body of 'reliable' graduate students. So, once again, dire catastrophe had been narrowly averted, for if I had not been able to give at least a part of one of my thirty lectures, which the Japan Society for the Promotion of Science and Mombusho had jointly sponsored, both Yamaguchi and the University would have lost irreplaceable face, and no doubt I should have been deemed to have done likewise, despite the fact that I had more than enough face—or at least cheek—to survive unscathed.

As I had hitherto spent only half of my scheduled time in and around Hiroshima, where clearly my lecture course had now come to an untimely end, it was agreed that I should visit other universities within accessible range. So I accepted an invitation from the University of Matsuyama City, where Professor Omitsu offered to arrange for me to be taken in a Cessna light aircraft for a flight over some of the small but extremely intensively cultivated islands of Seto Naikai.

Before our flight began I was introduced to the pilot, who was said to be one of Japan's most distinguished surviving wartime flying aces—a real-life hero-god in fact—who seemed to be in nearly every respect except his physiognomy the very embodiment of a typical R.A.F. pilot. Just as we were about to take off, Omitsu said to me, 'Yesterday light aircraft like this crashed at Tokyo. All three people killed.' When I asked whether the crash had occurred on landing or on take-off, he replied: 'No, it fell out of the sky', towards which—*per ardua ad astra*—we now proceeded to climb, though only to an altitude of about a thousand feet as my purpose was to take some detailed photographs of these islands in which, so far as I could see, even the minutest piece of land was utilized.

Of the several universities I visited during this period of filling in time, all except the one at Matsuyama City were having serious student problems. This situation caused intense loss of face to the Matsuyama students, who were certainly doing their best to cause all the trouble they could, so as not to let their side down, though the relative calm here was clearly viewed with intense satisfaction, tinged however with a certain humility, by their teachers who obviously hoped that things would stay that way.

Meanwhile the University of Hiroshima could lay claim to full battle honours for the intensity of its student unrest, although among its eight thousand students only some two hundred were 'Maoist extremists' and between three and four hundred were said to be Communist sympathizers, a total which I found surprisingly small for a city which had relatively recently suffered the terrible fate of Hiroshima.

Nevertheless I took the precaution of rearranging the contents of my two suitcases and my overnight bag in a careful order of priorities based on the respective amounts of time that would be required to get out of the Guest House at short notice if the need arose. Thus with my overnight bag containing money, passport, tickets and other necessary documents, together with immediate toilet requisites, I could in a crisis shin down a drainpipe, nip out of the campus by the now familiar back door, grab a taxi to a hotel beyond the immediate range of the University, and there set up my own private headquarters from which, in due course I could reinfiltrate my lost territory and ultimately recover my two suitcases. After all, while Yamaguchi was on the staff of General Yamashita—the renowned 'Tiger of Malaya'—I had served on the staff of General Percival, the brilliant staff officer who had organized the almost miraculously successful retreat from Dunkirk, which seemed much more relevant to my own immediate needs. Fortunately the necessity for such dire measures did not arise, though in view of the killing of a policeman by students near Hiroshima, while I was there, I continued to lie low and keep my powder dry.

Since by now there was clearly no point in wasting my time in not lecturing at Hiroshima, I decided to go back via Osaka to Tokyo in order at least to have discussions with several friends in both places. Almost without exception all my university friends in whatever part of Japan I visited were understandably far more preoccupied with student problems than with their proper business of teaching and research, and their conversations kept returning obsessively to the unrest which showed no sign whatever of abating.

Nevertheless, when I mentioned to Yamaguchi that I was planning to leave Hiroshima as soon as possible, face reasserted itself and he suggested that before I left he would arrange for me to talk to a small but distinguished private audience in the City Hall, which would at least give me an opportunity to meet some of Hiroshima's leading citizens. I agreed at once to this proposal, and was very pleased to find a much closer similarity of views than I had expected on almost every topic we discussed. Unquestionably the City Fathers had measured up to the tremendous challenge which Hiroshima's recent history had presented, and I came away very much heartened by what I had learned.

To my surprise, however, as soon as the meeting came to an end I was presented with a cheque for a substantial sum as an honorarium for my talk. Since the reason why that talk had been given was because events had made it impossible for me to deliver even a single one of the thirty lectures that the Japanese authorities had so lavishly sponsored, I felt embarrassed at the thought of accepting any further payment and I told the chairman that, in these circumstances, I would prefer not to do so. As immediately became only too obvious, I realized that I had committed a major breach of etiquette: to refuse a gift from the City Hall could only be construed as an inexcusable insult to Hiroshima and its citizens, which of course was the last thing I had intended. So, after sounding out one or two people whom I had already got to know among those present, I asked if it would be acceptable for me to present the cheque instead to the Memorial Hospital for the victims of the atomic bomb raid on their city. Happily, this was eventually deemed acceptable, so I asked one of my friends to accompany me to the Hospital—which was just across the road from the University—and to direct me to the office where I could explain my purpose and make the necessary arrangements.

As it happened, the day I had unwittingly suggested was visiting day for relatives of the patients, and I could find no one in the office, and nobody else who could assist me in what I was trying to do. In desperation I—apparently the only non-Japanese there—walked into ward after ward without discovering anyone who could help, until, after giving up the attempt, I found the office door opening as I was about to pass it on my way out. So, after all, I was able to accomplish my little mission. The cheque was accepted graciously, and with a profound sense of relief I left the Hospital.

Yet, although I still retain in my memory a clear image of the entrance to the Hospital and the office I called at on the way out; and though I remember sharply the effect which the sight of the victims produced upon me at the time, I can recall no visual image whatsoever of the appalling sights which I know I saw. Presumably some inbuilt defence mechanism in my brain automatically blacked it out, and it has never come back. But obviously this defence mechanism is not available to the scores of relatives, whose memories are kept alive by their regular visits to this place of terrible suffering, to bring what comfort they can to those who have not yet died.

Nevertheless it would be wholly wrong for me to end my observations about Hiroshima on this note. Though time can never heal the physical sufferings of the victims, Hiroshima is far from being a city of gloom, let alone of despair. On the contrary, having first been almost totally destroyed, it has since been completely rebuilt, with spacious, tree-lined avenues, bright and shining new buildings, excellent shopping facilities, and a thriving economy based primarily on the automobile industry.

Indeed, a visitor coming to Japan from another planet might well single out Hiroshima as the most lively and cheerful city in the entire country, large enough to be a major regional centre and yet not too large to lose its strong and confident sense of community. Among the younger generation probably the most popular bar and dance hall, which I often visited for an evening snack when I was there in 1969, was called The New Hope. The name was well chosen, and wholly appropriate to the ethos of this indescribably brave and inspiring city.

*

To go from Hiroshima, in the throes of its student troubles to Tokyo on the eve of Okinawa Day, when it was still the unwritten duty of every young Japanese male to display his virility by demonstrating against the Americans for the reversion of Okinawa to Japan (this was to happen on 15 May 1972), was tantamount to jumping from the frying pan into the fire. But since I was unaware of the precise date of this exceptionally red letter day, I managed unintentionally to arrive late at night in Tokyo on the eve of the frolics. So when I went out for a peaceful stroll in the precincts of the Imperial Palace next day, which happened to be a Sunday, I was completely mystified to find gangs of workmen, under police protection, removing all the concrete paving slabs from the sidewalks flanking Tokyo's counterpart to the Mall, until someone explained to me that otherwise the students would be using these slabs—thoughtfully broken into smaller and more manageable portions—as ammunition in tomorrow's annual festivities.

Although, unlike most other foreign visitors, I thus got some brief advance warning of the antics to be expected on the great day, and so was able to take a few belated precautionary measures, I nevertheless got stranded in suburban Tokyo for several hours before I could persuade an unusually tough taxi driver to risk taking me back to the Dai Ichi Hotel where I was staying. As we approached Shimbashi station, on the opposite side of the street from the hotel, I saw phalanxes of students, wearing crash helmets and armed with long iron bars, fighting massed ranks of police on the elevated electric railway track, and on the bridge overlooking the entrance to the hotel, each side apparently trying to topple its opponents over the bridge into the busy and overcrowded street some twenty feet below.

When eventually I tried to get into the hotel I found all the recognized entrances blocked by high piles of sandbags, and I only succeeded eventually in gaining entrance, with the connivance of one of the hotel's catering staff, by climbing up a wooden plank and then sliding down the vegetable chute into the kitchen. As I cast off at the top of the slide I experienced a sudden flashback to Charlie Chaplin's *Modern Times*, and for a horrifying moment wondered whether there might be an automated chopper or slicer lying in wait for me down below. With unprecedented and unrepeatable agility I leapt from the slide as soon as I touched bottom and, after a hasty examination, succeeded in convincing myself that at least all the more indispensable parts of my anatomy had not been removed in the process.

However, several of the older guests in the hotel suffered considerable distress when the air-conditioning apparatus sucked large quantities of tear gas from the 'demo' outside into the hotel lobby, which caused so much discomfort and commotion that the apparatus had to be switched off, after which several people fainted from the excessive heat and stuffiness, though fortunately there were no more serious casualties.

Two days later, after Okinawa Day had run its customary chaotic and bloodstained course, the paving slabs were brought back to Tokyo, and those that were still usable were quietly re-laid as before, to the accompaniment of fulsome congratulations from the Tokyo newspapers for the tact and ingenuity of the police in handling this potentially explosive situation so effectively.

Since by now both my time and my patience were running out, I accepted an invitation to accompany my old friend, Professor Akira Watanabe, on a short tour of Taiwan, which neither he nor I had ever visited before, I am not sure which of us was the more surprised by the extraordinary warmth with which he, as a Japanese, was greeted wherever we travelled in Taiwan, especially when I recalled the far from friendly attitude I had seen many Koreans adopt towards their former colonial masters. In fact, however, the difference was easily explained. Korea, as a natural bridgehead into Manchuria, had from the outset of its period under Japanese rule suffered under the harsh and inflexible control of the Imperial Japanese Army, whereas Taiwan had experienced an altogether more tolerant and flexible style of government at the hands of the Japanese navy. Perhaps also the origin of the difference goes back even farther, for the Japanese army had been trained by Prussian officers, while the navy had been trained by the more easy-going British. Or at least I should like to think that had something to do with the matter, though the fact remains that soldiers the world over are apt to be more inflexibly minded than sailors, whose horizon is much wider and whose outlook accordingly tends to be more tolerant.

Thus my third period as a guest of the Japanese came to an end, but so far from having clarified the various ideas and impressions about the Japanese which I had formed and accumulated over many years, I now felt, if anything, more confused than ever. What on earth was one to make of such extraordinary people?

13. THE COST OF AFFLUENCE

'Take what you will,' says God; 'take it, and pay for it.'
Spanish proverb

The severe student unrest which I witnessed, notably in Tokyo and Hiroshima, reached its peak, there and in many other university cities in Japan, in 1969, some twenty-four years after that country's cataclysmic defeat in August 1945. During the preceding three and a half years of war Japan had lost more than two million lives, together with a quarter of a million square miles of territory—representing nearly half of its pre-war empire—and an even higher proportion of its dwellings, natural resources, industrial plants and other installations.

Yet, during the years between 1945 and 1969—less than a quarter of a century—Japan had made an almost unprecedentedly rapid economic advance which, in the extent of the transformation it has wrought in the lives of the Japanese people, may not unreasonably be compared with what Erwin Baelz called the *salto mortale* (which, *pace* the late Chairman Mao, may be freely translated as 'the great leap forward') from mediaeval Tokugawa to modern Meiji times.

To the ordinary Japanese man in the Ginza, immediately after the unconditional surrender which the nation had finally been driven to accept in August 1945, the outlook must have seemed almost unrelievedly bleak. For, besides the appalling human and material losses which they had sustained, the Japanese—whose Shinto traditions had taught them that not only their emperor but, though in a lesser degree, the entire Japanese nation were of divine origin—now for the first time in their history found themselves confronted with the stark reality of total defeat at the hands of ordinary mortals whom they had hitherto regarded as innately inferior to themselves.

Nor did the initial post-surrender policy of the Allied Occupation, which began in September 1945, seem to offer much encouragement, except for the rural population who benefited greatly from the Occupation's extremely well conceived Land Reform. For, by enabling a high proportion of the impoverished tenant farmers to acquire proper title to their holdings, the Land Reform brought distinctly better living standards to the countryside, which in pre-war days had been the principal source of extremist recruits to the army. For the rest, however, the thinking of the preponderantly American Allies, under the supreme command of General Douglas MacArthur, was dominated by the assumption that China, the member of the Allied partnership which had suffered by far the most severely at Japanese hands, must receive preferential treatment in rebuilding its shattered economy so that it might be speedily re-established as the leading power and geopolitical stabilizer of East Asia.

Clearly in these circumstances Japan would at best have to take second place, and although the Allies stated that adequate means of subsistence would be found for its people, they also made it clear that the military capacity of Japan to disturb the peace must be destroyed for ever. Indeed, as a foretaste of this, the Cairo Declaration of 1943 had already stipulated that the fruits of past Japanese aggression, not merely since 1941 but going back all the way to the Sino-Japanese War of 1894–5, must be restored to their rightful owners. And, presumably in order to make doubly certain, the Far Eastern Commission proposed to dismantle the greater part of Japanese heavy industry, much of which was to be used as reparations; and even the lighter industries were subjected to close Allied control. In the words of General MacArthur, Japan was advised to become 'the Switzerland of Asia', relying on the rule of international law for its security and concentrating on the production of militarily innocuous consumer goods in order to pay for such imports as it needed.

Meanwhile, however, the Occupation had in 1946 provided Japan with a new Constitution which, in sharp contrast to its inflexible Prussian-style predecessor of 1889, reflected something of both the democratic-monarchical traditions of Britain and the characteristic American emphasis on individual rights and freedom. Moreover, in stressing that the emperor was henceforward to be merely 'the symbol of the State and of the unity of the people', and that his position was derived 'from the will of the people', the new Constitution formally recognized the revolutionary change which defeat had already produced. For, in effect, the Emperor's readiness to divest himself of his supposed divinity effectively symbolized the termination of the traditional Shinto concept of the State.

Even more surprisingly, however, the new Constitution, besides seeking to promote the growth of individuality and democracy, also *inter alia* purported to turn Japan into a virtually pacifist state. Thus, under Article 9, the Japanese people formally and 'forever renounce[d] war as a sovereign right of the nation and the threat or use of force as a means of settling disputes'. Moreover, presumably as a precaution against any future backsliding, it was stated that 'land, sea and air forces will never be maintained', and the new regime's seriousness of purpose was further emphasized by the dismissal of many reactionary public officials and the execution of seven of the leading war criminals, including General Tojo who had formerly held the posts of Premier, Home Minister and Minister of War.

However, to coin a phrase, never is a short time in politics, and indeed within two years of the formulation of the initial post-surrender policy, the basic assumption on which it rested had already lost its validity. Thus, as the chaos in China deepened, and relations between the Soviet Union and the United States continued to deteriorate, the latter began drastically to rethink its entire East Asian policy. For already in 1947 the 'containment' doctrine was becoming fashionable, and General Marshall appeared to have concluded that little could now be done to prevent the political disintegration of China. On this assumption the best hope for containing Communism seemed to lie in building up Japan, with American economic aid and also, whenever appropriate, by providing it with naval and air support so that, as the geopolitical centre-piece of the offshore island chain stretching from the Kuriles and Saghalien to the Malaysian-Indonesian archipelago, Japan could replace China in the role of stabilizer of the Orient.

Nevertheless, if such a policy was to have any hope of success, it would be essential to provide the impoverished and dispirited Japanese as quickly as possible with the necessary means of earning an adequate livelihood. Moreover the problem was intensified by the fact that between 1945 and 1948 a mere three and a half years of the post-war 'baby boom' had raised the Japanese population total from seventy-two million to over eighty million, which was only ten million short of the supposed explosive point of ninety million, which had been forecast for 1957.

It was in these circumstances that in March 1948, following the mission of General Draper to Japan, the United States declared its intention to rebuild this shattered country as 'the workshop of the Far East', with an authorized steel output by 1952 of some 140 per cent of the 1930–34 level, along with a proportionate expansion in other major industries.

However, in view of the recent experiences of Japan's Pacific neighbours, it was scarcely surprising that several of these, notably

Australia, New Zealand and the Philippines, became seriously alarmed lest this new American policy might foreshadow another round of Japanese rearmament. Indeed, owing to the tense atmosphere which ensued, it was not until the United States had agreed to provide supplementary guarantees of support to these three Pacific states, that the Peace Treaty with Japan was finally signed at San Francisco on 8 September 1951 by forty-nine states which, however, did not include the Soviet Union.

Moreover, in order to allay the fears of the newly disarmed Japan, the United States had also to provide for its defence by means of a bilateral United States–Japanese security pact, agreed on 5 September 1951, whereby United States forces were to be stationed in the vicinity of Japan 'for the time being'. Two years later, in November 1953, this tense and protracted interlude finally came to an end as the United States, simultaneously seeking to complete its containment of the Soviet bloc while reducing its own heavy defence commitments, called upon Japan to rearm, and formally admitted that the decision to include Article 9—that Japan was to renounce war—in the Constitution had been a mistake.

Undoubtedly this extraordinary *volte face* in the Occupation's policy towards Japan marked a major turning point on the latter's road to recovery and rehabilitation. Nevertheless, although the Occupation authorities had done their best to fulfil their undertaking to provide Japan with adequate means of subsistence, the great majority of the Japanese population suffered severe food shortages and, as so often seems to happen in such critical circumstances, the crucial year—1945—yielded an exceptionally poor rice harvest and it was widely feared that up to ten million people might starve to death. Thanks largely to some 400,000 tons of rice being made available by the British and Commonwealth forces, the worst did not happen, but even so something akin to complete economic breakdown threatened in 1947. But in 1948 the situation began to improve, and by late 1951 industrial production had climbed back to the level of the mid-1930s, though general living conditions remained dispiritingly low.

Meanwhile, to the majority of the population the experience of defeat had been profoundly traumatic. For besides the unnumbered thousands of individuals who had suffered heartbreaking personal losses, the people as a whole had witnessed the collapse of the entire Shinto tradition which had hitherto provided the central core of the beliefs in which they had been brought up since childhood. Thus, among so volatile a people as the Japanese, it did not seem unreasonable to suppose that there was danger of a complete collapse of morale.

However, even if Shinto had failed, the age-old Confucian virtues of discipline, hard work, frugality, family loyalty and wider group solidarity held firm, and in common with innumerable other people, of diverse creeds and backgrounds, the Japanese had had ample opportunity to learn from bitter experience that sustained hard work directed towards a positive and rewarding goal is the most effective of all anodynes.

In the event, by what seemed to be a remarkably fortunate coincidence, what the Japanese people most urgently needed to do in order to regain their own material well-being and self esteem was to partake in the kind of programme which the Occupation's new industrial policy, following the Draper mission, had decided to implement. In effect, this policy involved a long overdue clearing away of the chaotic jumble of mostly small and by now antiquated and/or devastated factories which had sprung up since early Meiji times, and now needed to be rehabilitated or, more commonly, replaced by modern factories with up-to-date equipment.

Thus the way was prepared for what was to become known as 'the Japanese miracle' which in the space of less than thirty years had, through the intense and sustained effort of the literate and technologically skilled Japanese population, transformed this down-at-heel and broken-backed country of 1945 into one of the three or four topmost industrial powers in the world. It was in this context that the aged but ever optimistic and still curiously Anglophile former Prime Minister, Shigeru Yoshida, commented approvingly that 'God helps those who help themselves'. Whether it really was such divine intervention which provided Japan with a further economic boost in the form of the handsome profits it made from supplying 'special procurements' to the embattled United Nations forces in Korea, following the outbreak of war there in 1950, is perhaps another matter which may, however, have reminded Mr Yoshida of the very English hymn which begins:

> God moves in a mysterious way his wonders to perform;
> He plants his footsteps in the sea, and rides upon the storm.

More seriously, of course, many other factors played significant parts in the economic and psychological resurgence of Japan for, once the process of recovery had been set in motion, many new initiatives added to its momentum. Thus, in particular, each of a succession of Japanese Prime Ministers during the 1950s and 60s strove during his term of office to achieve a specific objective of major relevance to the nation's recovery and further advance, and although, so far as I know, there is no evidence to suggest that these various goals were thought of as constituent parts of an overall strategy, they did in fact follow one another in a remarkably logical fashion.

To begin with, Prime Minister Kishi concentrated on the fundamental problem of guaranteeing the long-term security of Japan by replacing the provisional security pact of 1951 with a formal Japan–United States Security Treaty in 1960. In turn such a policy, by enabling a still convalescent Japanese economy to keep its spending on armaments to a minimum, indirectly made a substantial contribution towards the achievement of the chosen objective of Prime Minister Ikeda's period of office between 1960 and 1964, namely the Income Doubling Plan which, for obvious reasons, enjoyed exceptionally wide popularity. Thirdly, since Japan had thus made good progress in providing for both its strategic and economic security, it now seemed wholly appropriate for Prime Minister Sato to focus his energies on removing the greatest remaining obstacle to the restoration of the nation's *amour propre* by pressing hard and long—as he did after 1964—for the reversion of Okinawa to Japanese sovereignty, an objective which was finally realized, to the accompaniment of nationwide rejoicing, in 1972. Thus, during the terms of office of Premiers Kishi, Ikeda and Sato, extending over a period of fifteen years from 1957 to 1972, the long-disappointed dreams of prosperity turned, slowly at first, but later with growing momentum, into tangible reality.

In the course of this period I was able to make extended visits to Japan both in 1961 and 1969, and during the intervening time the appearance and character of the country changed with astonishing rapidity. In 1961 only a relatively small percentage of Tokyo looked like a Western city, not least because it was still the normal practice—as it was in India—to use rickety bamboo poles as scaffolding for the unprepossessing and still mostly small box-like concrete buildings which seemed to be mushrooming chaotically all over the city. Yet in the late 1960s, amid the vast gaping holes which were being excavated and prepared as sites for new twenty- or thirty-storey office blocks, I was repeatedly at a loss to know where I was even within the downtown areas of Tokyo which I had known like the back of my hand a few years previously.

Nevertheless, as—at a phenomenal rate—more and more of these tall new buildings were completed, I was bound to admit that the overall impression was far more pleasing than I had expected it to be, and—even more significantly—the great majority of the people one saw in the street were not only much better dressed, but also appeared to be far healthier and much less strained than those I had been accustomed to see in 1961. Moreover, occasional spells of window shopping repeatedly revealed an extraordinary improvement in both the variety and the quality of the goods on display, most of which seemed to be at least comparable in quality to those on view in the corresponding shopping areas of London.

Still more surprising, whenever I was invited to visit Japanese friends, was my discovery of the astonishing array of consumer durables—including washing machines, radio and television sets, pianos, electronic organs and other musical instruments, slide projectors, and of course cameras—ciné and still—together with their multifarious accessories, as well as every other conceivable and inconceivable form of gadgetry. Perhaps most unexpected of all, however, was the excellent quality of the food, largely Western-style, including canned meats and fruit, homogenized milk—somewhat disconcertingly branded HOMO—sliced bread, and indeed virtually everything that one finds in an average middle-class British kitchen.

Only in one respect did the Japanese homes which I visited appear distinctly inferior to those I was accustomed to in Britain. But, to me at least, that respect—namely space—was all important. For besides the limits which shortage of space imposed on individual privacy indoors, it also virtually ruled out the possibility of possessing even the smallest of gardens, let alone a garage, except at considerable distance from home and even then the cost might well prove prohibitive

Obviously, however, the shortage of space at the individual level is a trivial matter when compared with the intensity of the pressure which already exists on the extremely limited extent of usable flat land at the national level. And unfortunately, by what seems to be a cruel irony the long overdue achievement of a steadily rising material standard of living for an increasingly high proportion of Japan's 115 million people inevitably imposes steadily growing pressures on the severely limited extent of the nation's land. For in fact what the Japanese, in common with most Europeans, have come to see as the model of a truly affluent life-style is the American image of a two- or multi-car family, living in spacious ranch-style housing, and indulging in innumerable kinds of outdoor activities, with related tennis courts, swimming baths and the like. And while all of this may be appropriate enough in a vast and still uncrowded half-continent, it is literally unattainable, except for a minute minority, in the incomparably smaller and infinitely more congested islands of Japan.

In these circumstances the decision in 1972 of a fourth Prime Minister, Kakuei Tanaka, to put forward a plan for remodelling the Japanese archipelago was certainly an extremely challenging one, though the idea had in part been anticipated, most curiously, by one suggestion for filling in the whole of Tokyo Bay with garbage which it was hoped would solidify under pressure and so provide a foundation upon which new factories could be erected. More significantly, however, the idea of remodelling the Japanese islands has been influenced by changing attitudes concerning territory, some indication of which may be inferred from views expressed by former Prime Minister Yoshida shortly before his death.

Essentially Yoshida argued that the generally accepted pre-war view —the view that a country with a large and expanding population needed a correspondingly large territory possessing substantial natural resources—was out of date and that, so far from being a liability, the smallness and narrowness of the Japanese islands constituted 'a blessing in disguise'. For indeed, not only has this 'thin, belt-like shape' meant that no part of Japan is more than fifty miles' straight-line distance from the coast, but even more significantly all the country's major industrial and port cities are situated within the coastal zone. Moreover, since the Japanese economy was already based primarily on using the nation's massive resources of high-quality labour to produce manufactured goods of all kinds for export overseas, immense economies could be achieved by almost completely eliminating the transport of bulky goods overland and relying overwhelmingly on seaborne transport to carry such goods between the major cities of Japan itself, as well as between Japan and its trading partners overseas.

Meanwhile the needs of the ordinary inter-city and commuter travellers have long been adequately provided for by the original trunk railway between Tokyo and Osaka, together with its feeder lines and other ramifications, while the spectacular *Shinkansen* line now provides high-speed passenger transport between Tokyo and Osaka, and beyond that to Okayama, and is also paralleled by a new express motorway which is already being extended beyond Osaka. However, Yoshida omitted to mention the other and much less pleasant side of the coin. For in concentrating on and subsequently expanding over such meagre coastal plains—mostly bay-head deltas—as Japan possesses, the major cities have by now swallowd up the greater part of these lowlands.

Thus the stage had now been reached at which over eighty per cent of the value of Japanese industrial production and a substantial majority of the Japanese population are concentrated within a narrow coastal zone, extending from the Kanto plain to northern Kyushu. This zone, which is known to Japanese geographers as the Pacific belt, contains the three major bay-head industrial regions of Keihin, Hanshin and Chukyo, centred respectively in Tokyo, Osaka and Nagoya, which together account for sixty per cent of the total value of the Japanese industrial output, and forty-seven per cent of the country's population. Or, to quote the even more striking estimate of former Prime Minister Tanaka, nearly one-third of the Japanese population is concentrated on one per cent of the land. Here, in fifteen words is epitomized the transcendental problem with which Japan is now faced.

This appallingly complicated problem, compounded as it is by the steadily mounting concentration of industry in the Pacific belt, has several facets, of which the most widely publicized, both in Japan and overseas, is environmental pollution which has already led to the emergence of certain hitherto unknown and extremely serious diseases. The first of these to be identified, in the 1950s, was Minamata disease, which produced paralysis and mental derangement, and was proved to have been caused by the contamination of fish by organic mercury discharged by an industrial effluent from a local factory in the vicinity of Minamata Bay in western Kyushu; and a similar but smaller outbreak of the same disease, likewise caused by organic mercury discharge, followed near the Agano estuary in Niigata Prefecture. Meanwhile another similarly dangerous illness, known as Itai-itai disease, caused by the discharge of cadmium from a mine in Toyama Prefecture, made its appearance in the 1960s. A somewhat less frightening but nevertheless extremely unpleasant complaint was the peculiarly severe form of asthma, known locally as *Yokkaichi Zensoku*, produced by inhaling sulphur dioxide in the heavily polluted atmosphere in the vicinity of the oil refining and petro-chemical manufacturing city of Yokkaichi.

In all of these four instances substantial damages were awarded to the victims, amounting respectively to 900 million yen, 270 million yen, 1,360 million yen and 200 million yen (approximately £2¼ million, £¾ million, nearly £3½ million and £½ million). Meanwhile the inhabitants of the larger conurbations frequently suffer the discomfort of photo-chemical smog resulting from exhaust fumes, particularly in summer, though the government's recently introduced controls on exhaust fumes have done much to counteract this problem. Clearly, although the victims of smog and similarly unpleasant conditions in the more congested cities normally obtain no financial compensation for these and other discomforts from which they suffer, the very large total of 2,330 million yen, which was awarded to victims of the serious pollution diseases already mentioned, is proof enough that a very heavy price—not only in cash, but even more so in human suffering—has had to be set against the saving in transport costs resulting from the 'disguised blessing' which Mr Yoshida claimed to see in the singularly svelte configuration of his homeland.

From such romantic and aesthetic considerations it seems appropriate to turn to the controversial problem of how so intensely congested a country as Japan can best attempt to preserve at least something of what remains of its scenery, much of which has long been recognized as being among the most beautiful in the world. Here there can be no gainsaying the acute dilemma which is posed by the fact that Seto Naikai—which Herbert Ponting described as 'the fairest stretch of water in the world'—has already suffered devastating despoliation, for the obvious reason that so vast and well sheltered an almost completely landlocked sea is, in purely utilitarian terms, a monumental natural harbour. Thus already several vast rectangular slabs of newly reclaimed and uniformly flat land—in some cases three or more kilometres long—have been created as sites for immense automobile factories, along this formerly exquisite coastline.

Moreover, an even vaster scheme of a somewhat similar sort—though fortunately not in an area of similar beauty—is envisaged for the construction of a mammoth floating international airport out at sea off Osaka City: 'Taking the shape of three massive interconnected aircraft carriers, with a deck area of more than half the size of Heathrow airport, the project could be completed in four years at a cost of £3,000 million, Japan's Association of Shipbuilders claims.' The plan, which has been submitted to the Transport Ministry at the Government's request, has two main objectives; to appease protesting environmentalists at Osaka's existing airport, and to help the shipbuilding industry through a recession. Officers of the Transport Ministry are said to think it possible that the Government may sanction the plan because of the violent demonstrations and protest movements that delayed the opening of Tokyo's new international airport at Narita for five years, at a daily cost of £60,000. (The protesting—which still continues sporadically although the airport has been officially opened—is mainly against the use of scarce farmland, although compensation has been paid.)

Although, so far as can be deduced from a short report, this project seems to pose no serious threat of further scenic despoliation and in fact appears greatly to reduce noise pollution in the Hanshin region, the strong emotional reactions to which it has given rise clearly illustrate the enormity of the problem with which Japan is faced by sharply conflicting interests in such an intensely congested country. Fortunately, however, growing public concern in recent years has done much to prevent the despoliation of the Japanese countryside and many areas of outstanding natural beauty have been designated as national parks. Here the main problem which remains is the frequently intense pressure of visitors during the tourist season, and indeed during 1973 the total number of individual visits to national and similar parks reached the remarkable total of 617 million.

Admittedly, when one is confronted by such comments as that of the *Japan Times* of 27 May 1968, to the effect that the new urban policy 'is also aimed at revamping the Japanese island chain to become a highly efficient, balanced, and extensive urban sphere', one may well wonder what has become of the intense and deeply ingrained Japanese sensitivity to the unique natural beauty of their homeland, though against the background of the nineteenth-century desecration of so much of Britain's own finest scenery it ill behoves a British visitor to criticize the Japanese, whose problems in this respect are far greater than ours.

Fundamentally it is a case of 'needs must when the devil drives', but even so the Japanese have by no means lost their traditional love of natural beauty. On the contrary, indeed, they have shown a sturdy initiative in their attempts to preserve their much loved countryside, and I recall with particular delight the occasion when on a lovely spring morning (10 April 1969) I read in my *Japan Times* that, following growing evidence of widespread local concern, the Utsonomiya District Court had ruled that 'preserving a stand of 350- to 400- year-old cedars is more important than widening a road to smooth traffic in Nikko'.

Moreover the new Environment Agency established by the Japanese Government has repeatedly intervened to prevent schemes which have threatened areas of outstanding scenery, most notably by preventing the building of a proposed new road through the southern Japanese Alps because it threatened the survival of a 500-year-old forest, and under the Nature Conservancy Law of 1972 all schemes for constructing new industrial areas must include assessment of the implications of factory development for the natural landscape.

Nevertheless, in their obsessive desire to keep ahead in the industrial race, the Japanese authorities have again expressed concern at the possibility that the population may begin to decline after the year 2005, by which time the total is expected to have reached some 122 million, or over twenty million more than in 1974. And since the drift from agriculture and the countryside continues unabated, the Tokaido zone, which in 1970 contained thirty million people is now expected to become a 'giant corridor of growth' which will contain between eighty and ninety million people by the end of the present century.

Meanwhile, as Mr Tanaka's plan for the remodelling of the Japanese archipelago has been in abeyance since his resignation from the Premiership in 1974, the crucial problem of explosive urban growth becomes ever more intractable. Already in a public opinion survey of 1969, 'only 31 per cent of those interviewed thought that Japan would be a nicer place to live in in another 20 years' time' (cited by Hide Ishiguro in 'Will success spoil the new Japan?', the *Observer* colour supplement, 16 February 1969), and it is difficult to believe that a similar survey today would express any greater optimism on this score.

Such considerations as these inevitably raise what is probably the most disturbing aspect of all, namely the psychological problems exemplified by both the 'economic animals' of the older generation and their often disenchanted and in many cases alienated offspring. So far as the former are concerned the explanation is not difficult to find. Having been suddenly deprived, by a uniquely devastating war, of much—if not all—of what they had hitherto valued or at least taken for granted, members of this generation faced the grim choice of either giving up in despair at what seemed an impossible struggle, or else of making an almost superhuman effort to rehabilitate themselves economically. Very much to their credit, it would seem that the majority chose the latter alternative, and seized every opportunity they could to 'work their passage' back to what they regarded as at least a tolerable standard of living.

Not surprisingly, however, amid the appallingly dreary wastelands of ruined cities which, even before their destruction, had rarely been places of beauty, many such people became obsessively concerned with their own material advancement. As such, moreover, these 'economic animals' were all too readily despised by their children, for whom what should have been the springtime of life seemed far more like the longest and bitterest winter of discontent and, in the prevailing absence of any positively inspiring system of beliefs, many undoubtedly became almost completely deracinated.

Nevertheless the 'Japanese miracle' provided irrefutable proof of the intensely disciplined hard work of innumerable members of two overlapping generations of Japanese, whose achievements truly merit Christopher Wren's epitaph: *Si monumentum requiris, circumspice.* Unquestionably this magnificent performance owed much to traditional Japanese group solidarity, and above all to the corporate sense of loyalty to the firm to which one belonged, the classical expression of which is the much quoted daily song of Matsushita Electric:

> Let's put our strength and mind together,
> Doing our best to promote production,
> Sending our goods to the people of the world,
> Endlessly and continuously,
> Like water gushing from a fountain.
> Grow, industry, grow, grow, grow!
> Harmony and sincerity!
> Matsushita Electric!

Unfortunately, however, while the Japanese excel in such group performance, especially when it is felt to be directed towards the achievement of a national goal, they are liable to lose confidence when left to their own initiative. This tendency is understandably more pronounced among the student generation, partly because of their immaturity and lack of worldly experience, but even more so because of the excessive pressures to which the intensely competitive educational system subjects them.

Admittedly, the major reforms instituted under the Occupation included a thorough overhaul of the traditional educational system, involving a complete reorganization of the school curriculum along American lines and a drastic revision of predominantly tendentious textbooks, particularly those relating to history, politics and ethics. However, while the academic content of Japanese education was substantially improved by these reforms, they were far from satisfactory in other respects. Thus the sudden American-style proliferation of new 'universities', by the simple device of nominally upgrading numerous teacher-training and technical colleges, did not conduce to the maintenance—let alone the improvement—of academic standards in the country as a whole. Thus although the policy undeniably provided many more low-level university places, and accordingly made it fashionable for almost every aspiring teenage student to seek at all costs to obtain such a place somewhere, its net effect has been to intensify Japan's notorious and indeed pernicious educational rat-race.

So far as the teenage generation of students is concerned, the goal of the most ambitious is to obtain entrance either to Tokyo University, or to one of a handful of other big-city universities, whose fees are relatively low, thanks to government or municipal subsidy, or else—if their parents can afford it—to gain admittance to one of the several private universities, most of them in Tokyo. Nevertheless, so great is the demand for higher education that only a small minority even of those who have been assiduously prepared at school for entry into one of the better universities—whether private or public—can seriously expect to obtain the kind of post to which they aspire. Theoretically the selection process works on the principle of the survival of the fittest, but the questions 'fittest for what?' is apt to remain unasked and therefore unanswered, and meanwhile many keen and potentially able students burn themselves out in the thankless struggle to succeed in a country which, at least until very recently, has been short of virtually everything except people.

Moreover the situation is far more disturbing than the foregoing remarks may seem to imply. For the term 'student generation' includes children as well as adolescents, as was tragically emphasized by the death in October 1977 of a ten-year-old schoolgirl, who jumped from her bedroom window on the fourteenth floor of a Tokyo block of flats, where the police later found a pathetically tell-tale pile of unfinished homework.

As reported by Peter Hazelhurst in *The Times* of 2 November 1977, this young schoolgirl was 'a victim of the pressure of Japan's highly competitive and draconian educational system which is expected to push child and teenage suicides to a record level of about 800 this year, according to the projections of a report by the national police.' Moreover, Hazelhurst's grim report goes on to cite the view of some Japanese sociologists that many nine- and ten-year olds are forced to study fourteen hours a day and are developing such adult diseases as ulcers and hypertension. Nor is this surprising in the light of a report that some 'children on the outskirts of Tokyo start the day at 4.30 in the morning to attend special private lessons. At 8 a.m. they join formal school classes. Later in the afternoon they travel across the city to study at private *jukus* (cramming schools) and after a two-hour journey home they complete their homework by 11 p.m.'

Clearly Japanese public opinion is now becoming increasingly alarmed by the intolerable pressures to which many presumably over-ambitious parents are misguidedly subjecting their children, as may be inferred from Hazelhurst's quotation from a recent issue (October 1977) of the daily newspaper *Yomiuri Shimbun*: 'Japan's fiercely competitive school system is generally regarded as the primary culprit in causing young people to throw away their lives. In Japan the road to worldly success is tied directly to passing examinations in prestigious schools and universities. Most students are therefore forced by their parents to attend schools after hours.'

In view of the well-known Japanese fondness for children, such pressure on the part of parents is all the more difficult for Westerners to understand, though it is certainly consistent with the tendency already noted among the Japanese to go to extremes in their pursuit of whatever objective monopolizes their attention. At the present time the over-riding objective is to overtake the West to become the pacemakers of the twenty-first-century world. But now that the great majority of Japanese no longer live in poverty, or even in straitened circumstances, is it really necessary for them to subject young children to such excessive working hours (if not to similarly squalid working conditions) as those to which Freda Utley drew attention forty years ago?

Unquestionably affluence, like everything else, has—in one way or another—to be paid for. But surely the least sensible way of paying for it is by driving one's children to suicide.

14. MORE SINNED AGAINST THAN SINNING?

He that is without sin among you, let him cast the first stone.

John: 8:7

Today, nearly a third of a century after the ending of the Pacific War, the sense of revulsion produced in the West by the accounts of Japanese atrocities, particularly in their P.O.W. camps in East and South-east Asia, has largely—though by no means entirely—abated, and a new and chastened Japan is widely and rightly accepted as a member of the world community (though, along with Germany, not yet of the United Nations). Nevertheless the popular images, both of wartime and pre-war Japan, continue to cause uncertainty and resentment in many people who fear that, notwithstanding its virtual demilitarization, Japan remains a peculiarly unpredictable and potentially dangerous nation, which has already aggressed against its neighbours no less than five times during the past eighty-three years. In these circumstances the question inevitably arises: is Japan an incorrigibly expansionist nation, or has it finally settled down to an enduring policy of friendly relations with its neighbours?

Certainly, against the background of its own unique experience as a victim of nuclear warfare, there is good reason to believe that Japan's military and territorial ambitions are a thing of the past. Nevertheless, it is equally obvious that Japan intends to play a far more significant role in the world of the twenty-first century than it has done heretofore. In short, it remains a dynamic and thrusting nation, and as such may not be the easiest of neighbours to live with, even within the expansive spaces of the vast Pacific basin, with its enormous commercial and industrial opportunities. Above all, it is this apparently innate restlessness and instability of the Japanese that has caused so much trouble in the past, and not least so because they themselves have often seemed wholly oblivious to the reactions which they produce in others.

However, this is not the whole of the story, and against Japan's recent record of repeated aggression, during the late nineteenth and the first half of the twentieth century, must be set the fact that before 1894 there was a gap of over three hundred years in the history of Japanese aggression, between the Sino-Japanese War of 1894–5 and the unsuccessful attempt by Hideyoshi to conquer China, likewise via the Korean peninsula, in 1592.

During these three extraordinary centuries in which Japan had remained almost completely isolated from the outside world, reliable information about the condition and evolution of the Japanese polity and society was extremely sparse. Nevertheless some fascinating glimpses may be obtained from Hugh Murray's remarkably penetrating appraisal contained in his *An Encyclopaedia of Geography*, published in 1834, twenty years before the signing of the Treaty of Kanagawa which, in response to the initiatives of the American Commodore Perry and the Russian Admiral Putyatin, finally prised the door of Japan at least partially open again. The following brief extract may be allowed to speak for itself:

> The national character is strikingly marked, and strongly contrasted with that which generally prevails throughout Asia. The Japanese differ most especially from the Chinese, their nearest neighbours, notwithstanding the resemblance in form and lineaments. Instead of that tame, quiet, orderly servile disposition, which makes them [the Chinese] the prepared and ready subjects of despotism, the Japanese have a character marked by energy, independence and a lofty sense of honour. Although they are said to make good subjects, even to the severe government under which they live, they yet retain an impatience of control, and force of public opinion, which renders it impossible for any ruler wantonly to tyrannise over them . . . their manners are distinguished by a manly frankness, and all their proceedings by honour and good faith. They are habitually kind and good-humoured when nothing occurs to arouse their hostile passions, and they carry the ties of friendship even to a romantic height. To serve and defend a friend in every peril, and to meet torture and death rather than betray him, is considered a duty from which nothing can dispense. Good sense is considered, by Thunberg, as a prominent feature; and it appears particularly in their dress, which they seek only to render substantial and suitable, despising those glittering ornaments which are so eagerly sought over all Asia. The greatest defect seems to be pride, which runs through all classes, rises to the highest pitch among the great and leads them to display an extravagant pomp in their retinue and establishment, and to despise everything in the nature of industry and mercantile employment. It has the still worse effect of giving rise, on any injury, real or

> supposed, to the deepest and most implacable resentment. This passion, which decorum and the rigour of the laws prevents from breaking into open violence, is brooded over in silence, till the opportunity of vengeance arrives. Forced often to bend beneath a stern and powerful government, they are impelled to suicide, the refuge of fallen and vanquished pride. Self-murder here, like duelling in Europe, seems to be the point of honour among the great; and the nobles, even when condemned to death by the sovereign, reserve the privilege of executing the sentence with their own hands.

Since, in view of its date, this analysis must have been based essentially on second-hand information, obtained in ways like those of modern 'China watchers', peering into this secluded country from outside, and relying largely on intensive perusal of such records as remained of the travels of the German physician Engelbert Kaempfer and the English pilot Will Adams, it is all the more remarkable that Murray's account seems in many ways so remarkably up to date in its observations and judgements.

By way of comparison with this early nineteenth-century assessment, it is useful to note the findings of an opinion survey conducted by the Japanese Ministry of Education in 1974. Thus, for example, in that year—as twenty years previously—the overwhelming majority of respondents stressed the importance of service to one's superior, and placed in the same sequence the four most important moral principles: filial duty, the repayment of favours, respect of people's rights, and respect of freedom. But although twenty years earlier, 'the Survey showed pronounced optimism about the humanity of the Japanese, more than half of the respondents in 1974 said that their quickly attained affluence had deprived them of their humanity, while making their lives more convenient.' Moreover, when asked what they considered to be the strongest point of the Japanese, the largest number opted for 'diligence', and the next largest for 'tenacity', whereas their weakest point was considered by the greatest number to be 'the tendency to panic easily', which was followed by the 'insularism' of the Japanese. (Robert Whymant, 'The Japanese—the superior race' the *Guardian*, 4 May 1974).

Certainly many Japanese do still tend to suffer from a rather inhibiting mental insularity, doubtless resulting at least in part from the relative isolation of their homeland from most other parts of the world. But of far greater significance has been the way in which this geographical isolation has served to perpetuate both archaic feudal styles of living—such as that enshrined in the samurai code of Bushido, 'the way of the warrior'—and, more fundamentally, in the curious jumble of animist beliefs which have gone to make up Shinto, 'the way of the gods'.

While undoubtedly Bushido was distinguished by certain positive ethical principles—such as stoicism, defence of the weak and consideration for a defeated enemy, together with sundry professional and artistic accomplishments—the outlook of the samurai remained essentially that of the warrior rather than of the thinker, and in spirit it had far more in common with aboriginal Shinto than with Buddhism and Confucianism which had already reached Japan via Korea, during the latter part of the first millenium A.D. Unfortunately, however, while the Japanese absorbed an infusion of Confucianism and acquired a veneer of Buddhism, it was Shinto which was most deeply rooted in the Japanese psyche, and the prevailing life-style of mediaeval rural Japan served to reinforce that tendency.

To most Westerners traditional Shinto seems to be either completely naive or totally incomprehensible, or possibly even both, but some comments on 'Shinto, the original faith of Japan' by one of Japan's greatest scholars, the late Dr Inazo Nitobe, are certainly revealing:

> Though the race is endowed with a deep sense of reverence, the Japanese have no genius for dogmatization—that is, for putting into a system the vague yearnings and experiences of communion with the unseen Power immanent in the universe. Shinto is an embodiment of their unique jejune aspirations. They enjoy the pulsations of Nature and Nature's mysterious vitality, but they have never formulated their observations into a credo. They crave for the Absolute and satisfy their craving by a crude animistic or animatistic worship. Their idea of sin is physical uncleanness. Their first and last idea is to get rid of pollution, and if by thus seeking purity other things shall be added unto them, well and good. . . . Their life is almost vegetal. Truth and righteousness are qualities of the cleanness of the spirit to be secured by lustration. The vocabulary of Shinto is extremely limited, showing paucity of ideas.

While trying to make appropriate allowances for the great cultural differences between East and West, I must admit that I find Shinto disturbingly primitive, and indeed it seems doubtful whether it would have survived into modern times but for the extreme isolation in which the Japanese people lived for so long, while the great neighbouring civilizations of China and India, with their wide-ranging—if necessarily tenuous—contacts with the outside world produced such infinitely more mature and sustaining doctrines as Confucianism, Taoism and Buddhism. Moreover, there seems to be a significant parallel between the introversion of Shinto in mediaeval Japan—which by the fifteenth century had self-consciously withdrawn from the great Chinese world order—and that of the roughly contemporary and similarly retarded pagan mythology of the proto-German peoples, living in comparably inhibiting isolation amid the primeval beech forests (whose German name Büchenwälder has obvious overtones to those who remember the Third Reich) of Central Europe, beyond the outermost limits of Romano-Christian civilization.

Certainly among both peoples there has been a noticeable and seemingly psychopathic tendency to glorify gory hand-to-hand fighting and neurotically romantic love, on occasions such excesses culminating in tragic suicide pacts. Likewise both the Japanese and the Germans seem to be exceptionally susceptible to the emotions aroused by evocatively beautiful scenery and music. Whether these apparently very similar psychological characteristics of the modern Japanese and Germans explain why, in the 1974 survey referred to earlier, the Japanese placed the Germans second to themselves as the most excellent people in the world, I do not know. But I certainly find it difficult to believe that it is purely coincidental that these two undeniably great nations, with their exaggeratedly romantic tendencies to evade the humdrum realities of everyday human existence in order to wallow in fantasy worlds of their own immature imagining, have been responsible for precipitating the two most devastating wars in the whole of human history.

Nevertheless to write thus is not necessarily to imply that there is some inborn and irremediable flaw in the make-up of either the Japanese or the German peoples. Indeed, a much more obvious explanation would seem to lie in the possibility that the similar historical experiences of prolonged isolation on the part of both peoples, during the critical formative periods in the evolution of their respective cultures, has led to an imbalance between their emotional and intellectual development. In any case, however, other factors must be taken into consideration; and probably the most significant of these, in the specifically Japanese context, has been the obsession with the group at the expense of the individual.

In origin this primary emphasis on the group seems to be derived—though with some distortion—from the fivefold Confucian relationships, respectively between emperor and subjects; parents and children;

husband and wife; elder brother/sister and younger brother/sister; and teacher and disciple. In the original Chinese-derived Confucian system these five pairs of relationships, in each case between superior and inferior in status, worked on the inherently civilized and mutually tolerant principle that the superior should extend guidance and benevolence towards the inferior, who in turn would reciprocate by appropriate deference and obedience. However, the less historically mature and hence more inflexibly minded Japanese tended, virtually from the outset, to formalize these fivefold relationships into a rigidly hierarchical and constraining system whose principles had to be firmly and deliberately instilled into the younger generation by their parents. And, as time went on, similarly constraining and hierarchical formalization came to be extended into almost every aspect of Japanese social life and behaviour.

Thus, for example, it has long been decreed that, except in extremely rare and special cases, every Japanese citizen must, throughout his entire life, remain within the social class into which he was born (of course, crowding into restricted areas makes some such policy necessary). Or, to paraphrase the appropriate Japanese usage, everyone must know and keep to his proper—that is, his pre-ordained—place within the rigid confines of the 'web society'. And, carrying this obsession with organization and regimentation to the limits of absurdity, the authorities even laid down specified dates upon which all Japanese were required by law to make prescribed changes in the clothing they wore so as to conform with the expected seasonal changes in the weather. Instinctively, but not accidentally, one is reminded of Jerome K. Jerome's comment in *Three Men on the Bummel* on the German government's attitude to its citizens: 'Just get yourself born, and we'll do the rest.'

Such all-pervading formalization as that to which the Japanese people were subjected was bound in the long run to produce not merely social inflexibility but social fossilization. Indeed, particularly during the two and a quarter centuries of the Tokugawa Seclusion, the whole social structure of Japan appears to have been ossified into total immobility, a condition which, it would seem, must sooner or later prove fatal to the body politic.

Whatever virtues the Japanese authorities may have hoped to inculcate in their people by stripping them of all individual responsibility through intensive and sustained indoctrination in traditional values, the process must inevitably have been thoroughly destructive of individual self-confidence, let alone constructive initiative. Yet in fact that was precisely its intention. As the distinguished psychoanalyst, Dr James Clark Moloney, said in his book *Understanding the Japanese Mind*:

> The government insists upon disindividualization; at birth a person is expected to become nothing at all (*mimpi*). He is directed to respect authority (*kanzan*). He is trained to obligate himself obsequiously to the father (*ko*) or to any father or parent substitute (*oya bun*), or to the emperor (*chu*), or the emperor's way (*kodo*). He is required to become a god (*kami*) or to fulfil the way of the gods (*shinto*). He ceases to be an individual, performing *giri* (an elaborate institution requiring him to behave in a prescribed fashion expressive of his nationalism) to his empire and doing what is expected of him (*jicho*).

Against this background it is no wonder that, by Meiji times, the Japanese as a people had become notorious for their sense of inferiority and their apparently compulsive addiction to copying other people's achievements rather than pioneering new ways for themselves. And these tendencies have certainly been intensified by the almost complete absence of any countervailing process of mutual education through contact with other, less introverted neighbouring peoples, such as happened—greatly to its advantage—in Western Europe.

However, the apparently incomprehensible policy of trying indefinitely to freeze the *status quo* should not be attributed to pathological stupidity on the part of the Tokugawa Bakufu. Rather, almost certainly, it represented a serious—though ultimately counter-productive—attempt to constrain the Japanese people and society within the extremely narrow geographical limits of their effective national territory which, after 1637, had for all practical purposes been cut off from external relationships for some two and a quarter centuries. Thus, notwithstanding the palliative of *mabiki*, the pressure continued to increase, and the outcome seemed bound to be violent, as indeed—in a minor way—it proved to be, though the operative step came not from within but from the Americans, who first forced their way into this almost totally secluded country in 1853.

Nevertheless, neither the uninvited action of Commodore Perry from without, nor the internal reactions to it, culminating in the Meiji Restoration of 1868, wholly resolved the problem. For although the Japanese have repeatedly stressed that what happened in 1868 was not a revolution but a restoration (of the emperor to his proper—as opposed to his purely nominal—role) the fact remained that such a restoration was not enough, and a revolution—at least in mental attitudes—would sooner or later be needed.

Fundamentally the problem was that, whereas in the West industry and technology were outgrowths of a richly matured civilization, which had also nurtured the arts and political philosophy as well as the sciences and technology, no such rationally-based and well-rounded civilization existed in Japan. Here traditional animistic Shinto, patchily overlain by superficial deposits of Confucianism and Buddhism, could not possibly, of itself, have generated a scientific or a technological revolution. On the other hand, however, it was perfectly possible to train individuals, with no previous scientific education, to drive and maintain powered vehicles and to operate a wide range of military hardware and other kinds of gadgetry with reasonable success.

For this reason, therefore, once the Japanese armed forces had seen for themselves the immense superiority of nineteenth-century Western weaponry over their own of pre-Meiji times, there was no practical obstacle to its adoption by either the army or the navy. And since, after the alarm occasioned by the manifest superiority of Perry's 'black ships', the Japanese were anxious at all costs to keep up with the times, priority in modernization was unhesitatingly given to the armed forces, and in particular to the army, which conveniently provided opportunities for the employment of former samurai who had been displaced by the formal abolition of feudalism in 1871. Thus a strong element of continuity was preserved between the deeply traditionalist Tokugawa and the new Meiji Japan, though in fact its roots went down even deeper into the very subsoil of traditional Shinto mythology.

It was in such unprecedented circumstances that the effective rulers of Japan, with no proper grounding in modern political philosophy and only superficial first-hand experience of the outside world, had somehow or other to find their bearings and begin to chart their course in almost totally unfamiliar surroundings. Thus it was not surprising that, while technological innovation—not only in the increasingly powerful armed forces, but also in manufacturing and transport industries—began very quickly to change the outward appearance of Japan, in matters of government the rulers opted instinctively for caution and continuity of tradition. Hence the fundamental character of the country's institutions was only slowly and peripherally modified, as may readily be inferred from both the very restricted powers which the Constitution of 1899 granted to the Diet, and from the supposedly forward-looking but in fact distinctly traditionalist *Imperial Rescript on Education*, of 1890:

Know Ye, Our Subjects: Our Imperial Ancestors have founded our

> Empire on a basis broad and everlasting, and have deeply and firmly implanted virtue. Our subjects, ever united in loyalty and filial piety, have from generation to generation illustrated the beauty thereof. This is the glory and fundamental character of our Empire, and herein also lies the source of our education. Ye, our subjects, be filial to your parents, affectionate to your brothers and sisters; as husbands and wives, be harmonious; as friends, true; bear yourselves in modesty and moderation; extend your benevolence to all; pursue learning and cultivate the arts and thereby develop intellectual faculties and perfect moral powers; furthermore, advance public good and promote common interests; always respect the Constitution and observe the laws; should emergency arise, offer yourselves courageously to the State and thus guard and maintain the prosperity of our Imperial Throne, coeval with heaven and earth. So shall ye not only be our good and faithful subjects, but render illustrious the best traditions of your forefathers. The way here set forth is indeed the teaching bequeathed by our Imperial Ancestors, to be observed alike by their descendants and the subjects, infallible for all ages and true in all places. It is our wish to take it to heart in all reverence, in common with you our subjects, that we may all thus attain to the same virtue.

Although the *Imperial Rescript on Education* tells us little about education in the sense in which that word is used in the West, it unconsciously reveals a great deal about the way in which the Japanese were still thinking more than twenty years after the Meiji Restoration. Particularly significant in this regard is the reference to 'our Imperial Throne, coeval with heaven and earth', a concept which was elaborated in 1937 in a highly tendentious publication of the Japanese Ministry of Education entitled *Kokutai No Hongi—The Cardinal Principles of the National Entity of Japan.* From this we learn:

> That our Imperial Throne is coeval with heaven and earth means that the past and the future are united in one in the 'now', that our nation possesses everlasting life, and that it flourishes endlessly. Our history is an evolution of the eternal 'now', and at the root of our history there always runs a stream of eternal 'now'.

Moreover:

> Since ancient times the spirits of the deities of our country have fallen into two groups: the spirits of peace (*nigi-mitama*) and the spirits of warriors (*ana mitama*). Where there is a harmonious working of the

> two, all things under the sun rest in peace, grow and develop. Hence, the warrior spirits work inseparably and as one with the spirits of peace. It is in the subduing of those who refuse to conform to the august influence of the Emperor's virtues that the mission of our Imperial Military Forces lies; and thus we see the Way of the warriors that may be called *Jimmu* (Divine Warrior).

Not altogether surprisingly, against this background of conflicting spiritual forces, the period from 1868 to 1945 was one of almost continuous instability and turbulence, reflecting what may not unreasonably be called the split personality of a Japan which was still deeply rooted in the primitive and utterly outdated past, and yet at the same time was not merely striving at break-neck speed to catch up with the Western world, but was also lecturing the latter on the shortcomings of its individualistic culture. Thus, in the words of *Kokutai No Hongi*, 'Our present mission as a people is to build up a new Japanese culture by adopting and sublimating Western cultures with our national entity as the basis, and to contribute spontaneously to the advancement of world culture.'

In contrast to the turgid tergiversations of *Kokutai No Hongi* it is appropriate to conclude this section by quoting the remarkably illuminating and perceptive analysis by Dr J. C. Moloney of the way in which the Japanese, at least until very recently, have tended to view their nation:

> The Japanese nation is not considered by the Japanese to be an aggregate of separate, distinct, and different individuals. Japan is thought to be a homogeneous entity. Perhaps this could best be understood by thinking of Japan itself as being a super-individual. No majority of Japanese could alter this position. They could not alter the form nor the type of government. Because of its implications for the future, this type of thinking is ominous, and perhaps more of us should be aware of it. We should think about the fact that the Japanese government is not constituted as an instrument to serve the Japanese people. Instead the Japanese people are considered instruments to serve the Japanese government. The popular rights of the Japanese people (*minken*) are subordinated to the nationalistic institution (*kokken*) epitomized in the regality of the emperor.

In seeking to understand why the Japanese have evolved in this curious and to many Westerners virtually incomprehensible way, it may help first to try to look back briefly at the unfolding sequence of their chequered history from the standpoint of the Japanese themselves.

From its origin as a national entity, Japan as a relatively small and very secluded country, was acutely conscious of being completely overshadowed by China which, as early as T'ang times, from 618 to 907 A.D., was an immense, prosperous and populous land, with a highly developed civilization. As such, it had long regarded itself as 'the only sun in the sky' and the centrepiece of the Chinese world order which already encompassed—at least nominally—the greater part of the territories which, over a thousand years later, the Japanese came to call 'Greater East Asia'.

By comparison with Imperial China, mediaeval Japan—small, territorially fragmented, and inward-looking, had scarcely advanced culturally beyond the rudimentary level of aboriginal Shinto. Moreover, while, from its peripheral position on the edge of the Pacific, Japan deferentially revered China as 'the great land beyond the seas', even to the point of remodelling itself on the pattern of T'ang China, the Japanese people continued to be despised and ridiculed by the Chinese as a manifestly inferior race. However, beginning in the late fourteenth century, the Japanese, from their small and already incipiently congested islands, turned with growing confidence to maritime pursuits, which for a time included piratical raids along the China coast, though later the emphasis switched to the establishment of outposts of traders in various parts of the Nanyo or, to give it its modern name, South-east Asia. Although these activities had been partly stimulated by contact with the more advanced seamen of Portugal and Spain, whose ships and firearms—as well as their Christianity—greatly impressed the Japanese, the latter, in a characteristic surfacing of their sense of inferiority, retreated into virtually complete seclusion from the outside world in 1637.

Hitherto, therefore, apart from sporadic piracy, such as many offshore islanders—not excluding the British—have tended to indulge in, and the abortive attempt by Hideyoshi—curiously foreshadowing that of the Imperial Japanese Army in 1894—to invade China through Korea in 1592, the Japanese nation could scarcely be accused of excessively aggressive tendencies, at least before Commodore Perry's action, in forcing an entry into Japan in 1853–4, introduced the Japanese to Western ways of behaviour, to which in due course they responded.

In fact the decisive response came from the Emperor Meiji himself, whose Charter Oath of 1868, besides providing for the formation of a deliberative assembly, and the decision of all measures by public opinion, also stated that 'the uncivilized customs of former times should be broken through; the impartiality of justice displayed in the workings of nature be adopted as a basis of action; and intellect and learning should be sought for throughout the world' in order to establish the empire on sound foundations.

Unfortunately these excellent intentions were not always reciprocated. For, virtually from the outset, many of the most promising Japanese pupils were humiliated by the condescending racialism of Western—particularly British—'experts', which served only to intensify the already deep sense of Japanese resentment. Moreover this situation was further exacerbated by the subsequent attempts of other Western powers implicitly to prevent Japanese immigration into their territories. Meanwhile, covertly and calculatedly, the Japanese militarists worked out their own response to Western imperialism, and began to put it into practice.

Having been indoctrinated into believing that, as semi-divine and hence invincible beings, the Japanese were destined to rule the world, they made their plans accordingly. As an offshore island nation, Japan must first acquire a bridgehead on the continental mainland, and for this purpose Korea, an introverted tributary state of China since 1637, seemed almost to have been providentially designed. Accordingly, by 1876—a mere eight years after the Meiji Restoration—the Japanese succeeded in opening Korea to trade, and thereafter, by carefully contrived and skilful intriguing, they managed, at least nominally, to establish its independence from China, while in reality obtaining *de facto* control over it themselves. Thus the way was prepared for the Sino-Japanese War, beginning in 1894, whereby Japan, having invaded the mainland via Korea, proceeded to defeat China, hitherto the greatest power in Asia, in 1895.

By this swift and—to most observers—unexpected victory, Japan displayed its superiority, as a young, vigorous and up-and-coming power, over the old, infirm and apparently decadent China. Flushed by this success, Japan proceeded to extract from China the strategic Liaotung Peninsula (which to its intense humiliation Japan was immediately forced by the Triple Intervention of France, Germany and Russia to retrocede to China), the island of Taiwan and a large indemnity which enabled it to finance the building of the great steel plant at Yawata. In thus establishing itself as a major industrial power, Japan was able greatly to increase its naval strength to a level which made it fit to be ranked as partner of the United Kingdom in the Anglo-Japanese Alliance of 1902. Thus enhanced, both in power and esteem, Japan quickly acquired the confidence it needed before daring to attack

Tsarist Rusia in order to prevent the latter from attacking China before the Japanese themselves were ready to do so in 1904–5.

So, successively mutilated and softened up, China could now be prepared for its further reduction to the status of a *de facto* Japanese satellite, a process which was initiated via the Twenty-one Demands presented to China by Japan on 18 January 1915. Once again the way had been assiduously prepared, and within less than a month of the outbreak of the First World War on 28 July 1914, Japan invaded the German Concession of Kiaochow in Shantung—the third of the three strategic peninsulas encircling the maritime approaches to Peking (the others being Korea and Liaotung). Thus hemmed in, China was forced to accept the first four groups of Japan's demands, though the fifth group was toned down by British intercession. Nevertheless China's weakness was not abated, and in February 1931 Japan forced China to relinquish its Manchurian provinces which were then revamped as the Japanese puppet state of Manchukuo in 1932, and in 1937 an essentially similar process of politico-cosmetic surgery was performed on what was left of China.

Both geopolitically and economically the Japanese take-over of Manchuria marked a crucial turning point for, with the acquisition of its vast resources of coal, iron, and foodstuffs, Japan was now in a position to contemplate taking on the United States, the United Kingdom, and the Netherlands, whose combined dependencies in South-east Asia contained valuable resources of tropical produce and, above all, of oil, without which it would be impossible to maintain the necessary land, sea and air communications to hold Greater East Asia together, before finally embarking on the culminating conquest of the rest of the world.

Only at this final stage did Japan fail. But then, like the house builded upon the sand, it fell; and great was the fall thereof. These portentous biblical words have been used deliberately in order to emphasize that, although the most obvious cause of the defeat of Japan was the unprecedented destructive capability of Allied air power, culminating in the nuclear attacks on Hiroshima and Nagasaki, there was also an inbuilt and profound weakness in the Japanese state itself. For, rooted as it had hitherto been in the primitive mythology of Shinto, devoid of either ethical or philosophical structure, the Japanese polity provided a wholly inadequate foundation for a modern industrial state, and indeed continued to present the greatest of all obstacles to Japan's achievement of true maturity as a nation.

As one looks back over this extraordinary sequence, from the sedately Sinophile stage of the Nara period, between the fifth and the seventh centuries A.D., through the subsequent cycles of intermittent internal turbulence, followed by the strangely ill-judged and wellnigh disastrous two and a quarter centuries of the Tokugawa Seclusion from 1637 to 1868, and thence to the increasingly hectic seventy-seven years which culminated in the catastrophe of 1945, two conflicting themes may be discerned. First, in their relations with the outside world, the Japanese—at least until the early 1890s—seem on balance to have been more often sinned against than sinning. But secondly, in allowing themselves to be led astray by their own militaristic fanatics, they became their own worst enemies.

Between 1868 and 1905 the processes underlying these two themes became intertwined and, following its annexation of Korea in 1910, Japan seemed to be set irresistibly on course for unlimited territorial expansion. Thus the scene was prepared for the outrageous havoc and carnage of the insolently miscalled 'China Incident' which, incidentally, lasted from 1937 until it merged with the Second World War in 1941. It was against this background that, initially in China and subsequently in other parts of eastern and south-eastern Asia, the Japanese came to acquire their terrible reputation for callous and infamous cruelty which, even now, they have not succeeded in living down.

Today, half a lifetime after I came out of the last of the various Japanese P.O.W. camps in which altogether I spent exactly three-and-a-half years, I frankly do not know whether further discussion of Japanese wartime atrocities serves any useful purpose other than that of reminding succeeding generations that human beings—in their tens and perhaps hundreds of thousands—most certainly did sink to levels of behaviour which remain as a standing disgrace to all mankind. No doubt, for those unnumbered victims who suffered most traumatically, it may be kinder to follow the Japanese proverb 'Move not that which is still' or, adopting its English counterpart, to let sleeping dogs lie. However, partly because many friends who know that I have been writing this book seem to be primarily concerned to discover what I have to say on this intensely emotive subject, and more importantly, because a Japanese ex-prisoner of the British—who, like me, is a university professor—has himself written at length about what he considers to be the even worse cruelty of the British towards the Japanese (Yuji Aida, *Prisoner of the British*), I feel that I have a particular obligation to accept this challenge, as I propose to do forthwith.

In attempting this daunting task one must begin by recognizing that both the historical and geographical circumstances and—to a lesser extent—the behaviour of the particular Japanese units involved—differed significantly between one place and another. For this reason the brief account which follows concentrates on examples drawn from two markedly dissimilar cases, namely the 'China Incident' and the Imperial Japanese Army's P.O.W. camps along the Siam-Burma railway, though my own first-hand experience is limited to the latter. Nevertheless, since there is a common psycho-political background to the entire sequence of Japanese atrocities during the 1930s and 40s, it is necessary briefly to recall it.

As was explained in chapter nine, the explosive impact of the unexpected Japanese victory over Russia in 1905 produced repercussions which rapidly reverberated throughout Asia, and thereafter over much of the rest of the world as well. Thus, for the first time in history it had been demonstrated that even a relatively small Asian power like Japan could defeat so vast a Western power as the sprawling Tsarist Empire (though, of course, the Tsarist Empire was seriously overextended and very inefficiently organized). In such wholly unprecedented circumstances it suddenly began to seem conceivable—at least to the Japanese who had achieved this almost unbelievable victory—that the entire global balance between the white and the non-white peoples might be within sight of being overturned.

Yet while Japan was still basking in the euphoria of its victory over Russia, the British, by means of the Anglo-Chinese Wars of 1839–42 and 1856–60, had shatteringly undermined the established position of China, hitherto the undisputedly pre-eminent power in the entire Orient. By the Japanese, already half anticipating the prospect of leading the East to claim its rightful position *vis à vis* the West, the totally unforeseen disintegration of Imperial China could be viewed either as an appalling setback to the East as a whole, or—if China really was incapable of resuming its traditionally pre-eminent role—as a never-to-be-repeated opportunity for Japan itself to replace China as the supreme power in the East and, in so doing, to hasten the fulfilment of its divinely ordained mission to conquer the world.

In the event, since China, under the decaying rule of the Manchu Dynasty prior to 1912, and thereafter under successive 'revolutionary' regimes ending with Chiang Kai-shek's Nanking Government of 1928–37, never succeeded in effectively reorganizing itself, the Japanese took it upon themselves to knock their formerly revered 'elder brother' into shape. While the extremity of the brutality with which they attempted to do so may be explained in terms of the intense contempt which the ever-thrusting Japanese felt for this supposedly erring and degenerate member of the family, such brutality cannot by any rational standards be excused, as the following accounts and comments from Lord Russell of Liverpool in his book, *The Knights of Bushido*, relating to what came to be known as the 'Rape of Nanking', in December 1937, will make all too clear:

> As the Japanese 'Central China Expeditionary Forces' approached Nanking early in December 1937 more than half the population fled the city. . . . The Japanese troops were then let loose like the hordes of Genghis Khan to ravish and murder. . . . Small groups of Japanese soldiers roamed all over the city night and day. Many were crazed with drink, but no attempt was made by the commander or the officers to maintain discipline among the occupying forces. Soldiers marched through the streets indiscriminately killing Chinese of both sexes, adults and children alike, without receiving any provocation and without rhyme or reason. They went on killing until the gutters ran with blood and the streets were littered with the bodies of their victims. . . . At the lowest computation twelve thousand men, women and children were shot or done to death during the first three days of the Japanese occupation. Rape was the order of the day, and resistance by the victim, or by members of her family who tried to protect her, meant almost certain death. Girls of tender years and old women, neither were spared. Neither youth nor age was respected, and the evidence given before the Tokyo Tribunal by eye-witnesses of the abnormal and sadistic behaviour displayed by the ravishers defies description and is quite unprintable.

By the time General Matsui arrived in Nanking four days after the entry of his troops, 'at least one hundred and fifty thousand innocent inhabitants had been massacred'. However,

> . . . on the day after his triumphal ceremonial entry into the city he held a religious service in memory of the dead and issued this statement: 'I extend much sympathy to millions of innocent people in the Kiangpei and Chekiang districts who have suffered the evils of war. Now the flag of the Rising Sun is floating high over Nanking, and the Imperial Way is shining in the southern parts of the Yangtse-kiang. The dawn of the Renaissance of the East is on the verge of appearing. On this occasion I hope for reconsideration of the situation by the four hundred million people of China.'

By comparison with the behaviour of the Japanese forces in China, whose peoples they despised, their record in the prisoner of war camps along the Siam-Burma railway was in some respects recognizably less appalling. Most obviously this was because in such exclusively male communities as P.O.W. camps the opportunity for committing the kind of pathologically obscene atrocities which were perpetrated by the Imperial Japanese Army in occupied China did not arise. However, such opportunities did exist—and were seized, with a vengeance—in the 'civilian labour camps' whose unprotected inmates comprised both sexes, and children as well as adults. And there the record was every bit as outrageous as that in Nanking and elsewhere in China, the only significant difference being that the numbers involved in the civilian labour camps were smaller.

Secondly, presumably because the Japanese engineers were acutely aware of the extent of their dependence on Allied prisoners—especially officers—for the completion of the more complicated tasks involved in railway construction, especially the building of the larger bridges, they seem to have made some attempt to husband this irreplaceable reserve of appropriate skills by providing the officers with somewhat less inadequate rations and medical attention than those made available for the unfortunate 'other ranks'.

Finally, since the Japanese officers greatly enjoyed our theatricals and similar performances—whether or not they understood them—they made some attempt to moderate their behaviour and that of their troops, so that our weekly shows should not be interrupted or terminated. And, since we all recognized the great contribution which such entertainments made to the maintenance of morale, the British and other Allied camp officials tacitly concurred in this policy. In short, a *modus vivendi* of sorts was maintained, though except perhaps on 'Kurisumasu' (Christmas) Day and Navy Day—our two annual holidays—it was precariously poised and no love was lost between the high and low contending parties.

Since in chapters two to five inclusive I have already written about conditions in our P.O.W. camps, first in Changi (Singapore) and later in various parts of Thailand, I shall leave my account to speak for itself. But the motivation of Japanese behaviour still calls for fuller explanation, and so I shall begin by considering the remarkable explanation proferred by Professor Aida to explain the behaviour of his fellow Japanese prisoners of war in Ahlone Camp, in Burma, immediately after the end of the war.

In essence Aida's argument seems to be that the atrocities committed by Japanese captors were merely spontaneous outbursts caused by a kind of panic reaction to wartime carnage, on the part of a people who—supposedly unlike the British—were not accustomed to the sight of blood. For my part, however, I find it impossible to regard this as other than the most transparent of rationalizations, probably conditioned by excessive exposure to everyday Japanese propaganda with its repeated reference to the 'red-faced, whisky-swilling Anglo-Americans'. Although it may appear frivolous of me to say so, I cannot remember a single instance of a Japanese refusing either a steak or a glass of whisky, nor, more seriously, do I recall ever having seen any members of the Imperial Japanese Army upset by the sight of Allied blood, which was certainly spilt in the more brutal assaults on their prisoners. But I strongly suspect that far more such blood flowed as the direct result of the hysterical frenzies *deliberately worked up* by our Japanese captors preparatory to carrying out such punishments as that of being 'severely beaten to death'.

It is at this point that the gulf between the Japanese and ourselves seems to become virtually unbridgeable. To the Japanese whom I encountered in our P.O.W. camps this kind of deliberately self-induced hysteria, culminating in orgies of beating, seemed to be generally accepted as normal by our captors, whereas among the vast majority of Westerners such behaviour is automatically assumed to be either a symptom of a degree of mental disorder which should automatically debar the individual concerned from military or any other kind of service, or else—and most shamefully—as evidence of a total lack of self-discipline, presumably resulting from inexcusably incompetent upbringing by the individual's parents.

Yet implicitly Professor Aida seems to regard lack of self-control as a valid excuse for irrational and irresponsible behaviour. Indeed he goes so far as to argue that what he regards as the callousness—though I would call it the frigid self-control—with which the British dispensed the justice of the military law was even harder to bear than the unpredictable outbursts of berserk fury by Japanese army personnel which culminated in some of their worst atrocities. I can only say that it must be a very strangely distorted view of life which permits a human being to prefer being beheaded, or bayoneted through the eyes or stomach, to a few minutes—or even a couple of hours—of withering but controlled contempt.

How, then, is one to account for such appalling behaviour? And how, if at all, can it be reconciled with the other side of the Japanese character, with its exceptional devotion to children, its intense appreciation of natural beauty, and above all its extraordinary capacity for friendship, not least for its enemies of yesteryear? Certainly this dichotomy is apparent to both Japanese and non-Japanese, as may be inferred from the ever growing list of such book titles as *The True Face of Japan* (Nohara), *Behind the Japanese Mask* (Craigie), *The Chrysanthemum and the Sword* (Benedict), *Facing Two Ways* (Ishimoto), *Japan's Feet of Clay* (Utley), *Japan Unmasked* (Kawasaki), and *The Kimono Mind* (Rudofsky), to say nothing of the latent possibilities of *Queer Things about Japan* (Sladen, 1903).

Here I can offer little beyond a few random speculations which go back to my earliest days in Changi P.O.W. camp, immediately after the fall of Singapore in February 1942. Already by that time I had been struck by the coincidence of two comments by Nohara, respectively that the Japanese were 'a nation of children at play', and that the processes of logical thought were anathema to the Japanese, who preferred to trust their own intuitive reactions. To me it seemed obvious that these two characteristics were intimately inter-related, and also that both were derived from the fairy-tale world of Shinto which seemed to be totally devoid of any rational sense of causation.

Meanwhile, in living and working side by side with—at least nominally adult—Japanese in our camp, I had been astonished to discover that, although they had been effectively taught to believe in their superiority, as semi-divine beings, over all other races, most of them remained tortured by intense feelings of racial inferiority *vis à vis* their Western prisoners who, for all practical purposes, were now no more than slave labourers of an Oriental despotism. Moreover, from their endless repetition of such comments as 'Japan soja bery smoru man, but prenty worku; Engrish soja bery big man but smoru worku; no good danna', and from our glimpses of their English-language newspapers, whose headlines informed us, for example, that 'Six-foot U.S. airman weeps in captivity' and 'Long-legged Anglo-Saxons live on beef and whisky', I at last began to realize how intensely the Japanese had been humiliated by contemptuous comments on their own diminutive stature.

Perhaps the most unintentionally revealing of all the Japanese morale-boosting propaganda which we encountered was an article, in one of their English-language magazines, entitled 'The Perfect Human Figure'. Accompanied by numerous diagrams, and arguing in astonishingly laborious fashion from analogy with birds, fish, reptiles and mammals, the author claimed to have worked out the precise dimensions of the ideal human being (sex somewhat surprisingly unspecified) before going on to point out that these data corresponded almost exactly with the average figures obtained from recruits to the Imperial Japanese Army, while members of all other races, and particularly the Anglo-Americans, failed dismally on nearly every count!

Thus, ridiculous as it may seem to those unfamiliar with things Japanese, I gradually came to believe that the root cause of Japan's apparently irrational, perverted and megalomaniac phases of behaviour lay in the interaction of three curiously ill-assorted factors: to wit, Shinto, seclusion and shortness; and that the most serious of these—by far—was Shinto, which had so tragically retarded and distorted the development of the Japanese character.

Even for ordinary mortals the prolonged succession of denigration, ridicule and contrived snubs to which, mostly for absurdly trivial reasons, innumerable Japanese individuals have been subjected, must surely have constituted a deeply traumatic experience. But for a people who, down the ages, have been brought up from infancy to believe that they were in some mysterious way descended from the gods and, as such, were intrinsically superior to all other races of mankind, the cumulative effect of this experience may well have gone beyond normal trauma to the point at which it threatens to undermine the whole personality. And if this could happen at the individual level, it seems not only possible but even probable that, given the traditional Japanese obsession with the primacy of the group over the individual, whole units of the armed forces may have been similarly disorientated under the influence of falsely prestigious fanatics, a development which, in turn, might go far to account for the more psychopathic atrocities already referred to above.

It was with such speculations as these in my mind that, on the troopship which brought me back home to England in the late autumn of 1945, I first tried to sort out the tangle of conflicting impressions which I had formed about the Japanese military personnel whom I had encountered while in captivity. Manifestly there was much truth in Nohara's characterization of the Japanese as 'a nation of children' for, in terms of social age, that was precisely what so many of them seemed to be. And almost certainly this was attributable to the intellectually retarding influence of Shinto. But no less certainly—at least as I had observed them—they were not by any stretch of imagination 'children at play'. Admittedly, many of my fellow prisoners found that it was easiest to get along with our captors by treating them as youngsters, for clearly their sudden enthusiasms and wild tempers—often accompanied by fisticuffs, followed by apparent bursts of repentance, when they would buy their victims a cup of coffee, not so much from any sense of having done wrong but merely in order to satisfy a rather pathetic craving to be liked—all seemed to accord with this interpretation.

Yet, beyond any doubt, one could not regard as normal individuals such teenagers, or young men in their twenties, who were so pathologically irritable, unstable and repressed, presumably as a direct consequence of their peculiarly brutal and misguided military training. In short, these newly trained members of the Imperial Japanese Army, who instantly reminded me of junior-school bullies, could most appropriately be described as overgrown problem children. Thus it was that the first article I ever wrote on a Japanese theme was entitled 'The Japanese as Problem Children', which appeared in the *Political Quarterly*, volume 17, 1946.

That, of course, was over thirty years ago, and during the intervening decades the whole nature of Japanese life and society has been transformed almost out of recognition, thanks above all to the steadfast, sagacious and surprisingly sympathetic policies which were pursued under the Allied Occupation. Fortunately, moreover, the Occupation's concurrent processes of disarmament, democratization and the demythologizing of the Japanese polity have meanwhile been greatly assisted by contemporary developments in other fields. In the first place the appalling stupidity and arrogance revealed by the catastrophic miscalculations of the military leadership have virtually destroyed the former widespread adulation of the militarists and so smoothed the path to nationwide acceptance of demilitarization. Secondly, and perhaps more fundamentally, the massive and continuing drift of population from the countryside to the towns and cities is steadily undermining Shinto and all that goes with it for, as an essentially rural fertility cult, Shinto has nothing of value to offer to an already overwhelmingly urbanized and industrialized Japan, now racing rapidly towards the twenty-first century.

Thirdly, hand in hand with urbanization, the spectacular rise in living standards has had a revolutionary effect on both the minds and the bodies of the generation of Japanese born since the 1950s and now passing through that most crucial of all stages, from adolescence to maturity. For besides being spared the horrors and privations of the war years, these young Japanese of the first post-war generation have been raised on a far more nutritious and better balanced diet—including satisfying quantities of meat, milk, butter and other similar items previously almost unknown to the majority of the Japanese population. And, much to the surprise of all concerned, the members of this new generation of Japanese are, on average, some three to five centimetres taller than their parents, and in most cases possess longer and straighter legs. Since, over many years, I have become convinced that, to victims of racialist denigration, shortness of stature is apt to be at least as acute a source of embarrassment as pigmentation, and since I also believe that the process which in 1883 Yoshio Takahashi referred to as 'the improvement of the Japanese race' is now taking place, primarily for the dietary reasons he advocated (though without recourse to the mass intermarriage with Anglo-Saxons which he also proposed), I predict that, within the next two or three decades, the inhibiting sense of physical inferiority which has haunted so many Japanese for so long will have become a thing of the past.

Nevertheless, by far the most important of all factors making for renewed confidence in established values is the strength and resilience of the Japanese family system, based as it is on the Confucian virtues of filial piety, discipline, frugality, and hard work. Yet this too is changing, and distinctly for the better. For, thanks to the Occupation's enlightened policy regarding individual rights, the new generation of Japanese wives and mothers who have achieved liberation without having had to turn themselves into fanatics in order to do so, have begun slowly, steadily and skilfully to smooth away the excesses of traditional Japanese masculinity. Moreover, assisted by a panoply of modern domestic appliances, modern Japanese women are now able to devote even greater care than their predecessors did to the bringing up of their smaller families, both as domestic communities and as individual and hence unique persons, each according to his or her own tastes and talents. Thus freed from excessive traditional encumbrances, the new-style women of the new Japan are now at last seizing the opportunity to use to the full their unrivalled intuitive talents for home-making in the fullest sense of that term.

Curiously, but appropriately, this brings me back to the people whom I, as a brash young P.O.W., once condescendingly referred to as 'problem children'. Specifically I used that term to refer to the relatively youthful members of the Imperial Japanese Army, who often caused us a great deal of annoyance, and at times considerably more than that. In a real sense, moreover, the entire generation of Japanese males who grew to manhood in the politically turbulent late 1930s and 40s were at least in some measure adversely affected by that experience, and, as such, tended to exhibit some of the characteristics of problem children. Yet, thanks to the much more enlightened spirit which increasingly pervades Japan today, the problem of the 'problem children' now seems to be solving itself. In the article which I wrote on this theme, at the turn of the year from 1945/6, I ended with these words: 'Problem children need careful handling, unstinted patience, and unremitting forgiveness. But they are often exceptionally gifted, and capable of great achievements. And, given the right treatment, they sometimes make good.'

Now, at the end of the last of my three diverse experiences as a guest of the Japanese, I have been privileged to see for myself that the erstwhile 'problem children' have indeed been given the right treatment, that their talents have matured with the using, and that—to an extent which goes far beyond all expectations—they have more than made good.

APPENDIX

PROCLAMATION OF THE GENERAL OFFICER, IMPERIAL JAPANESE ARMY, IN COMMAND ALL BRITISH P.O.W. CAMPS IN THAILAND.

On assuming command of the local group of P. of W. Camps, the Lieutenant-Colonel I.J.A. made the following speech:

Today were opened the Branch Barracks of the Prisoners' Barracks in Thailand, and I am glad that I was appointed the Commander of this Camp. From now I will give you the instructions of the Commander in Thailand.

The instruction of the Commander of the Prisoners' Camp in Thailand.

I am glad that I was appointed to the Commander of the Prisoners' Camp in Thailand, and I can engage in establishing the new order of the world.

According to the various reports from the prisoner and the result of my observation about your present circumstances, I understand that you are all engaged in your working parties sincerely, and the condition of your health is good also.

This is the reasonable result of a great nation like England, I think.

I recall that it is stated clearly in the International Law to impose labour upon the prisoners, and I believe that labour is the most effective way to keep your health.

Well, in Nippon, there is existing morality, well known as 'Bushido' from the ancient time, and our nationality was cultivated for the sake of this morality and became the great nation like today.

And the soul of 'Bushido' is carrying out its duty to the best of its power.

I wish to lead you relating to practise your duty by means of the above explained.

You must understand this purport and must devote your best to your labour. If anyone does not obey our order he will have a severe punishment; *but* if you obey our order carefully, I will give you the best treatment that a great nation can give, if possible.

Henceforth, I wish you faithfully to work more and more to bring the good results.

(signed) SHOWA NEN
Commander of the British Prisoners Camp in Thailand

20th August, 1942 Brigadier SASA (Agent)

BABY GO TO SLEEPO SONG
(see pp. 82–3)

A lullaby for a Co-prosperous child
('The Japanese are forever committing acts of peace.')

Banzai, banzai, little Nip
How we love your comradeship;
With what skilled celerity
You build up co-prosperity.

Speedo, speedo, tired Thai
You must work as well as I;
Cutting down the big bamboo
To let the Nippon culture through.

Worko, worko, Tamil coolie
Nippon will not treat you crooly.
She's proud to see you play your part
And has your interests close at heart.

Chunkul, chunkul, mild Malay
In the Great East Asia way.
Nippon's watching while you toil,
Wresting victory from the soil.

Choppo, choppo, little Chink,
Do you ever stop to think
That though she comes with sword and flame
Nippon loves you just the same?

Moshe, moshe, Buddhist Burman
Listen to a Shinto sermon:

Bushido, that's the Warrior's Way,
Means all men work, for damn-all pay.

Careful, careful, canny Korean
Don't let them see you've found a durian;
In Greater East Asia there's lashings of loot
You tend the tree but they eat the fruit.

Slappo, slappo, stalwart Sikh,
Are you still as smooth and sleek,
As in the days that used to be
Before Dai Nippon set you free?

Kuru, kuru, English shoko,
Too much resto, too much smoko;
Charge to win your soul's salvation
In the seventh incarnation.

Sleepo, sleepo, little man
Leave it all to great Japan
May her heroes never cease
Committing glorious acts of peace.

Banzai—'Long live the Emperor'
Chunkul—a hoe, to hoe
Moshe, moshe—Hello (as used over the telephone)
Shoko—officer
Kuru—'D'you hear?'

COLONEL NAGATOMO'S SPEECH ON ASSUMPTION OF DUTY AT THANBYUZAYAT, BURMA.

Instructions to Prisoners in No. 3 Branch, Thanbyuzayat, delivered by Colonel Y. Nagatomo at different camps in Burma between October and December 1942.

It is a great pleasure to me to see you in this place as I am appointed chief of War Prisoners Camp in obedience to the Imperial Command issued by His Majesty, the Emperor.

The Great Asiatic War has broken out due to the rising of the East Asiatic nations whose hearts were burnt with the desire to live and preserve their nations on account of the intrusion of the British and Americans for past many years.

There is therefore no other reason for Japan to drive out the Anti-Axis powers of the arrogant and insolent British and Americans from East Asia in co-operation with our neighbours of China and other East Asiatic nations and to establish the Greater East Asia Co-prosperity Sphere for the benefit of all human beings and to establish everlasting peace in the world.

During the past few centuries Nippon has made extreme endeavour and has made sacrifices to become the leader of the East Asiatic nations who were mercilessly and pitifully treated by the outside forces of the Americans and British, and Nippon without disgracing anybody has been doing her best up to now for fostering Nippon's real power.

You are all only a few remaining skeletons after the invasion of East Asia for the past few centuries and are pitiful victims. It is not your fault but till your government do not wake up from the dreams and discontinue their resistance all of you will not be released. However I shall not treat you badly for the sake of humanity as you have no fighting power at all. His Majesty the Emperor has been deeply anxious about all the War Prisoners and has ordered us to enable opening of War Prisoners camps at almost all places in the southward countries. The Imperial thoughts are unestimable and the Imperial favours are infinite and as such you should weep with gratitude at the greatness of them and should correct or mend the misleading anti-Japanese ideas.

I shall meet with you hereafter and at the beginning of the opening of the office I require you to observe the 4 following points.

1. I heard that you complain about the insufficiency of various items. Although there may be lack of materials it is difficult to meet your requirements.

Just turn your eyes towards the present condition of the world. It is entirely different from the pre-war times. In all countries and lands all materials are considerably short, and it is not easy to obtain even a small piece of cigarette or a small matchstick, and the present position is such that it is not possible even for needy women and children to get sufficient food.

Needless to say therefore that at such inconvenient place even our respectable Imperial Army is also not able to get mosquito nets, food-stuffs, medicines and cigarettes freely and frequently. As conditions are such, how can you expect me to treat you better than the Imperial Nippon Army. I do not persecute you according to my own wish and it is not due to the expense but due to the shortage of materials at such distant places. In spite of my wishes to meet your requirements I cannot do so with money. I shall however supply you if I can do so with my best efforts and I hope that you will rely on me and render your lives before me.

2. I shall strictly manage all of you. Going out, coming back, meeting with friends, communications, possession of money, etc. shall of course be limited. Living manners, deportment, salutation and attitude shall be strict and according to the rules of the Nippon Army because it is only possible to manage you all who are merely rabbles, by the order of military regulations. By this time I shall issue separate pamphlets of House Rules of War Prisoners and you are required to act strictly in accordance with these rules and you shall not all infringe any of them by any means.

3. My biggest requirement from you is escape. The rules for escape shall naturally be very severe. This rule may be quite useless and only

binding to some of the War Prisoners, but it is most important for all of you in the management of the camp. You should therefore be contented accordingly. If there is a man here who has at least one per cent of a chance of escape we shall make him to face the extreme penalty. If there is one foolish man who is trying to escape, he shall see big jungles toward the east which are absolutely impossible for communication, towards the west he shall see the boundless ocean, and above all, in the main points of south and north our Nippon Army is staying and guarding. You will easily understand the difficulty of complete escape. A few such cases of ill-omened matters which happened in Singapore shall prove the above and you should not repeat such foolish things although it is a last chance after great embarrassment.

4. Hereafter I shall require all of you to work as nobody is permitted to do nothing and eat as a present. In addition, the Imperial Nippons have great work to promote at the places newly occupied by them and this is an essential and important matter. At the time of such shortness of materials, your lives are preserved by the Military and all of you must reward them with your labour. By the hand of the Nippon Army railway work to connect Thailand and Burma have started, to the great interest of the world. There are deep jungles where no man comes to clear them by cutting the trees. There are also countless difficulties and sufferings but you shall have the honour to join in this great work which was never done before and you should do your best efforts. I shall check and investigate carefully about your non-attendance. So all of you except those who are really unable shall be taken out for labour. At the same time I shall expect all of you to work earnestly and confidently every day. In conclusion I say to you 'Work cheerfully' and from henceforth you shall be guided by this motto.

The above instructions have been given to you on the opening of War Prisoners Camp at Thanbyuzayat.

COLONEL NAKAMURA'S SPEECH ON RAILWAY CONSTRUCTION WARDOM, JANUARY 1943

Instructions given to P.O.W. on my assuming the command.

I have pleasure to lead you on the charge of last stretch of Railway Construction Wardom with the appointment of present post. In examination of various reports, as well as to the result of my partial camp inspection of the present conditions, am pleased to find that you are, in general, keeping discipline and working diligently. At the same time regret to find seriousness in health matters.

It is evident there are various cases inevitable for this end, but to my opinion, due mainly to the absence of firm belief as Japanese Health Follows Will and 'ceases only when enemy is completely annihilated'.

Those who fail to reach objective in charge by lack of health or spirit is considered in Japanese Army as most shameful deed. 'Devotion till death' is good yet still we have the spirit 'Devotion to Imperial cause even to the seventh turn of life in incarnation', the spirit which cannot become void by death. You are in the act of charge in colleague with the Imperial Japanese Army. You are expected to charge to the last stage of this work with good spirit, by taking care of your own health. Besides that you are to remember that your welfare is guaranteed only by obedience to the order of the Imperial Japanese Army. The Imperial Japanese Army will not be unfair to those who are honest and obey them, but protect such. You are to understand this fundamental Japanese spirit and carry out the task given you with perfect ease of mind under protection of Imperial Japanese Army.

Given in Kanchanaburi, January 26, 1943.

Colonel SIJUO NAKAMURA, Commander P.O.W. Camp.

HEALTH FOLLOWS WILL

('Those who fail to reach objective in charge, by lack of health or spirit, is considered in Japanese Army as most shameful deed. "Devotion till death" is good yet still we have the spirit "Devotion to Imperial cause even to the seventh turn of life in incarnation", the spirit which cannot become void by death.') Lieutenant-Colonel Nakamura

'Vitamins are luxuries. . . . I have a cure for dysentery. It is work.' Lieutenant Nobisawa, Camp Medical Officer, Imperial Japanese Army

Charge onwards, my prisoners, and be of good cheer,
Dai Nippon's discovered the world's panacea—
No patented powder, no potion, nor pill,
But simply the formula, 'Health follows Will'.

When pricked by a mischievous mossy's proboscis
That's full of malaria's dispiriting doses,
Though retching with rigors, you're not really ill,
For in Greater East Asia, 'Health follows Will'.

Should a swift epidemic of cholera appal
By the cartloads of corpses that rot as they fall,
Take heart and remember that cholera will kill
Only sceptics who're doubtful that 'Health follows Will'.

If a ravenous ulcer has guzzled your thigh,
And it has to come off, or you'd otherwise die,
Your survival depends not on surgical skill,
But on your conviction that 'Health follows Will'.

When luxurious vitamins fail, you may soon
Have a belly blown up like a barrage balloon;
But so long as there's rice, keep on eating your fill,
And say with each shovelful: 'Health follows Will'.

And when dysentery amoebae are driving you nuts,
While they're worming their way through your gangrenous guts,
Though doctors despair, there's hope for you still
If you're filled with the spirit of 'Health follows Will'.

But if by some quite inexplicable freak,
Though the spirit is willing, the flesh should prove weak,
What comfort to think, as you draw your last breath,
That this spirit will NOT become void by your death!

MESSAGE TO THE TRANSPORT COMPANY

This time Mr Terekadi and I, instead of Mr Watanabe, practise the transporting service with motor cars as the master of your Company. At the beginning of this work I think to express my thoughts to you. You and I met on the battlefield as enemy each other. But it was the collision between the two countries. This fact does not mean that there were private enmity and hate between you and us. Now we shaking hands each other are not enemy already. We are mysterious friends that have met here by mysterious Providence. So we want to do anything with you as good friends. I tell you the instructions addressed to you by our Commander, Colonel Ikari, as follows:—

1. You should be absolutely obedient to the order of the Japanese soldiers.
2. We treat you according to the warrior spirits—Bushido. You must fulfil your duty faithfully. Therefore we do not force you to be obedient to us by violence.

Bushido, the way of the Samurai, has much contents, but now I show you an expression of them as follows:

It is to be kind to the enemy of yesterday. In old time of Japan a General who had sea-shore as part of his territory sent much salt to his enemy in mountain where people could not get salt. Bushido spirits resemble the Knight spirits of your country.

Our real heart is Bushido. But now the great war is in progress and so the materials to treat you are not sufficient, accommodation is poor. As here is battlefield, please excuse us. But to conquer the present unhealthy conditions, the bad camps, insufficient bedding, poor food, etc. you must take care of your own health as much as you can.

I think you do not like to work with us who were your enemies of yesterday. But when you do not use your energy that God has given you and your ability that you have gotten by your long diligence, spending your every day in vain, you have no excuse to God. And it is not good for your health to spend all days inactively. So that thinking upper matters you must work every day in high spirits.

Next I tell you my longings:

1. To prevent against dangers. As we use motor cars every day we must presuppose the occurrence of accidents. You and we equally have the native land, the parents, the wife, children, and when the war is finished you work for your country in your country and for mankind. Your bodies are very important. So you must keep off being wounded by accidents. The route of our transporting is not so long that the efficiency of one day does not depend on so much the speed of the cars. Then please drive with the speed of about 30 m.p.h.

2. To treat kindly the machines. Materials have hearts. If a machinist does not love a machine, it will be broke soon, on the contrary he loves the machine, it will be used in a long time. You must love a machine and set it to work in good condition for a good while.

3. Be frugal of materials. Example, oil. It belonged to you yesterday but now it belongs to us. But after all it has been given from Heaven. So if we use it in vain we must be called traitors who acts against Heaven. We want you to use all materials effectively.

(Signed) L. FUKUDA. [undated]

BIBLIOGRAPHY

Aida, Yuji, *Prisoner of the British*, translated by Hide Ishiguro and Louis Allen, London 1956

Baelz, Erwin, *Awakening Japan*, edited by Toku Baelz, translated by E. and C. Paul, New York, 1932

Barber, Noel, *Sinister Twilight*, London, 1968

Beasley, W. G., *The Modern History of Japan*, London, 1963

—— (ed.), *Modern Japan: Aspects of History, Literature and Society*, London, 1975

Benedict, Ruth, *The Chrysanthemum and the Sword*, London, 1947

Coast, John, *Railroad of Death*, London, 1946

Craigie, Right Hon. Sir Robert, *Behind the Japanese Mask*, London and New York, 1945

Curzon, Hon. George N., *Problems of the Far East*, London and New York, 1896

Dening, Sir Esler, *Japan*, London, 1960

Dyer, Henry, *Dai Nippon*, London, 1904

East, W. G., O. H. K. Spate and C. A. Fisher (eds), *The Changing Map of Asia*, London, 1971

Enright, D. J., *The World of Dew*, Tokyo and London, 1955

Fuller, J. C. E., *The Second World War*, London, 1948

Gibney, Frank, *Five Gentlemen of Japan*, London, 1953

Gowing, Margaret, *Science and Politics*, London, 1977

Grew, Joseph, C., *Ten Years in Japan*, London, 1944

Gunther, John, *Inside Asia*, London, 1939

Ishii, Ryoichi, *Population Pressure and Economic Life in Japan*, London, 1937

Kawasaki, Ichiro, *Japan Unmasked*, Tokyo, 1969

Moloney, James Clark, *Understanding the Japanese Mind*, New York, 1954

Nitobe, Inazo, *Japan, Some Phases of her Problems and Development*, London, 1931

—— *The Soul of Bushido*, London and New York, 1905
Nakabashi, T., *Kokoku Sakuron (Policies of National Expansion)*, Tokyo, 1913
Nohara, Komakichi, *The True Face of Japan*, London, 1936
Norman, Henry, *The Peoples and Politics of the Far East*, London, 1895
Ponting, Herbert G., *In Lotus Land Japan*, London, 1910
Reischauer, E. O., and J. K. Fairbank, *East Asia: The Great Tradition*, London, 1960
Reischauer, E. O., J. K. Fairbank and Albert Craig, *East Asia: The Modern Transformation*, London, 1965
Rudofsky, Bernard, *The Kimono Mind*, London, 1965
Russell of Liverpool, Lord, *The Knights of Bushido*, London, 1958
Simson, Ivan, *Singapore: Too Little, Too Late*, London, 1976
Stoddard, Lothrop, *The Rising Tide of Color*, New York, 1922
Storry, Richard, *A History of Modern Japan*, London, 1960
Takahashi, Yoshio, *Nihonjinshu Kairyoran (The Improvement of the Japanese Race)*, Tokyo, 1883
Toland, John, *The Rising Sun*, New York and London, 1971
Tracy, Honor, *Kakemono*, London, 1950
Trewartha, Glenn T., *Japan: A Geography*, London, 1965
Utley, Freda, *Japan's Feet of Clay*, London, 1936
Whitecross, Roy H., *Slaves of the Son of Heaven*, Sydney, 1951
Yoshida, Shigeru, *The Yoshida Memoirs*, London, 1961
—— *Japan's Decisive Century 1867–1967*, London and New York, 1967
Zinsser, Hans, *Rats, Lice and History*, Boston, 1935